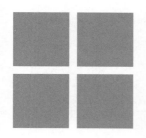

TEACHING HISTORY CREATIVELY

Edited by

Hilary Cooper

Routledge
Taylor & Francis Group

LONDON AND NEW YORK

First published 2013
by Routledge
2 Park Square, Milton Park, Abingdon, Oxon OX14 4RN

Simultaneously published in the USA and Canada
by Routledge
711 Third Avenue, New York, NY 10017

Routledge is an imprint of the Taylor & Francis Group, an informa business

British Library Cataloguing in Publication Data
A catalogue record for this book is available from the British Library

Library of Congress Cataloging in Publication Data
Teaching history creatively / edited by Hilary Cooper.
     p. cm.
  1. History—Study and teaching (Elementary)—Great Britain. 2. Creative
thinking—Study and teaching (Elementary)—Great Britain. 3. Creative
teaching—Great Britain. I. Cooper, Hilary, 1943–
LB1582.G7T43 2013
372.890941—dc23   2012026706

ISBN: 978–0–415–69884–9 (hbk)
ISBN: 978–0–415–69885–6 (pbk)
ISBN: 978–0–203–07481–7 (ebk)

Typeset in Times New Roman and Helvetica Neue by
Book Now Ltd, London

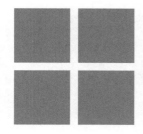

CONTENTS

CONTENTS ▨ ▪ ▪ ▪

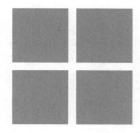

ILLUSTRATIONS

TABLES

ILLUSTRATIONS ■ ■ ■ ■

FIGURES

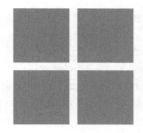

CONTRIBUTORS

Hilary Cooper is Emeritus Professor of History and Pedagogy at the University of Cumbria. She undertook her doctoral research into Young Children's Thinking in History (London University Institute of Education 1991) as a practising primary school teacher, before becoming a lecturer at Goldsmith's College, London University, then moving to Cumbria in 1993. She is a Fellow of the Historical Association and has published widely; her publications have been translated into Spanish, Romanian, Portuguese Turkish, Russian and French. She is co-editor, with Jon Nichol, of the *International Journal of History Teaching Learning and Research* and been a key note speaker at many international conferences, in Europe, Turkey, Russia, Australia and Brazil.

Cherry Dodwell has worked on a range of courses at the University of Exeter as a drama specialist – currently on the Creative Arts Masters and the PGCE programmes. She is an experienced teacher who has worked with all age ranges from five-year-olds to adults. She runs workshops to promote drama in schools as well as courses at the University for Gifted and Talented children. She has worked as an organiser developing International Conferences for practitioners involved both in Researching Drama and Theatre in Education (Conferences based at University of Exeter) and the History Education International Research Network (conferences based at universities in Istanbul, New York, Belfast, Braga and Curitiba). Her publications include: 'Building relationships through drama: the Action Track Project research in drama education', *The Journal of Applied Theatre and Performance*, Vol. 7, No. 1 (2002); 'Drama and storytelling: creative approaches for teaching historical, geographical and social understanding', *Primary History,* Autumn (2009); and 'Citizenship, history and the enquiring mind: innovations using drama methodology', *International Journal of Historical Learning, Teaching and Research (IJHLTR)*, Vol. 9, No. 2 (2010).

CONTRIBUTORS ▦ ▦ ▦ ▦

Penelope Harnett is Associate Professor in Education at the University of the West of England, Bristol. She has researched and published widely in the field of primary education, with an especial focus on history and citizenship education. She preceded Jon Nichol as editor of *Primary History*. Her most recent publications include *Understanding Primary Education: developing professional knowledge, skills and attributes*, Routledge (2008); *Exploring Learning Identity and Power through Life History and Narrative* (with A. Bathmaker), Routledge (2010).

Linsey Maginn trained as a specialist history teacher in primary education at the University of Cumbria. She taught in a large urban, primary school in Manchester, before teaching in Edinburgh. She is a member of the Historical Association Primary Committee. Linsey has special interests in local history and in teaching history in multicultural classrooms.

Hugh Moore is a Senior Lecturer in primary history at the University of Cumbria. He is a former museum educator and a specialist in ancient history, with an interest in the use of sources and artefacts in the classroom. His publications include: 'Ancient History, things to do and questions to ask', in *Exploring Time and Place through Play* (H. Cooper, ed.) London: David Fulton (2004); 'Who Are We', in *Cross Curricular Approaches to Teaching and Learning* (C. Rowley and H. Cooper, eds) London: Sage (2009); 'Teaching World War 1 and Teacher Professional Development', *Primary History* Issue 54, Spring (2010).

Jon Nichol has been involved in cutting-edge developments on the theory and practice of history teaching since the early 1970s. From 1991 he co-edited the Nuffield Primary History project for teaching National Curriculum History to 5–11-year-olds. For the past 4 years he has been editor of the Historical Association's journal, *Primary History*, the country's leading publication in this field.

Sue Temple taught across the 3–11 age group in primary schools in the North East of England for many years. She is a Senior Lecturer in primary history education at the Carlisle Campus of the University of Cumbria. She is a member of the Historical Association Primary Committee and a regular contributor to the journal, *Primary History.* She is currently working on her PhD, exploring teaching history to children with Special Educational Needs.

Sarah Whitehouse is a Senior Lecturer at the University of the West of England, Bristol, where she teaches history education to undergraduate and post graduate students. Her current research is in the area of teacher subject knowledge and the pedagogical subject knowledge of trainee teachers.

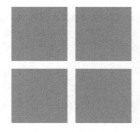

SERIES EDITOR'S FOREWORD

Over the last two decades, teachers in England, working in a culture of accountability and target setting, have experienced a high level of specification both of curriculum content and pedagogy. Positioned as recipients of the prescribed agenda, it could be argued that practitioners have had their hands tied, their voices quietened and their professional autonomy constrained. Research reveals that during this time some professionals have short-changed their understanding of pedagogy and practice (English *et al.* 2002; Burns and Myhill 2004) in order to deliver the required curriculum. The relentless quest for higher standards and 'coverage' may well have obscured the personal and affective dimensions of teaching and learning, fostering a mindset characterised more by compliance and conformity than curiosity and creativity.

However alongside the standards agenda, creativity and creative policies and practices also became prominent and a focus on creative teaching and learning developed. Heralded by the publication *All Our Futures: Creativity, Culture and Education* (NACCCE 1999), this shift was exemplified in the Creative Partnerships initiative, in the Qualifications and Curriculum Authority's creativity framework (QCA 2005) and in a plethora of reports (e.g. Ofsted 2003; DfES 2003; CAPEUK 2006; Roberts 2006). It was also evident in the development of the Curriculum for Excellence in Scotland. The definition of creativity frequently employed was creativity is 'imaginative activity fashioned so as to produce outcomes that are both original and of value' (NACCCE 1999: 30). Many schools sought to develop more innovative curricula, and many teachers found renewed energy through teaching creatively and teaching for creativity.

Yet tensions persist, not only because the dual policies of performativity and creativity appear contradictory, but also because the new National Curriculum draft programmes of study in England at least afford a high degree of specificity and profile the knowledge needed to be taught and tested. We need to be concerned if teachers are positioned more as technically competent curriculum deliverers, rather than artistically engaged, research-informed curriculum developers. I believe, alongside Eisner (2003) and others, that teaching is an art form and that teachers benefit from viewing themselves as versatile artists in the classroom, drawing on their personal passions and creativity as they research and develop practice. As Joubert observes:

> Creative teaching is an art. One cannot teach teachers didactically how to be creative; there is no fail safe recipe or routines. Some strategies may help to promote creative thinking, but teachers need to develop a full repertoire of skills which they can adapt to different situations.
>
> (Joubert 2001: 21)

However, creative teaching is only part of the picture, since teaching for creativity also needs to be acknowledged and their mutual dependency recognised. The former focuses more on teachers using imaginative approaches in the classroom in order to make learning more interesting and effective, the latter, more on the development of children's creativity (NACCCE 1999). Both rely upon an understanding of the notion of creativity and demand that professionals confront the myths and mantras which surround the word. These include the commonly held misconceptions that creativity is connected only to participation in the arts and that it is confined to particular individuals, a competence of a few specially gifted children.

Nonetheless, creativity is an elusive concept; it has been multiply defined by educationalists, psychologists and neurologists, as well as by policy makers in different countries and cultural contexts. Debates resound about its individual and/or collaborative nature, the degree to which it is generic or domain specific, and the difference between the 'Big C' creativity of genius and the 'little c' creativity of the everyday. Notwithstanding these issues, most scholars in the field perceive it involves the capacity to generate, reason and critically evaluate novel ideas and/or imaginary scenarios. As such, I perceive it encompasses thinking through and solving problems, making connections, inventing and reinventing and flexing one's imaginative muscles in all aspects of learning and life.

In the primary classroom, creative teaching and learning have been associated with innovation, originality, ownership and control (Jeffrey and Woods 2009) and creative teachers have been seen, in their planning and teaching and in the ethos which they create, to afford high value to curiosity and risk taking, to ownership, autonomy and making connections (Cremin 2009; Cremin et al. 2009). Such teachers, it has been posited, often work in partnership with others: with children, other teachers and experts from beyond the school gates (Cochrane and Cockett 2007). Additionally, in research exploring possibility thinking, which it is argued is at the heart of creativity in education (Craft 2000), an intriguing interplay between teachers and children has been observed; both are involved in possibility thinking their ways forwards and in immersing themselves in playful contexts, posing questions, being imaginative, showing self-determination, taking risks and innovating (Craft et al. 2012; Burnard et al. 2006; Cremin et al. 2006). A new pedagogy of possibility beckons.

This series Learning to Teach in the Primary School, which accompanies and complements the edited textbook Learning to Teach in the Primary School (Arthur and Cremin 2010), seeks to support teachers in developing as creative practitioners, assisting them in exploring the synergies and potential of teaching creatively and teaching for creativity. The series does not merely offer practical strategies for use in the classroom, though these abound, but more importantly seeks to widen teachers' and student teachers' knowledge and understanding of the principles underpinning a creative approach to teaching. Principles based on research. It seeks to mediate the wealth of research evidence and make accessible and engaging the diverse theoretical perspectives and scholarly arguments available, demonstrating their practical relevance and value to the profession. Those who aspire to develop further as creative and curious educators will, I trust, find much of value to support their own professional learning journeys and enrich their pedagogy and practice and children's creative learning right across the curriculum.

TERESA CREMIN

Teresa Cremin (Grainger) is a Professor of Education (Literacy) at the Open University and a past President of UKRA (2001–2) and UKLA (2007–9). She is currently co-convenor of the BERA Creativity SIG and a trustee of Booktrust, The Poetry Archive and UKLA. She is also a Fellow of the English Association and an Academician of the Academy of Social Sciences. Her work involves research, publication and consultancy in literacy and creativity. Her current projects seek to explore children's make believe play in the context of storytelling and storyacting, their everyday lives and literacy practices, and the nature of literary discussions in extracurricular reading groups. Additionally, Teresa is interested in teachers' identities as readers and writers and the characteristics and associated pedagogy that fosters possibility thinking within creative learning in the primary years. Teresa has published widely, writing and co-editing a variety of books including: *Writing Voices: Creating Communities of Writers* (Routledge, 2012) *Teaching English Creatively* (Routledge 2009); *Learning to Teach in the Primary School* (Routledge 2010); *Jumpstart Drama* (David Fulton 2009); *Documenting Creative Learning 5–11* (Trentham 2007), *Creativity and Writing: Developing Voice and Verve* (Routledge 2005); *Teaching English in Higher Education* (NATE and UKLA 2007); *Creative Activities for Character, Setting and Plot, 5–7, 7–9, 9–11* (Scholastic 2004); and *Language and Literacy: A Routledge Reader* (Routledge 2001).

REFERENCES

Arthur, J. and Cremin, T. (2010) (eds) *Learning to Teach in the Primary School* (2nd edn), London: Routledge.

Burnard, P., Craft, A. and Cremin, T. (2006) 'Possibility thinking', *International Journal of Early Years Education*, 14(3): 243–62.

Burns, C. and Myhill, D. (2004) 'Interactive or inactive? A consideration of the nature of interaction in whole class teaching', *Cambridge Journal of Education*, 34: 35–49.

CapeUK (2006) *Building Creative Futures: The Story of Creative Action Research Awards, 2004–2005*, London: Arts Council.

Cohrane, P. and Cockett, M. (2007) *Building a Creative School: A Dynamic Approach to School Development*, London: Trentham.

Craft, A., McConnon, L. and Mathews, A. (2012) 'Creativity and child-initiated play', *Thinking Skills and Creativity*, 7(1): 48–61.

Craft, A. (2000) *Creativity Across the Primary Curriculum*, London: Routledge.

Cremin, T. (2009) 'Creative teaching and creative teachers', in A. Wilson (ed.) *Creativity in Primary Education*, Exeter: Learning Matters, pp. 36–46.

Cremin, T., Burnard, P. and Craft, A. (2006). 'Pedagogy and possibility thinking in the early years', *International Journal of Thinking Skills and Creativity*, 1(2): 108–19.

Cremin, T., Barnes, J. and Scoffham, S. (2009) *Creative Teaching for Tomorrow: Fostering a Creative State of Mind*, Deal: Future Creative.

Department for Education and Skills (DfES) (2003) *Excellence and Enjoyment: A Strategy for Primary Schools*, Nottingham: DfES.

Eisner, E. (2003) 'Artistry in education', *Scandinavian Journal of Educational Research*, 47(3): 373–84.

English, E., Hargreaves, L. and Hislam, J. (2002) 'Pedagogical dilemmas in the National Literacy Strategy: primary teachers' perceptions, reflections and classroom behaviour', *Cambridge Journal of Education*, 32(1): 9–26.

Jeffrey, B. and Woods, P. (2009) *Creative Learning in the Primary School*, London: Routledge.

Joubert, M.M. (2001) 'The art of creative teaching: NACCCE and beyond', in A. Craft, B. Jeffrey and M. Liebling (eds) *Creativity in Education*, London: Continuum.

National Advisory Committee on Creative and Cultural Education (NACCCE) (1999) *All Our Futures: Creativity, Culture and Education*, London: Department for Education and Employment.

Ofsted (2003) *Expecting the Unexpected: Developing Creativity in Primary and Secondary Schools*, HMI 1612 [Online]. Available at: www.ofsted.gov.uk (accessed 9 November 2007).

Qualifications and Curriculum Authority (QCA) (2005). *Creativity: Find It, Promote It! – Promoting Pupils' Creative Thinking and Behaviour Across The Curriculum At Key Stages 1, 2 and 3 – Practical Materials For Schools*, London: QCA.

Roberts, P. (2006) *Nurturing Creativity in Young People. A Report to Government to Inform Future Policy*, London: DCMS.

PREFACE

AIMS OF THIS BOOK

We hope that our book will inspire readers with evidence that history is an exciting and worthwhile subject, which can be taught in creative ways and so foster creativity in learners. It aims to generate readers' confidence in planning their own creative approaches, by setting out clearly the processes of historical enquiry, demonstrating how these are integrally linked with key criteria of creativity and in addition, to help readers to employ those features of creativity not specifically linked to historical enquiry but which relate to ethos and teaching strategies relevant to teaching history.

A TIMELY BOOK

History

It was the stated aim of the National Curriculum (DfEE 1999) that the aims and values of history education in the primary school are for children to learn to answer important questions, evaluate evidence, identify and analyse different interpretations of the past, to substantiate arguments, debate and make judgements. Broadly, research has found that this curriculum was successful, that teaching and learning in history was good and that history was one of the most extensively taught of the non-core subjects, enjoyed by teachers and pupils (Alexander 2010; Ofsted 2011; Historical Association 2011; Cannadine *et al.* 2011). However, it found that many primary practitioners, because of other pressures on their time and in addition, little initial training in history or opportunity for continuing professional development, have limited understanding of the skills of historical enquiry (Ofsted 2011; Historical Association 2011). Nevertheless Cannadine *et al.* (2011) recommended building on what has been achieved.

Creativity

In the mean time a growing body of research and literature has emerged which examines the nature of creativity in the classroom, how it can be promoted and why it is important. It identifies the various aspects of creativity: asking questions, possibility thinking, imagination, risk-taking, how creativity relates to knowledge and is promoted by classroom ethos. Recently neuroscience has endorsed these criteria. Interestingly there is almost no research relating creativity to history. This book argues that history and creativity are interdependent. It explores precisely how they are linked and demonstrates the links through case studies.

History and creativity

In 2012 the Department for Education responded very positively (DfE 2012a) to the recommendations of a review by Darren Henley on Cultural Education in England (DfE 2012b). This set out a clear argument for the importance of the arts and humanities in the educational entitlement of all children and realistic suggestions about how this can be organised, funded and evaluated. Creativity and history feature significantly in the rationale. The report states that cultural education includes archaeology, architecture and the built environment, archives, galleries, heritage and museums (para. 1.5, p. 30). Visits to such places, it claims, can 'deepen children's understanding of the world around them and provide fresh insights into their studies (2.6), 'can be habit forming for the rest of a young person's life' (3.2) and are a vital part of any child's education. In paragraph 3.14 the report says that this is especially important in heritage and history 'where the subject could otherwise be reduced to the accumulation of facts rather than also including the acquisition of the understanding of historical contexts' and (3.26) it states that the coalition government has 'a commitment to improving standards in the teaching of history'. This, it claims, involves fostering creativity in cultural learning in every child's education and that those who advocate a pure knowledge agenda fail to value the skills and experiences that engagement with cultural activities can bring to a child's education', whereas creativity is in fact a synthesis of the two schools of thought (3.27).

Henley's report states that one of the advantages, for history, is that it gives young children a sense of place and of identity, an appreciation of the environment in which thy live and of their place in it, whereas a disconnection from a young person's built environment can have significant adverse consequences (3.34–5). History also exposes children to the best creativity from times gone by (3.32).

STRUCTURE OF THE BOOK

Part I sets out the context for the following chapters. Chapter 1 explains why history and creativity are inextricably interdependent and Chapter 2 argues that history, creativity and constructivist theories of learning are also interdependent, and so demonstrates how children can learn the processes of historical enquiry from the beginning and in increasingly complex ways. In Part II each chapter provides vivid and rich examples of the creative use of sources, and of strategies to create interpretations. Part III puts these case studies in a broader context: exploring creative ways of making local, national and global links and of creating an innovative whole school approach to planning. The final chapter describes how Sybil Marshall, who began teaching in a village school in the 1950s, became inspired to teach history creatively.

Hilary Cooper

REFERENCES

Alexander, R. (ed.) (2010) *Children, their World, Their Education: Final report and recommendations of the Cambridge Primary Review*, London: Routledge.

Cannadine, D., Keating, J. and Sheldon, N. (2011) *The Right Kind of History*, London: Palgrave Macmillan.

DfEE (Department for Education and Employment) (1999) *National Curriculum for England and Wales: a handbook for primary teachers in England*, London: DfEE.

DfE (Department for Education (2012a) *Cultural Education in England: an independent review for the Department of Culture, Media and Sport (DMCS)*, London: DfE.

Department or Education (DfE) (2012b) *The Government Response to Darren Henley's Review of Cultural Education,* London: DfE.

Historical Association (2011) *Primary History Survey (England),* 3–11, London: The Historical Association.

Ofsted (Office for Standards in Education) (2011) *History for All: History in English Schools 2007–2011*, www.ofsted.gov.uk/publications/090223.

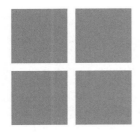

ACKNOWLEDGEMENTS

The authors would like to thank the many people who have contributed to the case studies in this book. They include colleagues and pupils in schools: Philipa Statter, staff and children from Shield Road Primary School, Filton, Bristol and Bannerman Community School and Children's Centre, Easton, Bristol; Susie Weaver, acting headteacher, Maeve Dorrian, history coordinator and all the staff and children at Ashley Down Infants School; children from Hanham Abbots Junior School, Bristol, The Tynings School, Bristol and Christchurch C of E VC Junior School, Bristol; Claire Coleman and Brook Street Primary School, Carlisle; Petteril Bank Primary School, Carlisle and Garry Schofield and staff at Irk Valley Community Primary School, North Manchester.

We are grateful to the colleagues and student teachers involved, including: Iona Edmonds and Henry Whitehouse, Sally Bassett, Sue Hughes, Mark Jones, Mandy Lee, primary post graduate students and Year 1 humanities students at the University of the West of England, Bristol. We are indebted to colleagues at the Carlisle Archive Centre, to Tom Robson and to Dawn Hurton, Heather Tipler, project co-ordinator and evaluator of the projects described in Chapter 4, and to storyteller Dominic Kelly. Cherry Dodwell is grateful to Jon Somers, who first introduced her to using a local story for classroom drama, as part of a research project and all the Exeter children on the course, 'Looking at landscape'.

Finally, as editor, I thank my colleagues who contributed chapters for this exciting and innovative book, based on their continuously imaginative work with students and teachers, for their support and engagement and, in spite of very heavy workloads, for meeting the deadlines.

PART I

THE ESSENTIAL INTEGRATION OF HISTORY AND CREATIVITY

Creativity –
involves.
generating
ideas

WHY MUST TEACHING AND LEARNING IN HISTORY BE CREATIVE?

Hilary Cooper

> There is no history of mankind. There is only an indefinite number of histories
> of all kinds of aspects of human life.
>
> Karl Popper (1945)

In this chapter we shall begin by considering what is understood by the concept of
creativity. Then we shall examine the processes of historical enquiry, how they involve
all the aspects of creativity which have been identified and why it is essential for
young children to engage with historical enquiry at an appropriate level.

WHAT IS 'CREATIVITY'?

'Being creative' is often associated with the arts, for example with dance, music, painting, or with great original thinkers such as Einstein or Tolstoy. However, over the past
thirty years there has been a great deal of educational research exploring what is meant
by 'creativity' and how it can be fostered. There is still no single definition; discourse
about creativity is continuously evolving. But there is a consensus about the key components of the concept and agreement that creativity involves generating ideas. These
may be ideas new to human history at the 'high creativity' end of the creativity continuum or simply ideas new to a person's previous way of thinking. It is agreed that
everyone can, to some extent, be creative. This is what Craft describes as creativity
with a little 'c' to distinguish it from 'high creativity' (Craft *et al.* 2001: 45–61). It is
generally agreed that it is possible to learn to be creative (Craft and Jeffrey 2008), that
creativity can apply across the curriculum (QCA 2005) and involves multiple intelligences (Gardner 1999). So what are the key components of creativity?

Identifying areas of enquiry, defining problems, asking questions

First, creative thinking depends on taking time to reflect, being curious, recognising, identifying and accepting problems. This leads to identifying and asking open questions to investigate problems, which may raise new questions (Gardner 1999; Craft 2004). Asking problematic questions requires being open to new information (Langer 1997), the tenacity to pursue questions, and also being prepared to accept possible failure in finding a solution.

Possibility thinking

Responding to such questions requires possibility thinking (Craft 2002). Possibility thinking involves open-mindedness. It is the ability to consider a variety of different possible responses or perspectives in answer to a question, a problem or a situation. This lies at the centre of creative thinking. Possibility thinking includes the ability to hypothesise, to consider alternative possibilities, to 'suppose', to ask 'what if?'. Possibility thinking brings together other aspects of creativity because considering alternative interpretations must have a perceived goal; it is not aimless. Generating creative ideas may lead to creative behaviour and creative action, experimentation and innovation (Levin and Nolan 2004). Langer (1997) calls possibility thinking 'mindful learning', which he says is a state of mind. The mindful learner reflects on subject matter while processing the information and sees it from different perspectives, which means the learning is absorbed and can be used in a new context, so that learners are empowered to make the learning their own.

Imagination

Possibility thinking involves the imagination to envisage a variety of possibilities, with the intention of finding solutions. So imagining and being imaginative are essential for creativity (Craft 2002). To imagine something is to create a mental image, picture, sound or feeling in your mind. It is a thought process that establishes a new idea – seeing other possibilities. Imaginative activity is fashioned so as to produce outcomes that are original and of value (NACCCE 1999: 29). It allows learners to conjecture a world different from their own.

But what is imagination?

Passmore (1980) makes a distinction between imaging (some form of mental representation), imagining (supposing that something is the case, hypothesising or empathising with another's perspective), and being imaginative (generating a novel outcome). It has been claimed that imagination is superior to the intellect because it makes it possible to form new thoughts, build up new worlds. 'The objects of imagination are created, not discovered; it is disciplined, not fanciful' (Kenny 1989: 114). Being imaginative involves going beyond the obvious and seeing more than is initially apparent or interpreting something in a way that is unusual. To proceed imaginatively is to be creative (Elliott 1971). If an enquiry is concerned with people, imagination will include empathy, the capacity to imagine, based on what is known, how someone else may behave, think and feel in a given situation. Scruton (1974) differentiates between imaging and imagining, which are mental acts, and being imaginative, which need not be and may result in a product.

Risk-taking

Considering possible ambiguities through imagination uncertainty, to consider surprises rather than expect wh choices depending on the knowledge available. Possi dence and a 'can-do' approach to learning.

Collaboration?

There has been some analysis of the ways in which di ratively can foster creativity through communication. Sonnenburg (2004) defines a specific kind of communication system from which collaborative creativity emerges. It starts with a problem and, if successful, results in a novel product, for example a theory, drama or work of art. She claims that this model should cover all kinds of collaboration, in all kinds of product creation. Sonnenburg analyses this process. She says that creative collaboration works through developing a shared understanding. Only thoughts which are spoken are important in the collaboration. Questions are important. Communication coordinates the single contributions. This speeds up new ideas. Everyone must contribute, in verbal, face-to-face communication.

Leach (2001) sees creative learning as a social process which can be expressed in team work and communities. Research by Bredo (1994), Lave and Wenger (1991) and Rogoff (1999) also analyses learning as a situated social practice, depending on interaction and communication. They argue that creativity depends on interaction with others and with materials, in social settings. However, Craft (2005) recognises the importance of both individual creativity and collaborative creativity.

Reaching conclusions?

There is a variety of views about whether creativity must lead to an outcome or product. The National Advisory Committee on Creative and Cultural Education (1999: 29) defined creativity as imaginative activity, fashioned so as to produce outcomes that are both original and of value. In their view creative ideas must be turned into action towards a goal. However, Elliott (1971: 139) considered that creativity is 'imagination manifested in any valued pursuit tied to an objective, but the process can be considered creative without necessarily making anything'. The processes are problem-solving and the making of an idea.

Fryer (2004) distinguishes between creative thinking, which generates new thoughts, creative behaviour, in which the first step is suspending judgement, and creative action, which results in experiment and innovation. Craft (2002: 82–3) proposes that being imaginative must involve some kind of outcome; 'there must be some public indication of some sort to show for it – a book, a decision, a behaviour, a poem'. But she suggests describing the outcome of creativity along a scale. At one end may be outcomes which are within the agent's head but not yet shared with others, for example, an idea. In the middle might be an outcome which has been expressed to others. At the other end of the scale might be a product which can be scrutinised.

Creativity and knowledge

The National Curriculum (QCA 1999: 11, 22) sees creativity as embedded in cross-curricular 'thinking skills' which can operate creatively in any knowledge domain. They are proposed as enabling pupils to 'generate and extend ideas, suggest hypotheses, apply imagination and look for alternative outcomes', so shaping one's identity through choices (p. 44). However, this presupposes an understanding of each domain or subject; creativity cannot be seen as knowledge free. Craft (2002) considers that a disposition to be creative must be domain dominated and that, although creativity involves possibility thinking and imagination, there are boundaries to being imaginative. Creativity is still governed by normative rules of what is appropriate.

Ryle (1979) claims that creativity involves 'knowing how', understanding the enquiry processes that lie at the heart of a discipline and 'knowing that', knowing about something. However, these usually go together. Creativity is not knowledge free. It presupposes some understanding of a subject. Even a child who is only beginning to master the processes and content of a discipline can nevertheless be creative. Piirto (1992) argues that we would expect different depths of understanding and knowledge, depending on a child's experience and ability. If we see knowledge as growth we would expect children to ask questions at a level meaningful to them. In a constructivist approach, which has much in common with the concept of creativity, learners' questions determine the lines of enquiry; they generate their own ideas and draw thoughtful conclusions. They construct and co-construct knowledge. Creativity shapes new knowledge by applying existing knowledge in new contexts. Dewey (1933), Montessori (2007/1949), and Kant (1989) all objected to the undisciplined exercise of fantasy but were in favour of the exercise of imagination within a discipline.

Overview of the concept of creativity

Key aspects of creativity have been identified. Overarching criteria are: recognising problems and asking questions which will help to address them. Doing so requires possibility thinking and imagination. Thinking in this way requires taking risks and accepting uncertainties, which needs the confidence. Creativity may benefit from collaborative enquiries. The process of enquiry may in itself be creative without necessarily reaching a conclusion. Nevertheless, knowledge and understanding the enquiry processes of a discipline is essential to creative thinking; it is not free-floating.

THE PROCESS OF CREATIVE THINKING: PSYCHOLOGY AND NEUROSCIENCE

It is interesting that recently neuroscience has endorsed aspects of creativity, previously based on observed behaviour, and shown how they occur in the brain.

Problem solving

Jung-Beeman *et al*. (2006), combined functional Magnetic Resonance Imaging (fMRI) and Electroencaphalographology (EEG) in the same study and found that the problem-solving process begins with intense mental search in the left hemisphere of the brain, but since there are far too many connections to consider, this phase leads to frustration and negative feelings. This is an essential stage because it signals that it is time to shift activity to the right side of the brain (just above the ear!) to explore more unexpected associations where thirty milliseconds before a new insight occurs, there's a spike of gamma-wave rhythm, which is the highest electrical frequency generated by the brain, although this first insight still needs to be refined. If there is no sudden insight we rummage through all the old filing cabinets in the right hemisphere until we generally end up with a conclusion, seen as a flicker of electricity inside the head.

Making connections

The ability to make separate ideas coexist in the mind is a crucial creative tool. Ideas come from the overlap between seemingly unrelated thoughts. Hume (1993/1777) described this as the essence of imagination. Gick and Holyoak (1980) say that the key element of this 'conceptual blending' is a willingness to consider information and ideas that do not seem worth considering, to free our minds to search for analogies, rather than concentrate on the detail. The notion of creativity as making connections occurs throughout this book.

A relaxed state of mind

Sandkuler and Bhattacharya (2008) demonstrated the importance of being relaxed, and also taking breaks from a focused enquiry. Then a steady rhythm of alpha waves ripples through the right hemisphere and we are more likely 'direct the spotlight inwards' towards the stream of remote associations coming from the right hemisphere. When we are focused and are thinking analytically this prevents us from detecting connections that lead to insights. Being relaxed and not afraid of taking risks or of getting things wrong enhances creativity because the dorsolateral prefrontal cortex (DLPFC), which is concerned with self-control, is deactivated and this leads to a surge of spontaneous ideas. On the contrary, the DLPFC remains active when an activity depends on memorization. Carson *et al.* (2003) found that the inability to focus helps to ensure a richer mixture of thoughts and 'eminent creative achievers'; instead of approaching a problem from a predictable perspective such people consider all sorts of far-fetched analogies. Creative individuals, they found, seem to remain in contact with information constantly streaming in from the environment.

Collaboration

A group is not a collection of individual talents but a chance for those talents to exceed themselves and produce something greater than an individual could achieve, providing that the right group of people collaborate, in the right way. 'Brain storming', for example, has been shown to be ineffective because it depends on an absence of criticism. Group activity, it has been shown, only becomes more than the sum of its parts if it includes debate and candid criticism of each other's ideas. This does not inhibit ideas but stimulates them, because it encourages us to fully engage with the ideas of others – because we want to improve on them (Nemeth 2004; Nemeth and Ormiston 2007).

I find this fascinating because it chimes so much with my experience in teaching history in primary schools long before the days of fMRI and EEG; the importance of creating a relaxed ethos, where no one was afraid to be wrong or to accept the criticism of others. This was demonstrated particularly in recorded, mixed ability, group discussions of historical sources, when no adult was present (Cooper 1991, 2012: 89–100). All the children participated confidently. They took each other's arguments forward and when a less able child made an inference that others thought was flawed, they would point out why. 'No Frank, that can't be right look, because … .' And most interestingly, the children's suggestions were far more numerous and more imaginative, yet perfectly plausible, making some creative connections between other knowledge from inside and outside school, in the groups where no adult was present, compared with discussions of the same sources when observed by the teacher. The importance of problem solving, making connections collaboratively, in a relaxed atmosphere which nevertheless encourages peer criticism, is underpinned my own teaching, and runs throughout the case studies in this book. There is a tension between this approach and an emphasis on 'being on task – never day dreaming', 'planning for progression' and prescriptive time management of tasks which needs to be resolved.

CREATIVITY IS INTEGRAL TO HISTORICAL ENQUIRY

So, having a broad understanding of the concept of creativity, let us see how and why creativity and history are essentially interdependent. There is no single 'grand narrative of the past'. Closed societies manipulate the past to tell the story they find most expedient. But the ways in which historians find out about the past in open societies creates many, equally valid histories, told from different perspectives, which are dynamic. They change with time, as new information is found and with the changing preoccupations of societies. It is essential that children, from the very beginning, engage with the processes of historical enquiry, in embryonic ways, in order to understand this. They need to learn to have reasons to support an opinion, to listen to what others say, and perhaps change their point of view or recognise that there is often no single right answer. This is important to social and emotional as well as cognitive development.

The following section explores the relationship between creativity and the ways in which historians find out about the past, in order to write accounts of the causes and effects of changes over time. In Chapter 2 we shall consider the implications of this for children's learning in history.

Creativity and history: defining areas of enquiry, identifying problems and asking questions

Defining areas of enquiry

Popper (1945) said that there is not one history but many histories. He went on to say that only one of these is political history. Over the past hundred-and-fifty years history has become defined as an academic discipline and its scope has continuously broadened. Historians select particular aspects of the past within which they define problems to investigate, since the scope of history is so vast. Hexter (1961) calls this 'tunnel vision' but, as Elton (1967: 15) argues, issues and problems demand some sort of tunnel for clarification; the past must be sorted into aspects to become not only manageable but meaningful. Historians select areas to investigate which are of particular interest to them and to the times in which they write. They may be in-depth studies or 'broad brush stroke'.

In doing so they are selecting a particular perspective or range of perspectives. 'There are no ways of dealing with history which are intrinsically superior to others. Political history ... is not necessarily more jejune than social history – the analysis and description of the ways men have lived together in ordered groups' (Elton 1967: 16). Historians may focus on groups of people (Chartists, Suffragettes), on events or people they regard as significant, or they may be interested in women's history, ethnic groups, classes (the rise of the 'middle class', or of the 'working class'), the history of childhood, economic, social, political, military history, local history, national, global, the history of art or music or science. At certain points these histories may become collated, from the perspectives of different historians.

Identifying problems

Within their chosen area historians identify problems to investigate. For example, Rowbotham (1973) recognised that the position of women in nineteenth-century England was being challenged; her enquiry focused on by whom and in what respects. Fryer (1989) posited that racism was nurtured by those in power in the British Empire and investigated the negative effects of this on the colonies and positive effects on

British industry. Ferguson (2011) begins with the question, why, beginning in 1500, did a few small countries in Western Europe come to dominate the world, and sets out to investigate the reasons. Schama (2000, 2001, 2002) lists a number of questions which begin this investigation: to whom do we give our allegiance and why? Where do the boundaries of our community lie: home, village, city, tribe, faith? Has British history unfolded at the edge of the world or right at the heart of it?

Asking questions

Creativity, we said, begins with recognising problems and asking questions to address them. Questions in history are concerned with the past, what past societies were like, similarities and differences between them, how and why changes occurred over time, and the effects of those changes. Collingwood (1939) clarified this process. He saw historical enquiry as beginning with a complex of ordered, specific questions, based on empirical evidence. Through practical application in the field of archaeology he worked out this process. He began with specific questions about sources, the significance and purpose of objects, whether they be buttons, dwellings or settlements, to the people who made and used them. The sequence proceeded from what we know, to what hypotheses we can make about the society that produced them. (How was it made? Why? What was it used for? By whom? Where was it found? Are there others? And so on.) For example, Roman shoes found at Vindolanda, the equivalent of shoes made by Gucci or Lobbe today, tell us something about the social and economic structure of the fort. A letter from a first-generation 'Dutch' Roman at the fort, written in Latin, asking for underpants and socks from Rome, tells us something about the economic and transport systems of the Empire and the attitudes of the Dutch tribes to cold, clothes and culture.

The third stage of developing the questioning is to ask what else we should we like to know, in order to support, extend or contradict our hypotheses. Collingwood, for example, knew, from evidence, that a Roman wall from the Tyne to the Solway existed. He guessed that its purpose was to form a sentry walk with parapets as protection against snipers. He wanted to know if there were towers as a defence against vessels trying to land between Bowness and St Bees, in order to support his hypothesis. A resulting search found that towers did exist but had been forgotten because their purpose was not questioned. Elton (1967) explained that understanding what a society was like at different times enables the historian to form hypotheses about the causes and effects of changes.

Creativity, sources and possibility thinking in history

There are, of course, facts in history. There are dates and names for which there is incontrovertible evidence. And 'without simple details of chronology, genealogy and historical geography, history would have no existence' (Elton 1967: 60). But as soon as more complex facts and events are involved, in many cases the evidence is not clear-cut. Elton gives the example of an historian totalling the income and expenditure of Lancastrian kings from the Exchequer rolls, which appear to provide factual information, but his conclusions are factually incorrect because he is unaware that the records contain quantities of repeated and fictitious entries. He cites another example of facts being problematic. A medieval chronicler reports the deaths of hundreds of men in a flood and identifies those he deems most important but others may have identified people who are now forgotten. History then is not simply a collection of facts which cannot be questioned. Elton concludes (p. 63) that 'History is an unending search for truth, with the only certainty that there will be more to be said and that, before long, others will say it'.

Evaluating sources

As Collingwood (1939) explained, historians find out about the past through interpreting historical sources, any traces of the past that remain. Sources may be artefacts or visual sources (photographs, paintings, cartoons). They may be music, plans, diagrams or sites, maps, statistics, oral or written sources. Written sources include documents, laws and literature, inscriptions, advertisements, speeches, newspaper accounts, letters, diaries, place-names, records.

It is clear already that these sources are of varying status; possibility thinking is called on to consider how valid or reliable a source is before it is interrogated further. Artefacts may have been made for cult, symbolic or ceremonial reasons, which we no longer understand. To what extent do portraits or backgrounds flatter the sitter? Are they symbolic? What are we meant to understand from portraits of Queen Elizabeth I? Why do people in Victorian photographs look so grim, so artificially posed, so well dressed? Were the pictures of Victorian working people staged? To what extent do the country dances and folk songs and ballads collected by Cecil Sharpe in North America at the beginning of the twentieth century or the gypsy music of Ravel or 'traditional Celtic lullabies' reveal genuine folk music? Who drew up a particular plan, map or diagrams and what was their motivation? What was the reason some statistics were collected? On what evidence and for what reason did someone give an account of a past event? What is the purpose of an inscription on a tomb stone or statue? Advertisements may tell us much, but what was their intended purpose? All writing was intended for a reader so what was the intention and how objective is the source?

Making inferences about sources: probability and risk-taking

Since evidence is often incomplete, historians find out about the past by asking questions and forming hypotheses about sources, which are valid if they are based on reasoning, conform to what is already known and if there is no contradictory evidence. Making inferences requires a high degree of probability thinking, of open mindedness, exploring and evaluating different possibilities and being able to tolerate uncertainty. There may be no single correct answer or there may be several different, but equally valid answers. For example, the four post holes in the centre of an Iron Age house plan may be to support the roof (Bersu 1940), they may surround an open courtyard where animals could be kept (Clarke 1960), or they may be a free-standing tower for repairing the roof (Harding 1974). It may mean accepting that there are things which cannot be known; for example we do not know how much of a new style of agriculture the Romans introduced into Britain, how it was related to the old and so how British communities related to Roman villas, since no examples of Roman field patterns have been identified (Richmond 1955). It is no use asking what medieval peasants thought about religion if the only sources we have are government sources, or asking what people's living standards were in a given place and time, if there are no figures from which to construct an answer.

Creativity, sources and historical imagination

It was said above that the process of imagining possibilities makes possible new thoughts, allows us to conjecture worlds other than our own, to create mental images, sounds, pictures, feelings. The object of what is imagined is created, not discovered. Historical imagination then is essential in interpreting sources: in making inferences about how they may have been made and used, by whom and what impact they may have had on the lives of the people who made and used them. It is essential too in filling in the gaps, in explaining a sequence of events, or the thoughts and feelings, which underpin people's actions.

After historians have interpreted sources they generally combine them to create an account, an interpretation. Because sources are incomplete it is necessary to 'fill in the gaps' where nothing is known. This may mean explaining a sequence of events, the behaviour of an individual or a group, or how people may have though and felt in the past, in societies with different value systems from those of the historian, because they had different belief systems, economic and political systems or knowledge bases from those of today. This does not involve free-floating imagination or projecting oneself into the past, or sympathising with people in the past. The historian cannot share the thoughts and feelings of people in the past but s/he can attempt to explain what these might have been. 'Historical imagination' also involves attempting to understand different points of view of people in the past.

Historians have an implicit understanding of historical imagination which is usually not adequately articulated. Kitson Clarke (1967) pointed out that 'men's actions can be the subject of detailed research but what went on in their minds can only be known from inference'. Elton (1970) saw historical imagination as, 'a tool for filling in the gaps when facts are not available'. Ryle (1979) saw it as a means of cashing in on the facts and using them: ammunition shortage and heavy rain before a battle cause an historian to wonder about the hungry rifleman and the delayed mule trains. Thomas (1983) says what interests him about the past is what ordinary people thought, felt and believed.

Collingwood (1939: 7) attempted to clarify the relationship between interpreting evidence and interpreting the thoughts and feelings of the people who created it. He says, for example, that we know that Julius Caesar invaded Britain in successive years.

We can suppose that his thoughts may have been about trade, grain supply or a range of other possibilities and that his underlying feelings may have included ambition or career advancement. Nevertheless it must be supposed that people in the past acted rationally, there must be no contradictory evidence, inferences must be supported by evidence and by what is known of the period. Is it possible? Is it likely? Historians must also attempt to understand what an historical source may have meant to people at the time. What, for example, was the status of a torc, dating from 1000 BC, discovered in a Wiltshire field? Was it a votive offering, or part of a funeral ceremony or was it simply stored for safe-keeping?

Elton says (1967: 64) that

> the discovery of truth requires … imaginative reconstruction and interpretation. Evidence is the surviving deposit of an historical event … the historian must read, not only with the analytical eye of the investigator but also with the comprehensive eye of the story teller.

This requires inferring what the evidence tells us, based on informed standards of probability and knowing how it fits together. 'The evidence' he says, 'need not, by any means, supply answers to all the questions the historian would like to ask' (ibid.).

Creativity and creating accounts or interpretations in history

Different views were expressed above about whether the process of creative thinking must necessarily lead to creative behaviour and a product. It has been argued that, in history, seeing problems, identifying questions, designing enquiries, selecting and evaluating the validity of sources and interpreting sources are all creative processes in their own right. But historians generally undertake these processes in order to construct an account, an interpretation of the past. Initially this is usually a written account but historians also deliver oral accounts on television, advise on film reconstructions, dramas and museum and heritage reconstructions and take part in discussions and debates, as a result of their research. These accounts, for all the reasons discussed above, result from creative behaviour and are the products of creative thinking. And as a result of the previous analyses, historians' accounts may vary but be equally valid. As Elton says (1967: 95):

> Certainly the fact that historians conjecture and imagine beyond what they hold in the hand, and that they are right to do so, will keep argument and controversy alive; but argument and controversy are themselves controlled by the historian's principles of learning … . There is no final end to the study of history; the true and complete past can never be described because not enough of it survives and because what survives must be interpreted by human minds.

'Every generation writes history from its own point of view and every historian worth reading has his mind filled with attitudes of his own' (p. 103). Of course historians read, compare and contradict each other's accounts, which for the reasons given above, will vary.

There have been some interesting recent examples of historians challenging previous interpretations. Although the Spanish Civil War has been extensively written about, Paul Preston (2012) has gone well beyond previous historians in his chilling and meticulous record of slaughter and in doing so has destroyed both left- and right-wing myths about it. Interestingly a Spanish publishing company, Glenat, instead of offering readers of its comics a politically correct view of the Civil War, in which general Franco's forces are shown as 'bad guys' and the defeated Republicans as heroes, has decided that people are ready to see the subject from different perspectives. Although the Civil War remains a politically sensitive subject there have also been films which have re-examined the subject, for example, *Pan's Labyrinth* (del Toro), *Land and Freedom* (Loach) and *Soldiers of Salamina* (Javier Cercas).

Alexander (2012) contests the view that the Cold War was a conflict between Communism and democracy, which risked the potential of a nuclear war and was a necessary contest from which the United States saved us. He argues that American intervention made the world much more dangerous and that the threat was never real. He claims that Stalin needed a buffer against Germany in Western Europe but had neither the resources nor the wish to conquer Western Europe or America and actively opposed Communist revolutions around the world.

The power of a controlling the master narrative is evidenced in France's recent censorship of the account of the end of the Algerian war, which had been commissioned from Guy Perville, Professor of Contemporary History at Toulouse University, to commemorate Algerian Independence. This was an objective account of how an agreement to end hostilities led to murders, kidnappings and terrorist attacks by a right wing French group, who wanted the country to remain under Parisian control. However, when the book was printed the Ministry of Culture depicted the process of decolonisation as a popular triumph (Sage 2012). Recent evidence that has emerged about the end of British rule in Kenya, for example, will now doubt give rise to new accounts.

An example of reinterpretation from further back in time is the destruction of the indigenous Polynesian population (the Rapa Nui) of Easter Island. It was thought that this was caused by the felling of the trees in making and transporting the iconic great stone heads, and that this caused the collapse of the ecology, food ran out, and the population turned to cannibalism. There is evidence to support this theory. The interpretation became a moral for our time; that the Easter Islanders, like us, became obsessed with producing ornaments and fripperies and depleted scarce resources in doing so. However, in 2011 a British archaeological expedition (Richards *et al.* 2011), disputed this interpretation and provided convincing evidence that the people adapted by inventing a way of irrigating the land using a sophisticated rock technology. It was contact with Europeans that brought disease and slavery and decimated the population.

It is currently particularly pertinent that children learn from the beginning how alternative interpretations are possible and that there is no master narrative which can be politically manipulated. Michael Gove told the Conservative Conference (2011) that he wanted 'our island story' at the heart of a revised history curriculum. The historian David Starkey has claimed that Britain is a white monoculture and that immigrants should assimilate accordingly (Hurst 2011). Richard Evans, Regius Professor of Modern History at Cambridge, has responded by describing this approach as myth and memory rote learning, to feed children self-congratulatory, narrow myths of history (www.centurion2.wordpress.com/starkey-is-a-white-monoculture).

Creativity and creating interpretations through narrative and museum displays

Narrative can be seen as a personal representation of a story or account of something that happened. By 'emploting' events into a narrative we turn them into realities which we can make sense of. Bruner (1996) agrees that narrative is important in the construction and assimilation of knowledge. However, he says that, in order for narrative to be effective as a meaning-making tool it has to be read, made, analysed, understood and discussed. The story is constructed from its various parts which leads to stories being interpreted, rather than explained.

Hooper Greenhill (1999) talking about the educational role of the museum, says that meaning-making involves an encounter between the past and the present, especially in museums, where meaning is constructed in relation to objects and specific sites. It is not ready made. Posing questions and exposing discontinuities is preferable to presenting a perfect narrative; discovering connections and answering questions leads to insight. History, of course, involves narratives, those constructed by experts as well as by learners, but they need to be analysed, questioned, explored, discussed and interpreted, in relation to previous knowledge and experience, if they are to 'make meaning'; they are not simply explanatory.

Creativity and knowledge in history

It was said above that creativity is domain related and that it is not knowledge free. It has been shown first that creativity in history depends on understanding the processes of historical enquiry, what Ryle called 'knowing how'. It requires knowing how to recognise problems, select enquiries, frame questions which are at the heart of the discipline, investigate them and combine them into accounts of past times. It has been argued that each of these aspects of history involves creativity; possibility thinking and imagination. And it has been shown that creativity in each of these aspects of history depends on knowledge; some knowledge of what might be problematic, of whether creative inferences about sources and of 'filling in the gaps' of an incomplete account and about motivation are valid, based on whether they conform with what is already known, knowledge of what is reasonable and likely and some understanding that people in the past may have had different attitudes, beliefs and values and why. It requires creativity in seeing connections between the many aspects of history and pieces of evidence in creating accounts. Creativity therefore also involves knowledge of the discipline of history, of the kinds of questions historians ask and how they answer them.

Examination of the processes of historical enquiry shows why content and process are interdependent and so why there can be no single, static view of the past. History is dynamic, it is controversial, multifaceted and inclusive. It is the product and reflection of an open society. As Popper says, there is an indefinite number of histories of human life.

REFERENCES

Alexander, A. (2012) *America and the Imperialism of Ignorance: US Foreign Policy Since 1945*, London: Biteback.

Bersu, G. (1940) Excavations at Little Woodbury, Wiltshire, *Proceedings of the Pre History Society* 5(6): 30–111.

Bredo, E. (1994) Reconstructing educational psychology: situated cognition a Deweyan pragmatism, *Educational Psychologist* 29(1): 23–35.

Bruner, J.S. (1996) *The Culture of Education*, Cambridge, MA: Harvard University Press.

Carson, S., Peterson, J. and Higgins, D. (2003) Decreased latent inhibition is associated with increased creative achievement in high functioning individuals, *Journal of Personality and Social Psychology* 85: 499–506.

Clarke, R.R. (1960) *East Anglia: ancient people and places*, London: Thames and Hudson.

Collingwood, R.G. (1939) *An Autobiography*, Oxford: Oxford University Press.

Cooper, H. (1991) Young Children's Thinking in History, unpublished PhD thesis, London University Institute of Education.

Cooper, H. (2012) *History 5–11*, London: Routledge, pp. 88–100.

Craft, A. (2002) *Creativity and Early Years Education*, London: Continuum.

Craft, A. (2004) Creative thinking in the early years of education, in M. Fryer (ed.) *Creativity and Cultural Diversity*, Leeds Creativity Centre Educational Trust.

Craft, A. (2005) *Creativity in Schools: tensions and dilemmas*, Abingdon: Falmer.

Craft, A. and Jeffrey, B. (2008) Creativity and performativity in teaching and learning: tensions, dilemmas, constraints, accommodations and synthesis, *British Education Research Journal* 34(5): 587–84.

Craft, A., Jeffrey, B. and Leibling, M. (2001) *Creativity in Education*, London: Continuum.

Dewey, J. (1933) *How We Think*, London: Harrap.

Elliott, R.K. (1971) Versions of creativity, *Journal of Philosophy of Education* 5(2): 139–52.

Elton, G.R. (1967) *The Practice of History*, London: Sydney University Press, Methuen.

Elton, G.R. (1970) What sort of history should we teach, in M. Ballard (ed.) *New Movements in the Study and Teaching of History*, London: Temple Smith.

Ferguson, N. (2011) *Civilisation: the West and the Rest*, New York: Penguin Press.

Fryer, M. (ed.) (2004) *Creativity and Cultural Diversity*, Leeds: The Creativity Centre Educational Trust.

Fryer, P. (1989) *Black People in the British Empire – an introduction*, London: Pluto Press.

Gardner, H. (1999) *Intelligence Reframed: Multiple Intelligences for the 21st Century*, New York: Basic Books.

Gick, M. and Holyoak, K. (1980) Analogical problem solving, *Cognitive Psychology* 12: 306–55.

Harding, D.W. (1974) *The Iron Age in Lowland Britain*, London: Routledge and Kegan Paul.

Hexter, J.H. (1961) *Reappraisals in History*, London: Longmans.

Hooper Greenhill, E. (1999) *The Educational Role of the Museum* (Leicester Readers in Museum Studies), London: Routledge.

Hume, D. (1993) *An Enquiry Concerning Human Understanding* (E. Steinberg, ed., reprinted from the posthumous edition of 1777), p. 11, Cambridge: Hackett Publishing Company.

Hurst, G. (2011) Starkey: Britain is a white 'mono-culture', *The Times*, 15 November.

Jung-Beeman, M. and Kounios, J. (2006) The prepared Mind: neural activity prior to problem presentation by sudden insight, *Psychological Science* 17: 882–980.

Kant, I. (1989) *On Education* (trans. A. Churchton), London: Kegan Paul, Trent Trubner and Co.

Kenny, A. (1989) *The Metaphysics of Mind,* Oxford: Oxford University Press.

Kitson Clarke, G. (1967) *The Critical Historian*, London: Heinemann.

Langer, E.J. (1997) *The Power of Mindful Learning*, New York: Addison-Wesley.

Lave, J. and Wenger, E. (1991) *Situated Learning: legitimate peripheral participation*, Cambridge: Cambridge University Press.

Leach, J. (2001) A hundred possibilities: creativity, community and ICT, in A. Craft, B. Jeffrey and M. Leibling (eds) *Creativity in Education*, pp. 175–93, London: Continuum.

Levin, J. and Nolan, J.F. (2004) *Principles of Classroom Management: a professional decision-making model*, 4th edn, New York: Allyn and Bacon.

Montessori, M. (2007/1949) *The Absorbent Mind*, Radford, VA: Wilder Publications. (Originally published by Dell, New York.)

National Advisory Committee on Creative and Cultural Education (NACCCE) (1999) *All Our Futures: creativity, culture and education*, London: Department for Education and Employment.

Nemeth, C. (2004) The liberating role of conflict in group creativity, *European Journal of Social Psychology* 34: 365–74.

Nemeth, C. and Ormiston, M. (2007) Creative ideas generation: harmony versus stimulation, *European Journal of Social Psychology* 37: 524–35.

Passmore, J. (1980) *The Philosophy of Teaching*, London: Duckworth.

Piirto, J. (1992) (2nd edn 1998) *Understanding Those Who Create*, Tempe, AZ: Great Potential Press.

Popper, K. (1945) *The Open Society and its Enemies* (5th edn 1966, reprinted 1973), Vol. 2: 270, London: Routledge and Kegan Paul.

Preston, P. (2012) *The Spanish Holocaust: Inquisition and Extermination in Twentieth Century Spain*, London: Harper Press.

Qualifications and Curriculum Authority (QCA) (1999) *The National Curriculum at Key Stages 1 and 2: a handbook for teachers*, London: QCA.

Qualifications and Curriculum Authority (QCA) (2005) *Creativity: Find it. Promote it! – Promoting Pupils' Creative Thinking and Behaviour Across the Curriculum at Key Stages 1, 2 and 3*. Practical Materials for Schools, London: QCA.

Richards, C., Hamilton, S. and Welham, K. (2011) *Rapa Nui Landscapes of Construction*, Arts and Humanities Research Council funded project.

Richmond, I.A. (1955) *Roman Britain*, Harmondsworth: Penguin.

Rogoff, B. (1999) Cognitive development through social interaction: Vygotsky and Piaget, in P. Murphy (ed.), *Learners, Learning and Assessment*, London: Open University Press.

Rowbotham, S. (1973) *Hidden from History*, London: Pluto.

Ryle, G. (1979) *On Thinking*, Oxford: Blackwell.

Sage, A. (2012) Don't mention the war – at least, much of it, *The Times*, 25 January: 31.

Sandkuler, S. and Bhattacharya, J. (2008) Deconstructing Insight: EEG correlates of insightful problem solving. PLoSONe 3 (1) www.plosone.org/article/info:doi/10.1371/journal/pone.0001459

Schama, S. (2000) *A History of Britain, Vol. 1: At the Edge of the World*, London: Ebury Publishing.

Schama, S. (2001) *A History of Britain, Vol. 2: British Wars 1603–1776*, London: Ebury Publishing.

Schama, S. (2002) *A History of Britain, Vol. 3: The Fate of Empire, 1776–2000*, London: Ebury Publishing.

Scruton, R (1974) *Art and Imagination: study in the philosophy of mind*, London: Methuen.

Sonnenburg, S. (2004) Creativity in communication: a theoretical framework for collaborative product creation, *Creativity and Innovation Management* 13(4): 254–62.

Thomas, K. (1983) *Man and the Natural World*, London: Allan Lane.

CHAPTER 2

SUPPORTING CREATIVE LEARNING IN HISTORY

Hilary Cooper

Chapter 1 explored what we mean by creativity and argued that creativity is an integral part of the process of historical enquiry. In this chapter we shall consider the ways in which constructivist theories of learning demonstrate that children *can* engage in the processes of historical enquiry identified in Chapter 1, in increasingly complex ways, and how teachers can support them in doing so.

CHILDREN CAN ENGAGE WITH HISTORICAL ENQUIRY

Young children can, in embryonic ways, engage with the same processes of enquiry as academic historians. All these processes require creative thinking. Creative thinking involves considering a range of possibilities, imagination, risk-taking, seeing connections and having knowledge, both of the questions to ask and how to answer them and of the content of history. The validity of the suppositions young children make will inevitably be constrained by their immaturity and limited knowledge. However, if young children learn to think in this way the possibilities they suggest will become increasingly informed and valid.

CONSTRUCTIVIST LEARNING THEORIES, CREATIVITY AND HISTORY

Piirto (1992), writing about creativity in any subject, said that we would expect children to ask questions at a level meaningful to them and to have a depth of knowledge and understanding consistent with their experience and ability. Constructivist theories of learning, applied to historical enquiry, have shown how children can engage in this process, in ways which continuously build on their knowledge and understanding (Cooper 1991).

Jean Piaget, possibility, probability and argument

Piaget's work on cognitive development, his general theory of assimilation, equilibrium and accommodation and his work on argument, on probability and on sets and sequence can all be applied to historical enquiry. Interpreting historical evidence involves internal argument and debate with others, testing deductions and inferences against evidence from other sources and accepting other points of view. It means supporting opinions with arguments, accepting that there is not always a 'right answer', that there may be equally valid but different interpretations and that some questions cannot be answered.

Piaget's theory that thinking develops through stages, which are qualitatively different, can be criticised but remains broadly relevant. It posits a sequence in the development of argument. Initially thinking is dominated by intuitive trial and error and by a child's own experiences and feelings. At the next stage, concrete operations, a child is able to take in information from the tangible world, fit it into his or her own mental patterns – adjusting these sometimes to accommodate new information – and so store it, in order to use it selectively to address problems. The child is therefore able to form a reasoned premise and support it with a logical argument. At the third stage of formal operations the learner can think in abstract terms (if … then, either … or, when … is not, both … and … and), to weigh all the possible variables in an argument.

Piaget's and Inhelder's work on probability (1951) shows that, initially a child sees no difference between chance and non-chance. At a concrete level there is increasing awareness of what we can know and what can be 'guessed'. At a formal level the learner can reason about what is the certain and what is probable. This work, however, was done using only concrete material.

Piaget's work on language (1926) and logic (1928) seems the most helpful to apply to thinking in history. In *The Language and Thought of The Child* Piaget says that, at the first level the child is not concerned with interesting others and can leap from a premise to an unreasonable conclusion. Next a child is able to form a valid statement of fact or description. This is followed by 'primitive argument' in which a statement, deduction or inference is made, which goes beyond the information given, but the explanation is only implicit. At the next stage a child can justify and demonstrate an assertion by using a conjunction (since, because, therefore) but does not succeed in expressing a truly logical relationship. In *The Judgement and Reasoning of the Child* (1928) Piaget says that children eventually arrive at 'genuine argument' through frequent attempts to justify their opinions and avoid contradictions and are able to use 'because' and 'therefore' correctly. At a formal level learners can consider incompatible propositions.

Piaget's pattern of reasoning cannot be consistently applied to historical evidence for a number of reasons. Piaget and Inhelder themselves found that levels of thinking depend on the complexity of the questions asked (Peel 1960). Beard (1960) showed that the child's interest and involvement are important and Isaacs (1948) found very young children capable of reasoned argument if they understood how to tackle a problem and were interested in it, as did Margaret Donaldson (1978).

Donaldson examined the dichotomy she observed between children's capacity for reasoning in informal, everyday situations and in contrived, research contexts. Her aim was to destroy the assumption that most people are incapable of developing 'the pleasures of the mind' beyond immediate personal experience. She found young children capable of deductive and inferential reasoning but that their problem-solving depends on the extent to which they concentrate on language. Piaget's own case studies suggest that suggestions and criticisms make learners more aware of the process of problem-solving and accelerate the process.

There is also evidence that children are able to understand different viewpoints at an earlier age that Piaget suggested. Flavell (1985) suggests that children are capable of making inferences which enable them to see other points of view if they can see the need to. Cox (1986) differentiates between visual perspective-taking, conversational role-taking and pictorial representation and finds that in each instance, young children appear to be underestimated.

Jerome Bruner, creativity and the role of the teacher

Bruner saw the role of the teacher as presenting the key concepts and questions of a discipline, in forms which enable children to engage with them at any age. This involves formulating questions appropriately, building on former knowledge, skills and concepts through a spiral curriculum, and scaffolding children's learning so that they learn the thinking process at the heart of a discipline, the questions to ask and ways to investigate them. This enables them to apply them to new material.

He says (1963) that the questions children are asked, if they are to acquire a deeper understanding of historical principles, must be neither too trivial nor too hard and must lead somewhere, and that this needs particularly sensitive judgement in history, which is characterised by uncertainty, ambiguity and probability.

The questions must be applied to carefully selected evidence so that general principles can be transferred from specific instances, connections can be made and detail can be placed in a structural pattern which is not forgotten (see 'Making connections', p. 7). He said (1966) that material should involve physical experience (a site visit perhaps or making a model), visual experience (pictures, maps, diagrams) and symbolic experience, (when concepts are organised in language, mathematics, or maps). He does not see physical, visual and symbolic contexts for learning as necessarily sequential. He says that a child must be given the minimum information, but emphasis on how to go beyond it. Having selected the experience, the materials and the question carefully the child must be taught how to answer it.

Lev Vygotsky, concepts and creative thinking

Learning new concepts specific to history requires imaging, imagining, possibility thinking, forming hypotheses and risk-taking. Vygotsky (1962) showed how concepts which belong to a particular discipline are explicitly learned. Specialised concepts in history may be procedural (for example evidence, cause, effect), they may be concepts used by historians to describe an era (Victorian, Roman), words not exclusive to but central to history (beliefs, communication, trade) or words used in history but no longer in everyday use (villa, cross-bow, fort).

Concepts are learned through trial and error. Concepts of, for example 'castle' are formed by mentally storing images of different castles, to which new examples can be added (or discarded) as the understanding of the shared characteristics of castles is refined. Is a Peel Tower (a fortified house in the Scottish borders) a castle or a house? Abstract concepts which cannot be stored as images are learned through forming a hypothesis of what the concept means. For example, given a collection of Neolithic artefacts a person needs to ask a sequence of questions. What is an axe, a scraper, a flake or an awl used for? Why? How? Therefore their common purpose to facilitate a task by limiting the energy required? So they are all 'tools'. What is a harpoon a bow, a spear used for? How? Why? Are their shared characteristics to kill? So they all weapons. Then to which group does this implement belong?

Collaborative learning

We saw in Chapter 1 that discussion and working collaboratively are widely seen as fostering creativity. Vygotsky (1978) saw learning as essentially a social process. He saw learning as promoted by working with others whose understanding is slightly more advanced, until they can work on the task independently. Many subsequent researchers have argued that cognitive growth comes about through social interactions, either as the result of conflict of viewpoint or the interaction of different cognitive levels.

HOW CAN TEACHERS DEVELOP A CREATIVE ENVIRONMENT?

The analysis of the concept of creativity, of the processes of historical enquiry and of constructivist learning theory, show that history is an ideal subject for developing creative learning, indeed that it must be taught in this way. Craft (2000: 74) says that the humanities provide a model of imagination and creativity because they are in the large part about understanding human experience and behaviour. History is an interpretive field. It is about interpreting evidence to piece together events and perspectives of people who, more often than not, lived before our own times. So it may be surprising that the considerable literature on creativity rarely mentions history. The next section then, is not concerned specifically with history but is necessary if creative teaching and learning in history to flourish.

Teaching creatively and teaching for creativity

Craft *et al.* (2001) make a distinction between 'teaching creatively' (using imaginative approaches, making learning interesting and effective) and 'teaching for creativity' which aims to develop creativity in the learner. This involves passing control to the learner, valuing learners' innovative contributions, ownership and control, encouraging questions, debating contributions and being a co-participant in the learning.

However, Craft and Jeffrey (2004) and Craft (2004) undertook research which analysed the relationship between 'teaching creatively' and 'teaching for creativity' and showed that they are interdependent. They examined the four characteristics of creativity and pedagogy identified by Woods (1990) (relevance, ownership, control and innovation), through observations and interviews with parents and children in an early-years setting. They found that if children saw the learning as relevant this led to their sense of ownership of their knowledge, of the learning process and of their skills and understandings. The school emphasised children's ownership of the curriculum, the knowledge to be investigated and the contexts in which teaching and learning take place; a framework for creative learning. This sense of ownership gave children a sense of control, which enabled them to be expressive and to think of possibilities in responding to problems. And relevance, ownership and control led to innovation. Craft and Jeffrey added a new concept; the involvement of the learner in making decisions about what knowledge is to be investigated, which raised the question of how the learning process could be evaluated.

Classroom ethos

Lucas (2001) suggests four conditions for creating an environment in which creative learning can thrive. Learners need to be challenged, have goals set and also set their own. Negative stress should be eliminated; feedback should enhance self-knowledge, self-esteem and motivation. Learners should learn to live with uncertainty. Teachers cannot have all the answers but can offer structures and processes for thinking. This requires confidence from teachers and learners. Lucas stresses the need to support individual interests and to respect individual learners. Jones and Wyse (2004: 5–6) say that in creative lessons there is a different kind of relationship in the classroom, one that is not about an authoritative figure who holds all the answers, resources and power but one which is based on mutual respect, trust and above all enquiry.

Fostering creativity

Many writers stress the need for teachers to share in the process of enquiry, to model curiosity. Teachers need to be active participants in experiences which are exciting and interesting and to provide an environment full of ideas, materials and resources. History is about other worlds and classrooms can create other worlds. Bage (2000: 26) says that, 'leading learners willingly into such worlds is a moral act of the highest order'. Questions which encourage opinion or require justification encourage alternatives and higher-order responses. Pupils should have the opportunity to formulate questions, especially at the start of a history-led project. Bage (2000) says that this provides them with a personal view and a constant point to which their study can be referred and provides the teacher with a wealth of material, if the questions are used as a basis for project content. The children ask the questions and together pupils and teachers begin to answer them. Bage says that such models emphasise the social, emotional and personal aspects of learning. Cropley (2001: 73) also points out that feelings are involved in creativity: 'curiosity, determination, fascination, excitement, satisfaction, pride, anticipation, elation'.

Similarly if we ask what learners want from the history curriculum their answers are likely to embody some of the classic reasons commonly supposed for learning history. Children need to negotiate the time scale and outcomes for an activity, whether it will be a short discussion or a lengthy role-play.

The way we listen is crucial too. Explaining something confirms what has been learnt and can lead to further thinking and extending ideas. We need to encourage learners, give them confidence to try, to think for themselves and to form independent judgements. We must also develop pupils' commitment and resilience, and encourage them to recognise that there may be more than one way to solve a problem or interpret a situation. Learners need time to reflect. They need opportunities to learn outside as well an in school.

Classroom organisation

Collaboration is frequently seen as generating creativity. Cropley (2001: 150–156) claims that a 'creative, group atmosphere allows learners to think and to work without stress and anxiety' because it is co-operative rather than competitive. There is considerable evidence that working collaboratively enhances learning (e.g. Alexander 2008). However, it is also important that there are periods of reflection as well as periods of activity.

A longitudinal study (Ng 2003) identified ways in which the instrumentalism of the 'reforms' of the 1990s could be mediated to develop creativity. Methods of doing this included: highlighting specific vocabulary and concepts, and providing a balance between direct teaching and individual and collaborative work and between knowledge passed on and what is found out. Teachers and children share and create knowledge together, developing an exploratory workshop culture of learning. Team identity is important, bringing teachers and learners closer by sharing and building on their common knowledge. This emphasises commonalities between them rather than differences. Teachers model thought processes. Knowledge is not explored but 'grappled with'. Taking account of learner perspectives was seen as a human rights issue. It is claimed (Woods and Jeffrey 1996) that these approaches, working with pupils from Years 1–6 in forty-eight schools, were effective in developing learner's awareness of the learning process and enabled them to articulate their perspectives concerning these processes.

REFERENCES

Alexander, R.J. (2008) *Towards Dialogic Teaching: rethinking classroom talk*, Thirsk: Dialogos.
Bage, G. (2000) *Thinking History 4-14: teaching, learning, curricula and communities*, London: Routledge.
Beard, R.M. (1960) Nature and development of concepts, *Educational Review* 13(1): 12–26.

Bruner, J.S. (1963) *The Process of Education*, New York: Vintage Books.

Bruner, J.S. (1966) *Towards a Theory of Instruction*, Harvard MA: Belknap Press.

Cooper, H. (1991) Young children's thinking in history, unpub. PhD Thesis, London University Institute of Education.

Cox, M.V. (1986) *The Development of Cognition and Language*, Brighton: Harvester Press.

Craft, A. (2000) *Creativity Across the Curriculum: framing and developing practice*, London: Routledge.

Craft, A. (2004) Creative thinking in the early years of education, in M. Fryer (ed.) *Creativity and Cultural Diversity*, Leeds: Leeds Creativity Centre Educational Trust.

Craft, A. and Jeffrey, B. (2004) Teaching creatively and teaching for creativity: distinctions and relationships, *Education Studies* 30(1): 77–87.

Craft, A., Jeffrey, B. and Leibling, M. (2001) (eds) *Creativity in Education*, London: Continuum.

Cropley, A.J. (2001) *Creativity in Education and Learning: a guide for teachers and educators*, London: Routledge Falmer.

Donaldson, M. (1978) *Children's Minds*, London: Fontana.

Flavell, J.H. (1985) *Cognitive Development*, London and New York: Prentice Hall.

Isaacs, S. (1948) *Intellectual Growth in Young Children*, London: Routledge and Kegan Paul.

Jones, R. and Wyse, D. (2004) *Creativity in the Primary Curriculum*, London: David Fulton.

Lucas, B. (2001) Creative teaching, teaching creativity and creative learning, in A. Craft and B. Jeffrey (eds) *Creativity in Education*, London: Continuum.

Ng, A.K. (2003) A cultural model of creative and conforming behaviour, *Creativity Research Journal*, 15(2): 223–33.

Peel , E.A. (1960) *The Pupil's Thinking*, London: Oldbourne.

Piaget, J. (1926) *The Language and Thought of the Child*, London: Routledge.

Piaget, J. (1928) *The Judgement and Reasoning of the Child*, London: Routledge.

Piaget, J. and Inhelder, B. (1951) *The Origin of the Idea of Chance in the Child*, London: Routledge.

Piirto, J. (1992) (2nd edn 1998) *Understanding Those Who Create*, Tempe, AZ: Great Potential Press.

Vygotsky, L.S. (1962) *Thought and Language* (ed. and trans. by E. Hanfmann and G. Vakar), London and New York: Wiley.

Vygotsky, L.S. (1978) *Mind in Society: the development of higher psychological processes*, Cambridge MA: Harvard University Press.

Woods, P. (1990) *Teacher Skills and Strategies*, London: Falmer.

Woods, P. and Jeffrey, B. (1996) *Teachable Moments: the art of teaching in primary schools*, Buckingham: Open University Press.

PART II

CREATIVE APPROACHES TO ASPECTS OF HISTORICAL ENQUIRY

CHAPTER 3

INVESTIGATING ACTIVITIES USING SOURCES

Penelope Harnett and Sarah Whitehouse

This chapter presents a range of ways in which children may be encouraged to develop investigations in different contexts and through using a range of sources of information. It begins by discussing opportunities for developing creativity within historical activities and draws attention to different models of curriculum planning and organisation which may support such learning opportunities. Attention is drawn to the importance of engaging children's interest from the out-set with stimulating activities, which fire children's imagination. Two case studies are presented. The first analyses historical learning occurring with Key Stage 1 children engaged in a history day at their local school. In particular, the chapter draws attention to the importance of play, the value of hands-on experience in handling artefacts and the use of language in enabling children to explain their ideas. Case study 2 focuses on a visit of Year 5/6 children from three local schools to the University of the West of England to investigate the experiences of children living during the Second World War. The value of using a wide range of resources is analysed, together with developing historical investigations, which draw on a range of cross-curricular skills and activities. The chapter concludes with some discussion of issues arising from the case studies, including teachers' roles, sup-porting child-initiated learning and curriculum integration.

ORGANISING OPPORTUNITIES FOR CREATIVITY IN HISTORY: MODELS OF HISTORY CURRICULUM PLANNING

Curriculum organisation may vary within different schools and it is worthwhile considering different ways in which curriculum organisation may support creative historical investigations. History lessons may be planned for every week through-out the year. In this case children are engaging with history on a regular basis and it is possibly easier to plan for progression, as children's progress may be evaluated more frequently. However, this approach does present challenges. Teaching history within an isolated lesson may reduce opportunities for developing cross-curricular work and is also very reliant on there being enough time, within the weekly timetable, to accommodate history alongside all the other curriculum subjects.

Some schools choose to focus on history for particular terms in their school year. This may provide opportunities for greater in-depth study and also for cross-curricular work. However, such an approach to planning may be criticised in that children may forget or lose interest in their learning in history if there are long periods of time between study.

'History Days' offer intensive and exciting opportunities to stimulate children's interest in history. A school may decide to enhance history provision by incorporating a themed week, or day, which can be used to raise the profile of history or to develop a specific focus. History Days (or weeks) may occur at the beginning of a history project and be used as a stimulus for children's future work. If such days are sited in the middle of a topic, they may reinforce children's existing learning and provide a stimulus for further enquiries. At the end of a history topic, History Days may be used for reviewing and celebrating what children have learned.

Whichever form of organisation schools choose to adopt, account needs to be taken of developing progression in children's historical experiences. Her Majesty's Inspectors indicate that planning for progression continues to remain a challenge for many schools and that, in history particularly, attention needs to paid to the development of children's chronological understanding (Ofsted: 2011). Curriculum planning should also provide opportunities for children's creative engagement with the past. The two case studies in this chapter illustrate how different schools utilised History Days to support their work with children.

A HISTORY FOCUS DAY AT ASHLEY DOWN INFANTS SCHOOL

Planning

In this case study a focus day was used to enhance the provision of history and develop opportunities for an enquiry approach to learning. Planning a focus day affords wonderful opportunities to challenge pupils and extend their historical understanding. Tutors from the University of the West of England worked with the history co-ordinator at Ashley Down Infants School and were able to provide resources and to discuss teaching approaches with her. The relationship between the university and the school is reciprocal and there is recognition of the different knowledge and skills that practitioners may have and of how together this knowledge can contribute to an enhanced learning experience for children.

The school aimed to develop children's historical understanding and questioning. Opportunities to encourage talk for learning and creative approaches were sought throughout the day. The theme of the focus day, whilst being interesting and meaningful for children, also related to the curriculum and was underpinned by the concepts, questions, skills and enquiry processes which are at the core of history learning (Cooper 2011). The process of historical enquiry was supported by an enabling learning environment, providing children with opportunities to experience events and different ways of life. At Ashley Down Infants School, the teacher wanted the children to become immersed in experiential learning and to approach history in a creative way. Arguably the word creative has many different interpretations and when beginning planning for the day considerations took into account how creativity can help shape new knowledge, by aiding learners to apply existing knowledge in different contexts.

The role of the co-ordinator in planning this day was a key factor in its success; it was an opportunity for her, not only to support staff, but also to develop her own ideas for planning and organising the curriculum (Mcilroy 2011). In this case the co-ordinator's passion and enthusiasm for the subject were reflected in the success of the day. Coordinating a subject gives a chance for teachers to enhance their own experiences by leading and supporting others, and by implementing their own visions for their curriculum area.

Getting started: Davis Jones visits Ashley Down Infants School

The day started with a whole school assembly. As the children filtered into the hall their attention was focused on a stage, which had been arranged to resemble an archaeological dig. This created a sense of awe and wonder as the children were excited and there was a tangible atmosphere of expectation. Once the children were settled, the Indiana Jones theme tune began to play, which added to the children's heightened expectation that something unusual was about to happen. Pupils' curiosity, interest and attention were evident. The history co-ordinator dashed through the hall, dressed as an archaeologist and introduced herself to the children as Davis Jones, a brother of Indiana Jones.

The children were informed that 'Davis Jones' was an archaeologist and there followed a series of questions, which built on the children's existing knowledge, to prepare them for the acquisition of new information. Questions were carefully scaffolded and the youngest children from the Reception class were able to participate. Their answers were used to develop discussion between the older children. Key vocabulary was introduced and reinforced as part of this process. Children were asked, what did an archaeologist do? Their answers included 'they dig for treasure' and 'they find things out about the past'.

Developing sustained shared thinking

Children were then invited to become archaeologists. A variety of artefacts had been 'buried' in a sand tray for children to find. This gave the children the opportunity to work as 'experts'. The most ordinary objects can yield much historical evidence and also serve as a stimulus for the imagination. Bage (2010) discusses the fundamental link between imagination and fostering historical understanding. We cannot know everything that happened in the past. Consequently imagination is very important to support the consideration of a range of possibilities and interpretations. A range of artefacts for exploration is a helpful stimulus for developing investigative learning. Objects are especially useful with younger pupils, whose reading and writing skills are still not well developed but who are able to use and develop their oral communication skills (Vella 2010). Sustained shared thinking was also developed when the teacher modelled thinking and encouraged further thinking, by building on the children's initial ideas (Siraj-Blatchford and Mayo 2012).

Artefacts included both old and new items, which were used to assess children's understanding of the past. A shiny necklace was perceived by some as being new while anything which looked worn or dirty was interpreted as old and was classed as from the past. Similarly, interesting views were expressed on the value of artefacts. Children gasped when the necklace was dug up – it was shiny and looked very precious. However, it is the objects which look dirty, broken or chipped which can often be of more value! The following example illustrates some of the challenges which children face in establishing the age of objects and how teachers may encourage shared thinking.

Teacher: How do we know if the artefacts are from the past?

Child A: They look old?
            (Child A notes that appearance is an important factor in determining age.)

Teacher: What does old look like?
            (Teacher moves the discussion on further to ask about the appearance of 'old'.)

Child A: Different from new, not shiny, sometimes ripped or torn.
            (Child A compares object to what it is not – before finding words to describe old.)

Teacher: Can anyone think of an example of something from the past that is shiny or does not look old?
            (Teacher encourages the children to extend their thinking on what constitutes old.)

Child B: What about gold and silver or necklaces and rings?

Child C: Yes they are shiny but they could look old.
(Children supporting each other with their ideas. Child C challenges Child A's earlier assumptions relating shiny to new objects.)

Teacher: Thank you, so artefacts can look old or new, then how can we tell if they are from the past?
(Teacher summarises the discussion so far and raises a further question to extend children's thinking).

Child D: We need to find out more about them – maybe look at them in more detail?
(Child D offers suggestions for further investigations.)

The teacher's questions enabled the children to pool their information. The teacher encouraged children by building on the information they provided, indicating the importance of listening to children's ideas and fostering an environment where children can be encouraged to develop their thinking skills. In this case children had the opportunity to generate and extend their ideas and to use their imaginations to consider alternative perspectives. Careful attention to the use of particular vocabulary enabled the children to become familiar with key words and reinforced the concept that artefacts are sources of information, which can be used to find out about the past.

Enthusiasm was maintained, as other children were encouraged to draw and take photographs of the artefacts. Magnifying glasses were also used to encourage the children to look closely at the objects and to become 'history detectives'. The children were introduced to different interpretations, as they listened to each other's views about the artefacts, as sources of information about the past. Not all children shared the same views and they were beginning to realise that they could draw on their own imaginations to think about the artefacts. The open-ended approach to this activity was crucial to support an understanding of different viewpoints.

History Day activities at Ashley Down Infants School

Following the visit of Davis Jones in their school assembly, the children returned to their classrooms to begin their creative History Day. Table 3.1 shows a plan of the day, which includes learning intentions and activities for each year group.

■ **Table 3.1** Plan for History Day

Year group	Learning objectives/ key questions?	Activities to investigate the learning objectives
Reception	How are nurses today different from and the same as nurses in the past? What else do we want to find out about? (opportunity for child-initiated learning)	Teacher input on the nurses from the past/artefact sorting into large hoops. Role-play to extend children's thinking about people's lives in the past
Year 1	Investigate the life of someone from the past. What do we know about this person from looking at the artefacts?	Suitcase activity – exploring a range of artefacts from a real person in order to find out and to suggest what the person was like
Year 2	What can we learn from fossils?	Observing and drawing fossils in order to discuss what they can tell us about the past

The Reception class

In the Reception class activities there was a balance between teacher input and child-initiated and child-led learning. When enquiries are child initiated or child led, learning outcomes are often likely to be more varied and adults may need to prompt, cue or question appropriately.

History and role-play

As part of a topic of work, 'People who help us', children had been looking at people's different roles within their community, which included the school developing links with parents and community members. The importance of linking children's work with the locality and community is well known. In *Children, Their World, Their Education,* Alexander (2010) argues that the local dimension is a meaningful starting point and recommends that a curriculum should have 30 per cent of its content rooted in the locality.

Before the History Day a parent, who works as a nurse, had been into school to discuss her work with the Reception class. This was crucial in developing children's understanding of the role of a nurse for the history activity, which focused on Florence Nightingale, since it permitted the children to compare and contrast the role of nurses 'now and then'. Florence Nightingale is an example of a significant person whom children could learn about at Key Stage 1, alongside the lives of artists, engineers, explorers, inventors, pioneers, rulers, saints and scientists (DfEE/ QCA 1999).

Children were introduced to the topic by discussing what they already knew about the role of nurses, from the recent visit to the class. The whiteboard was used to present information about Florence Nightingale and the work of present-day nurses. Children were encouraged to generate questions about the similarities and differences between these lives with talking partners, which gave them time to think and to rehearse their ideas before they shared them with the whole class.

Following the teacher's introduction a group of children initiated their own learning in the role-play area. Play is an important aspect of early-years education, since it provides opportunities for children to make sense of new information, as they rehearse new ideas and knowledge, including key vocabulary. Play supports both cognitive and social development. It is highly motivating and has self-directing qualities, where children may take more control of their own learning.

Within the role-play area, three children chose to take on the role of the injured soldiers, while others in the group decided to be nurses. The children adapted the resources available and used a variety of props in their role-play. While the nurses set about 'cleaning up' the area, the soldiers enthusiastically played the role of the injured. Some plastic food was used to feed the soldiers. One of the children had taken on the role of Florence and proceeded to inform the other nurses that this food was dirty and could not be eaten by the soldiers. It is evident from their play that these children had absorbed much information about Florence and were rehearsing what they had learned in their play. Children clearly demonstrated their understanding of the role of Florence Nightingale and continued their play by swapping roles and moving in and out of different time frames – acting out roles of both nurses in the past and contemporary nurses. Highly motivated, these children persisted with their role-play for some time, pursuing a specific storyline (Moyles 2010: 5).

Play is the work of children

The children's role-play was observed carefully by the teacher, who noted different features of the children's learning (Table 3.2).

■ **Table 3.2** Teacher's analysis of the role-play at the hospital at Scutari

---

Decision-making

Children selected their own roles. Some were nurses and some played the role of injured soldiers. Key decisions were made by individual children on when to clean the hospital and how to feed the patients. Children made decisions on when they began to feel better.

Motivation

The role-play occupied the children for over 30 minutes. They spent time looking for different props, suggesting scenarios which might occur and acting out different scenes. There was evident enjoyment in the activities and children spoke enthusiastically about their play at the end-of-day plenary.

(Continued)

▪ **Table 3.2** (Continued)

Using prior knowledge

Children demonstrated knowledge of nurse's work; they fed their patients using bowls and spoons and bandaged their patients' wounds. The hospital ward was swept clean with brushes and one nurse spent time dusting to ensure that there were no germs. Nurses supported injured soldiers who had hurt their legs with the aid of crutches.

Symbolic representation

Different toys were used to represent 'Jimmy the Tortoise' (Jimmy was a pet tortoise at Scutari hospital).

Problem-solving

An interesting conversation between two nurses involved them thinking about how they could cook the food so that it was hot for the patients. One child wanted to use the role play cooker – but another child felt that they ought to build a fire 'cos they'd didn't have cookers in the olden days'; another child went to telephone the doctor before realising that there would not be a telephone in the nineteenth century – the problem of contacting a doctor was not resolved.

Adapting resources

Many props were adapted from objects in the classroom (e.g. Florence's lamp was a small cardboard box with a hole in it).

Using key vocabulary

Children were using the past tense as they described what they were doing in their play; they demonstrated some quite complex sentence structures – 'they wouldn't have had a cooker then'.

Some unexpected outcomes

Incidental information about the hospital at Scutari was provided by the teacher, which included information about Jimmy, the pet tortoise in the hospital at Scutari, which the children found fascinating. (His shell can be seen in the Florence Nightingale Museum! www.florence.nightingale.co.uk/cms) The children used a range of cuddly toys to represent 'Jimmy' in the nineteenth-century hospital ward, which they created. The story of Jimmy is a powerful reminder that it is often the use of small details or incidental information which children find particularly interesting and fascinating and which provide useful starting points for their learning. It is useful for teachers to consider how they might capitalise on such interests as these to develop children's learning further.

Year 1, Marjorie's suitcase: who was Marjorie and what can we find out about her life?

This activity encouraged children to engage with many historical skills including interpretation, historical imagination, chronology and also supported talk for learning. The suitcase loaned from the University of the West of England was full of artefacts, which had belonged to Marjorie, a real person from the past. Using artefacts that belonged to someone helps children with their historical understanding, as it enables them to personalise their learning about the past and consider what the lives of different individuals may have been like. The children were shown the closed suitcase and discussed what might be inside. The teacher gave the children very limited information about the suitcase, except they were told that it contained items from someone who lived in the past. They were asked to find out what they could about this person. This use of enquiry focused the children on the task in hand and they were again encouraged to become 'history detectives' and to use the artefacts as clues to discover Marjorie's identity.

To whom does the suitcase belong?

The children worked in pairs and each pair was able to handle an artefact. Handling an object evokes a real sense of the past; someone in the past has touched and valued this object – the object would have felt the same when it was held by hands in the past as it does today. After exploration the pairs were encouraged to work together to find out more about the owner of the objects. The teacher's role was as a facilitator and she did not take part in the activity. The following transcript illustrates the sophistication of some of these children's historical thinking.

Children's ideas about Marjorie

Do you think it is a boy or a girl?

It is a girl because it has pretty things. *(Drawing conclusions from the information and justifying a conclusion.)*

Oh look it has a diary – I wonder if it has a name inside? *(Raising a historical question to promote further historical enquiry.)*

What do you think she did? *(Another historical question to promote further enquiries.)*

Maybe she worked in a shop isn't that one of the jobs that people used to do? *(Speculative language – use of the word maybe. Draws on existing historical knowledge to support an hypothesis.)*

Do you think she was famous?

Look at these gloves, do you think she would mind if we tried them on? *(Awareness that working with a 'real' person's objects and empathy with the owner of the objects – would she mind if we tried them on?)*

On they are really lovely – be careful though! *(Care taken in handling historic objects.)*

Look, here is an old book, it has a name in – I can't read this – the writing is really old but it begins with the letter M. Miss can you help me read this name – Marjorie, the suitcase belongs to Marjorie, but who was she? *(Draws conclusion about the name of the owner from historical source – raises further historical questions.)*

This activity was successful for a number of reasons. First, the approach adopted by the teacher in encouraging the children to find out who the person was absorbed the children. Second, the use of artefacts fostered children's curiosity, and lastly the collaborative approaches enabled children to talk through their ideas and work together to draw conclusions. This open-ended approach to interpretation and using imagination fostered creativity within the classroom.

Year 2: Using fossils

It is useful to help children to appreciate the 'bigger picture of history' where the earth's story is told from the beginning to the present day; exploring fossils from very long ago is a useful starting point. This investigation related well to the Year 2 children's current topic dinosaurs. A range of fossils was provided for exploration and also a variety of non-fiction texts, which the children made use of when they needed additional information. The children were provided with magnifying glasses to encourage their observational skills and to look for small details. Key vocabulary was introduced, including *ammonite*, *excavation*, *fossil*, *palaeontologist*, *archaeology* and *archaeologist*. It was evident that children were becoming familiar with this vocabulary, as they used it in discussions with their talking partners.

The magnifying glass for close observation work was crucial as it was through this the children were able to make detailed observations. Links were then made with their previous work on dinosaurs where they had explored a range of dinosaur skeletons or fragments of skeletons. The discovery of partial skeletons enabled the children to appreciate that we do not always have complete evidence about the past. Similarly, not all the fossils were complete and children had to use their imaginations to 'fill in' the missing pieces when they sketched their fossils.

Ashley Down Infants History Day – conclusions

Throughout the day children learned through first-hand experiences and were encouraged to engage in historical interpretation. Open-minded approaches to historical interpretation were in evidence and children were able to appreciate alternative viewpoints.

Handling and exchanging views on artefacts encouraged the children to learn how to think and communicate like historians, to consider different possibilities, defend their own points of view, listen to the views of others and perhaps understand that there is not always a known answer (Bage: 2010). Listening to children's conversations was also useful for assessing children's historical understanding.

CHILDREN VISITING THE UNIVERSITY OF THE WEST OF ENGLAND FOR THE 'BLITZ EXPERIENCE'

In contrast to the previous case study, the Years 5 and 6 children, who came to the University of the West of England for the 'Blitz Experience' had already learned a great deal about World War II in their own school. Their visit to the university was designed as an enrichment activity, which drew on what the children already knew and lead them on to further enquiries. Children were able to engage with a rich range of artefacts and sources of information and to become fully immersed in the experience. This provided them with opportunities to deepen their understanding of this period of time and to have a more holistic experience of what it might have been like living then. Ofsted comments on the success of such approaches, noting that 'Learning outside the classroom was most successful when it was an integral element of long-term curriculum planning and closely linked to classroom activities' (Ofsted 2008: 5).

The current National Curriculum (DfEE 1999) supports learning outside the classroom through school visits and much research indicates the benefits of such learning opportunities. The Council for Learning Outside the Classroom acknowledges, 'The "places" where learning happens can have a significant effect on how a young person engages with a subject or an idea' (2012). Visits outside the classroom encourage a focus on the processes of learning; knowledge is acquired through purposeful and meaningful activities which motivate and interest young learners.

Getting started: Preparation for the 'Blitz Experience' at the University of the West of England

Prior to the visit, detailed information was sent to schools about the purpose of the day. The children were asked to arrive in role; boys dressed in short trousers, girls in dresses and with items of other clothing, which they had researched as being typical of the period. The children were expected to research a 'blitz' packed lunch and bring it along for the day. Consequently, before the day had begun excitement was already generated and children's attention had already been drawn to aspects of children's lives in World War II, which were different from or similar to their own. Wearing different costumes helped the children get into role. Often the addition of an item of clothing, a hat or cloak, for example, or the possession of a particular artefact, may make someone act differently. In this case the children brought boxes for gas masks strung around their necks. They kept on losing them throughout the day, which was a reminder to them of how tedious it must have been for children in wartime to be continually checking that they had all they needed with them.

When the children arrived at the university they were met by the billeting officer, a member of staff dressed in uniform, who was flanked by trainees who were to work with the children during the day. The trainees were all dressed in wartime costumes, which related to the roles they were going to play. A roll call was held and the children were allocated to their different groups to begin the day's activities. Already therefore, before the activities had really begun, the children were beginning to recognise that they were going to be learning about a time different from their own.

Overview of the activities of the Blitz Day: planning with pre-specified learning objectives in mind

This project was planned to reflect the different types of thinking identified in Bloom's Taxonomy (see Figure 3.1), which are utilised in the PGCE Primary Integrated Learning Matrix at the University of the West of England (Table 3.3).

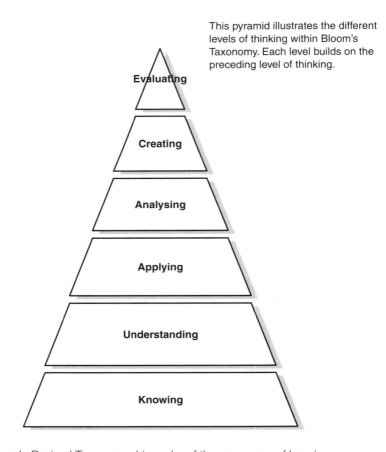

This pyramid illustrates the different levels of thinking within Bloom's Taxonomy. Each level builds on the preceding level of thinking.

Evaluating

Creating

Analysing

Applying

Understanding

Knowing

Figure 3.1 Bloom's Revised Taxonomy: hierarchy of the processes of learning

Source: Adapted from Atherton (2011)

Table 3.3 How students' learning in history can combine the processes of learning with the knowledge to be learned, in a cross-curricular way

BLITZ: Local history

PGCE Primary Integrated Learning Matrix

Subject specialism[a]	BLITZ workshops	Bloom's Taxonomy: Six thinking levels					
		Knowing	Understanding	Applying	Analysing	Creating	Evaluating
L&L, ML	Codes and Ciphers	Learn Morse code, semaphore from instruction and practice. Find out about the Caesar code and work at Bletchley Park	Receive non-verbal messages and interpret. Find patterns in codes and begin to understand substitution	Communicate in a range of ways using non verbal means. Send simple messages in Morse and semaphore	Explore a number of different codes and ciphers. Choose one and develop your own version	Imagine you are trapped in enemy territory. Send a message in your code in French/Spanish to the French resistance	Try to crack the code! Send a message successfully in Morse. Send a message in semaphore
CA, ML	Propaganda!	Find out about the Ministry of Information	Contrast and compare a wide range of wartime posters from great Britain, France and Germany, to begin to understand the meaning of propaganda and how posters and spoken messages convey meaning	Choose a poster theme. Choose images/fonts and sketch out your idea using block templates to help with layout. (Block templates are a range of shapes and sizes in card to help with positioning of text, images, etc.)	In pairs discuss each other's posters sketched ideas. Suggest improvements and modifications	Construct poster using your developed and modified ideas. • Colour • Fonts • Images • Messages	Display for other children to see. • Feedback/commentary • Yellow sticky stars/dots • Comment card

(Continued)

Table 3.3 (Continued)

Subject specialism[a]	BLITZ workshops	Bloom's Taxonomy: Six thinking levels					
		Knowing	Understanding	Applying	Analysing	Creating	Evaluating
S and D&T	Dr Carrot's Cookery Club	Recognise and name the range of vegetables used in wartime. Reflect on your likes and dislikes and the food you like to eat (familiar foods)	Begin to understand what is needed in a healthy diet comparing wartime rations to today's diet	Weigh and measure using scales, spoons and cups. Weigh dry and liquid ingredients. Apply bridge and claw methods to cut vegetable accurately and safely. Make soups and pies to wartime recipes	Explore recipes for wartime soups and pies. Identify the ingredients and their functions in the recipe and how they match to the 'eat well plate'. Identify key methods cooking: conduction, convection, radiation and microwave.	Design your own soup/pie recipe and make	Taste test food dishes and evaluate in a range of ways for taste, aroma, texture (mouth feel) appearance (TATA)
S and D&T	Make Do and Mend Workshop	The war effort. Squander bug. Mrs Sew and Sew. New from old	Clothes rationing. What was collected and recycled – compare and contrast to today. 6 R's	Recycle a sock to make a hat. Design and make a decoration for the hat badge or flower. Embroider initials or name	Sock material. Simple paper pattern. Sewing and construction methods	Hand sewing skills. Cutting. Machining	Model hats for others to see. 'Fashion Show'. Photo montage of hats
L&L	Evacuation	Why were children evacuated? Where did they go? (map). Oral histories	Evacuee suitcases. Reading from *Goodnight Mr Tom*	What would you put in your evacuee suitcase?	Exploration of contents. Use of contemporary images to help identify how the children felt	Imagine you have been evacuated – write a postcard home and post in letter box	Display of postcards for other children to read

Subject specialism[a]	BLITZ workshops	Bloom's Taxonomy: Six thinking levels					
		Knowing	Understanding	Applying	Analysing	Creating	Evaluating
H	Gas Masks, Shelters and Staying Safe	Find out about: The Anderson shelter The Morrison shelter Gas masks Personal protection	Spend time in the Anderson shelter to experience Blitz conditions (sound, darkness, cramped conditions)	Role play with air raid warden in costume The air raid	How safe were shelters? Did we need our gas masks? Using contemporary images of shelters to analyse and discuss above. How did they feel in the Anderson shelter?	What would you take to the shelter?	In pairs discuss the lists of items you would take to the shelter and why
S and D&T	Digging for Victory	Visit the Dig for Victory garden and find out about the planting schedule and crop rotation	Compare the range of crops with what is available today. Visit the herb bed and the flowery fringe. Why were they important?	Make simple digging tools to use in a garden or with a grow bag	Learn how to use a range of tools, equipment and the processes for working with resistant materials	Make a successful tool	Try out and test in the garden or on the grow bag
L&L, ML	The Street BLITZ Display	Watch and listen to the DVD about the Bristol Blitz	Handling the contemporary artefacts (clothes, plates, glasses, home front kitchen) and examining the photographs taken during the Bristol Blitz	Using the Home Front kitchen identify how it is different to the one at home. What can they see?	What did the Blitz mean to the people of Bristol?	Write a newspaper report of the Blitz imagining that you were an eye witness. Use the contemporary images to help you and use the factual information such as the number of people who lost their lives	Create the front page of the *Evening Post* using your accounts. Give out to the other children to read

(Continued)

■ Table 3.3 (Continued)

Subject specialism[a]	BLITZ workshops	Bloom's Taxonomy: Six thinking levels					
		Knowing	Understanding	Applying	Analysing	Creating	Evaluating
H	Lyon's Corner House	What were the Lyon's Corner Houses and why were they important in the war?	Wartime diet menus with traditional recipes and wartime recipes	Tea for Two Order from the nippy waitress and the wartime menu Table manners	Serving tea and taste-testing the sandwiches and cakes	Compare a wartime tea menu with a menu from a fast food cafe. Create your own menu	Evaluation card for the tea
CA	Local Defence Volunteers (LDV): The Home Guard	The role of LDV Issue of arm bands Warden's hut and office	Roles: Captain Sergeant Corporal Private Drill task with mock weapons	Air craft recognition task	Why was this war effort important? Who took part? How were they equipped? What did they do?	Wallscourt Home Guard LDV – write a short play to highlight the important work of the LDV. Perform and record play on DVD to show back at school	Aircraft recognition test

a CA: Creative Arts; D&T: Design and Technology; H: History; L&L: Language and Literacy; ML: Modern Languages; S: Science.

In preparation for the Blitz Day trainees had gathered a wide range of resources for children to work with and organised different learning areas throughout the Department of Education building. For example, one area became Lyon's Corner House, set out with tables and chairs. Tablecloths covered the tables, which were set out with tea sets, cake stands, menus and serviettes. Around the walls of the area, various posters warned customers of wartime dangers and how to take care of themselves. There were also pictures and photographs of wartime cafes. In another area, children were able to handle different household objects; scrubbing brushes, buckets and bars of soap; to read wartime comics and to play with old toys; to try on different uniforms and to work out how the air-raid siren worked. There were displays of children's clothes to look at together with photographs and posters. In one area children were gathered to watch a DVD of actual footage, taken of the Blitz in Bristol. Elsewhere a living room was created for children to unpack their evacuee's suitcase and to write a letter home to their parents. Outside there was a Dig for Victory garden with vegetables growing and at the bottom of the garden a fully equipped Anderson shelter.

The children were presented with a good range of resources, which the university had gathered to support learning about the Bristol Blitz. It is not always easy for schools to obtain artefacts, although many museums now have loan boxes to support learning in the classroom. For periods of history which are not so far away in time, parents, other family members and members of the local community may be able to lend particular objects. There is always the concern that objects might be harmed and it is important that children learn to respect and handle such objects carefully. Replicas of objects also might be used, which can lead to fascinating discussions with children about a new object showing signs of wear representing an old object made in the past!

Whilst the focus of the day was on the development of historical understanding, each activity also provided opportunities for learning in other subject areas. For example in Dr Carrot's Cookery Club, the children had to identify and discuss ingredients for soups and pies. They were taught how to chop food safely, to cook and to evaluate what they had made. Another group extended their knowledge of design and technology, as they made a small tool to use for planting seeds in the Dig for Victory garden.

In the Make Do and Mend Workshop, children made their own hand puppets from socks. They learned how to sew with simple stitches and how to stitch buttons on for eyes. All were engrossed in the activity and for several children it was their first encounter with needle and thread. The activity also provided opportunities for relaxed conversations about the War as the children sewed and discussed their designs.

I'm making mine with a long tongue 'cos it's very hungry and is going to eat everyone up ... it's going to start with yours [*lunges at another child's puppet*].

Mine's getting a tail, which it swings about to knock over anyone who gets in its way.

Do you think that they made puppets like this? If they didn't have many clothes p'raps they couldn't cut up their socks?

I'd miss my Xbox – do you think children living in the war would have liked Xboxes?

No – 'cos they didn't have playstations then.

But if they did – would they miss them?

We have here a conversation where children are in control of their talk and the subjects for discussion. Sewing the puppets in relaxed surroundings opened up different possibilities for children to consider what life might have been like during the war. The teacher was not prompting them. The questions, which the children raised, occurred naturally in their conversations. Importantly too, they were their own questions – deriving from a real desire of wanting to know the answer.

Developing children's sense of empathy

The activities were planned to enable children to experience a range of activities associated with daily life at the time. Making soups and pies, taking tea at the Lyon's Corner Cafe and visiting the Dig for Victory garden all provided opportunities for children to consider what food was available at the time. Tasting the wartime recipes was an effective way of helping children understand the challenges of cooking with limited ingredients and the strange flavours which were created – something which could never have been fully understood by simply reading about them in a book.

The Anderson shelter, which was set up in the university grounds, was equipped with blankets, water bottles, an oil lamp and some old comics to keep the children amused. At the sound of the air raid siren children squashed into the tiny space on the bed and the floor. It was anticipated that they would grasp some of the discomfort, which living and sleeping in the shelter involved. They did ... and they grumbled.

But they also thought it was fun! It was not possible to generate the real sense of fear which wartime children must have felt when they heard the bombs falling, the cries of people injured and the smell of the smoke and buildings burning. The question remains then – to what extent can those living in the present identify and empathise with those who lived in the past?

Not all historians believe that it is possible to empathise with the past (e.g. Jenkins and Brickley 1989; Jenkins 1991). Harris and Foreman-Peck (2004: 106–108) identify specific challenges in teaching empathy to children; namely children have less knowledge and experience to draw upon; they may be at a 'less advanced stage in their own moral development'; and third, 'they need a quite sophisticated grasp of historical evidence to see that some analogies are invalid'. However, despite these challenges, they do conclude that it is important for children to see 'things from someone else's viewpoint' and recommend that 'activities that engage and puzzle pupils are important'.

Thinking creatively about history and different literacy texts

During the day, children had opportunities to engage with a range of texts and to consider writing for different purposes. They looked at instructions and different forms of persuasive writing and propaganda. Children read information texts and identified significant points; they looked at how Michelle Magorian used words to describe the experience of evacuation in *Goodnight Mr Tom* (Magorian 1981), and discussed different texts on various historical sources available – menus, posters, adverts, food labels and army equipment.

This range of texts introduced children to the importance of context and provided opportunities for them to critically analyse their purpose and ways in which they had been constructed. In our twenty-first century lives we are surrounded by texts and images which permeate our thinking and ways of seeing the world. We do not always step back to analyse all the materials we are confronted with. In this respect, opportunities provided by historical texts may be useful in heightening our awareness and support critical engagement with contemporary contexts and media as well as texts constructed in the past.

REFLECTIONS AND QUESTIONS ARISING FROM THE CASE STUDIES

How was the children's initial interest stimulated?

The two case studies illustrate ways in which teachers sought to engage and to stimulate the children's interest in the activities which were to follow. The arrival of Davis Jones at Ashley Down Infants and dressing up in 1940s costumes served as hooks to inspire children to engage with the learning and to motivate them towards the different activities during the day. Other examples of stimulus materials might be an extract from a diary, a game, an artefact – indeed anything which gets the children interested and motivated in their future learning.

How can the tension between pupil-initiated learning and specified learning activities be resolved?

There is a perennial tension between identifying learning objectives in advance and trying to keep activities sufficiently open for children to be able to develop their own creative learning opportunities. This challenge has a long tradition in primary education dating back to the work of Jean Jacques Rousseau in the eighteenth century. In his book, *Emile*, Rousseau states that educators are always planning learning with the future in mind – towards the adult the child will finally grow up to be. He argues against this and claims that childhood is an important stage in development and that children should learn by finding out for themselves. Rousseau never claims that it was easy to undertake this form of 'natural education' but he emphasises that it is an important goal which should be attempted (Rousseau 1979).

Many educators have been influenced by Rousseau. Pestalozzi and Froebel both argue that learning should develop through close observation of the child and state the important role teachers have in guiding children through a range of experiences. Their thinking informed much of the progressive child-centred policies for primary-aged children in England in the twentieth century. So the Report of the Consultative Committee on the Primary School (Hadow Report) argues 'that no good can come from teaching children things that have no immediate value for them, however highly their potential or prospective value may be estimated', and states 'that the curriculum should be thought of in terms of activity and experience rather than of knowledge to be acquired and facts to be stored' (Board of Education 1931: 74–75). Over thirty years later, a similar philosophy was endorsed by the Central Advisory Council for Education, with the dictum, 'at the heart of the education process lies the child' (CACE 1967: para. 9).

However, there are challenges in developing curricula and learning solely on children's interests. Dewey (1990) reminds teachers that, whilst recognition of children's interest is necessary, it is also important to introduce children to particular subject knowledge created through the centuries, as humans have grappled with different problems and experiences. The teacher's role is one of providing a learning environment where children can engage in activities which lead them to utilise specific skills, to acquire particular knowledge and to have an understanding of its relevance.

Parallels may be drawn here with the structure of the National Curriculum (DfEE 1999), which describes how historical knowledge should be learned through the development of specific historical skills and concepts. So encouraging children to think 'historically' requires both the provision of historical knowledge and the acquisition of certain subject specific skills.

Integrating history with a range of subject areas

The key features of effective learning are the processes of learning (Figure 3.1) and the knowledge to be acquired. Table 3.3 shows how these key features were integrated in a topic on World War II. Bloom's sequence of levels may act as a guide and be useful both as a planning tool and as a tool for evaluation. To what extent may pre-specified learning outcomes support creativity?

The planning grid (Table 3.3) also illustrates how children's learning in history can be enhanced through a range of subject areas. In the past, history was often seen as a literary subject; children learned history through the stories in their reading books and through listening to teachers read them stories in the classroom. Indeed the advice offered by the Board of Education for teaching in 1927 observed that whether the subject was called history or literature was immaterial. It was the essence of the stories which was important (Board of Education 1927). Stories and narratives are important, but children are entitled to be introduced to a range of other sources of information to help them learn about the past as well. Moreover, as the grid illustrates, different subject areas may also contribute to children's historical understanding.

A key argument for developing an integrated curriculum is that children do not necessarily think in terms of subject areas and that knowledge cannot be so neatly compartmentalised. Prior to the introduction of the National Curriculum in 1991 there were many debates on how the curriculum might be organised in primary schools – through themes or topics; children's interests; around problem-solving or around key concepts (Schools Council 1983). A further influential document published by HMI in the series Curriculum Matters, *The Curriculum from 5–16* suggested that the curriculum should be planned around areas of learning and experience and elements of learning (DES 1985). The areas of learning were viewed as analytical, planning tools, representing different modes of knowledge and understanding, not necessarily subject related. They included: aesthetic and creative; human and social; linguistic and literary; mathematical; moral; physical; scientific and spiritual areas. Such ways of organising the curriculum however, were at odds with the subject based structure of the National Curriculum introduced in 1991 and gradually began to disappear. However, more recently, schools have been seeking more creative ways of integrating subjects and experiences (Harnett and Vinney 2008). Drawing on extensive research studies concerned with primary education, Alexander proposes that the curriculum should be planned with reference to aims concerning the individual, the self, others and the wider world, and to learning, knowing and doing. Alongside these aims, specific domains bringing together knowledge, skill, disposition and enquiry should be used as starting points for curriculum planning (arts and creativity; citizenship and ethics; faith and belief; language, oracy and literacy; mathematics; physical and emotional health; place and time and science and technology) (Alexander 2010: 265–66).

CONCLUSION

In this chapter we have considered case studies to develop different historical enquiries. Activities encouraged questioning and probability thinking; children were required to use their historical imagination and use language to explore different viewpoints. Ways in which creativity could be fostered through the learning environment were exemplified.

REFERENCES

Alexander, R. (ed.) (2010) *Children, Their World, Their Education. Final Report and Recommendations of the Cambridge Primary Review*, London: Routledge.

Anderson, L. W. and Krathwohl, D. R. (eds) (2001) *A Taxonomy for Learning, Teaching and Assessing: A revision of Bloom's Taxonomy of educational objective*, New York: Longman.

Atherton, J.S. (2011) *Learning and Teaching: Bloom's Taxonomy*. Online, UK: www.learning andteaching.info/learning/bloomtax.htm (accessed 3 October 2012).

Bage, G. (2010) History, artefacts and story telling in the 2011 Primary Curriculum, *Primary History* (54): 23.

Board of Education (1927) *Handbook of Suggestions for Teachers*, London: HMSO.

Board of Education (1931) *Report of The Consultative Committee of the Primary School* (The Hadow Report), London: HMSO. www.educationengland.org.uk/documents/hadow1931/index.html (accessed 17 April 2012).

Central Advisory Council for Education (England) (CACE) (1967) *Children and Their Primary Schools* (The Plowden Report), London: HMSO.

Cooper, H. (2011) Children's thinking: Development psychology and history education, *Primary History* (57): 8.

Council for Learning Outside the Classroom (2012) www.lotc.org.uk/what-is lotc (accessed 25 February 2012).

Department for Education and Employment (DfEE) (1999) *The National Curriculum. Handbook for primary teachers in England. Key Stages 1 and 2*, London: DfEE/QCA. www.education. gov.uk/publications/eOrderingDownload/QCA-99-457.pdf (accessed 24 April 2012).

Department of Education and Science (1985) *The Curriculum from 5–16. Curriculum Matters 2. An HMI Series*, London, HMSO. www.educationengland.org.uk/documents/hmi-curricmatters/curriculum.html (accessed 27 April 2012).

Dewey, J. (1990) *The School and Society* and *The Child and the Curriculum*, Chicago: Centennial Publications of the University of Chicago.

Harnett, P. and Vinney, M. (2008) What has happened to curriculum breadth and balance in primary schools? In Harnett, P. (ed.) *Understanding Primary Education. Developing Professional Attributes, Knowledge and Skills*, London: Routledge.

Harris, R. and Foreman-Peck, L. (2004) 'Stepping into other peoples' shoes': Teaching and assessing empathy in the Secondary History Curriculum, *The International Journal of Historical Learning, Teaching and Research* 4(2): 98–111. www.history.org.uk/resources/primary_resource_4858_150.html (accessed 30 April 2012).

Jenkins, K. (1991) *Re-thinking History*, London: Routledge.

Jenkins, K. and Brickley, P. (1989) Reflections on the empathy debate, *Teaching History* 55: 18–23.

Magorian, M. (1981) *Goodnight Mr Tom*, London: Kestrel Books.

Mcilroy, C. (2011) Planning for history: The coordinator's perspective, *Primary History* (57): 38–40.

Moyles, J. (2010) *The Excellence of Play* (3rd edn), Buckingham: Open University Press.

Ofsted (Office for Standards in Education) (2008) *Learning Outside the Classroom. How far should you go?* London, DfES. www.ofsted.gov.uk/node/2258 (accessed 24 April 2012).

Ofsted (2011) *History for All*, Available from www.ofsted.gov.uk/resources/history-for-all, publication 090223 (accessed 26 April 2012).

Rousseau, J.-J. (1979) *Emile, or On Education* (trans. A. Bloom), New York: Basic Books.

Schools Council (1983) *Primary Practice. A Sequel to the Practical Curriculum*, Schools Council Working Paper 75. London: Methuen Educational.

Siraj-Blatchford, I. and Mayo, A. (2012) *International Reader, Early Childhood Education*, London: Sage.

Vella, Y. (2010) Extending primary children's thinking through the use of artefacts, *Primary History* (54): 14–17.

USING ARCHIVES CREATIVELY

Sue Temple

INTRODUCTION

Children need to understand how real historians work, using actual sources, analysing these and making educated guesses about what they might mean. Often this takes the form of using artefacts and/or visiting a castle or historic house, for example. However, in order to support and deepen learning and understanding we should also be introducing children to source documents of different kinds. They should be introduced to how and why these documents were produced and by whom. Analysing the particular source then becomes easier as children are introduced to the idea of questioning the evidence they are presented with. This is not an easy skill for children to learn but they can begin to grasp these concepts if they are developed carefully and appropriately. Scaffolding the children's learning by introducing a small selection of carefully chosen archive documents can stimulate their curiosity and encourage them to develop enquiry skills in a context which is meaningful and relevant. If the documents are about local people, who lived in their village or city, their attention is all the more easily captured.

This chapter examines the value of using archive documents such as the census data, maps and plans, diaries, postcards, posters and other sources, to develop two very different projects. The first case study, working with Key Stage 2 children, was based on the former Fusehill Street Workhouse, which is now the University of Cumbria's main building in Carlisle. We shall also be exploring a project about Lady Gilford's House, now extended and renovated into a new Archive Centre (www.cumbria. gov.uk/archives/newrecoff/LGHdisplay). This is a project developed for schools by the Archive Office.

Accessing sources

'Before beginning a hunt, it is wise to ask someone what you are looking for before you begin looking for it' – as Winnnie the Pooh says (Powers 1995).

With the growth of the World Wide Web it is becoming ever easier to find archives online. However, these still tend to be documents which are of national importance rather than the written documents of the local people in your area. The best place to find archives like these is still your local archive office. Many people will not have used their local office but it is a treasure trove of interesting and informative documents, which have been collected together by the archive service. Thousands of documents are catalogued and stored in secure vaults, which are kept at the correct humidity and temperature to ensure a long life for these largely paper-based sources. Members of the general public can access these documents and photocopies or digital photographs can be taken to enable teachers to use the documents more easily back in their classrooms. Contact your local office before you visit, as they may need some form of identification to register you as a user, in the same way a library does. You can also talk to an archivist about what kind of documents you are particularly interested in and they will usually find you a variety and have these ready for your visit. Many offices have boxes with relevant documents already sorted, according to particular periods of history, for educational use; for example documents relating to the Victorian period or to World War II. These will usually be generic archives, so be sure to identify a particular local area or theme so that the archivist can access the most relevant sources for your purpose.

Although many of my trainees teachers studied A-Level history a large proportion had never been in an archive office. In Carlisle we are extremely lucky to have such a modern, well-equipped place to take pupils and trainees, which has its own large bright education room. However, smaller archive offices can have a real charm and atmosphere, which will appeal to some children more. My trainees are fascinated to realise that their local office can store such gems as the twelfth-century 'Dormont Book' – Carlisle's 'rules', which state for example, that no dead cats are to be put down the well and that you are not allowed to leave 'midden' waste (toilet waste) outside your door for more than 5 days. Children are able to handle documents that Elizabeth I or Henry VIII have actually signed – a real thrill for an historian!

But, despite all the advantages, we cannot just ignore the disadvantages. For a busy teacher it is time consuming and hard work to do the research and we do still need to ensure the children grasp the big picture, the larger scale of the issues. A focus on one small area or town still needs to be seen in the context of the whole country and what is happening elsewhere. It is also inevitable that sometimes you just will not be able to find the answer to a particular question – a dead end. My personal attitude is that accepting this is a life skill. We do not always find the answers we want and we need the ability to reconsider, reformulate the questions or find a new direction. This is an example of how children can learn about the nature of historical enquiries. Children need to learn the emotional resilience to cope with minor setbacks and obstacles.

The 3 R's of archive materials

Non-specialist primary teachers are sometimes overwhelmed and nervous of introducing archive sources into their classrooms as they are unsure how to access them, make them accessible to children and evaluate the documents themselves, never mind expect children to do this. I find the easiest approach is to think in terms of the 3 R's of archives. So consider, is the document:

■ Rich?
■ Reliable?
■ Relevant?

This gives us a straightforward framework to consider how useful a document may be. Some sources may be all three but this is unlikely.

■ Rich – does the document have a lot of detail or information? Will it help the children to understand a particular aspect in more depth or give more of an overview of the period? A relevant page from the census, a letter or diary entry, a map or plan might all provide the children with a lot of detailed information. For example a map of a particular area will show all the houses, public houses, banks, churches and schools. Evidence about leisure may be visible, for example bowling greens or picture houses. Factories, railways and roads are easily identified. Street names give further information and comparing an earlier and later map of the same area illustrates how an area changed during the intervening period. Educated guesses can then be made about why these changes may have happened.

■ Reliable – How reliable is this source? How accurate is it likely to be? (We can never know for sure!)? Is it likely to be biased? Who wrote it and why? Is it actually from the period you are examining or was it written afterwards or by someone who was not there? We tend to think of official documents as reliable but they are only as reliable as the person who wrote them, or the person who submitted the information. For example, for early versions of the census, people were employed to go round houses knocking on doors, asking the householder questions and recording the information given. However, householders could have genuine reasons for not telling the truth about the number of people who were living in a property, so even with an official record like this we have to retain an element of scepticism.

■ Relevant – Does this document give information about the local area, a local person or significant local event? Will it capture the children's interest and imagination? Does it give information which is valuable to this particular historical enquiry? Local newspapers can be useful here. Local libraries and/or archive offices will have microfiche versions of these, which can be accessed and a photocopy made. As newspapers are already printed, accessibility in terms of being able to read the document may not be as much an issue as a handwritten document might be.

There is a great variety in the types of archival documentation (Table 4.1) so it is best to discuss with your Archive Officer what is available and was what would work best for your class.

■ **Table 4.1** Examples of lesser used archive documentation

---

- Advertisements and posters
- Archaeological evidence
- Autobiographies
- Buildings
- Business records
- Catalogues
- Censuses of different kinds
- Chronicles, e.g. monastic
- Commissions such as royal and parliamentary investigations
- Council records
- Crime records such as charge books, prison and transportation records
- Deeds and charters
- Diaries
- Directories, e.g. trade directories
- Enclosure records and tithe records
- Estate agents' and auctioneers' documents
- Family and estate records
- Film
- Fiction such as references in novels and music
- Gravestones, memorials, inscriptions, statues
- Guide books and travellers' accounts, topographical records, county and town histories
- Letters
- Magazines, e.g. parish, school magazines
- Manorial and estate records such as accounts, court rolls
- Maps and plans
- Mass observation records
- Newspapers
- Oral testimony
- Pamphlets
- Parish registers and other parish documents
- Parliamentary records
- Photographs including aerial photographs
- Poor law records
- Place names
- Postcards
- Public health records
- Quarter session records
- Reconstructions
- School records, e.g. log books, registers, punishment books
- Surveys
- Tax and other financial documents – Domesday Book, lay subsidies, hearth and land taxes
- Transport records such as timetables, traffic figures
- Wills and probate records

Historical enquiry or being a history detective?

One aspect of teaching history that I find enthrals children is putting them in role as 'history detectives'. There is such a wide variety of documentation that has survived through the ages that we can help children to access and interpret. It does take time and effort on the part of the teacher to find, copy and sometimes translate but it is so worthwhile when you see the curiosity and enthusiasm from the children as they become involved an investigation of this kind.

Organising and planning a theme can be difficult, as there is always so much that could be included, but we need to choose particular aspects very carefully as children can get 'lost' in the vastness of history. We need to focus in, so that children can really explore an aspect in depth and come to a deeper understanding of how to 'do history'. Using local documents can help children identify, and identify with, some local characters. These are real people – maybe someone who lived in their street, went to their school, was in their local workhouse, for example. Younger children especially might still be struggling to understand that Florence Nightingale and Cinderella were not both fairy stories! We need to use materials that real people have written or documents written about them, to ensure they can begin to grasp the differences.

We need to grab children's attention, stimulate their curiosity and give them that thirst for finding out for themselves. As part of my job I visit schools watching trainees teach, as well as working with some practising teachers. It is so easy to teach a whole history-based project and not develop any real historical skills – watch some videos, read some books and use the Internet to do some games, do some writing and some art work, make a display, go on a trip (not an educational visit!) – job done! However, have you actually taught any real historical skills – Enquiry, Interpretation, Chronology?

It is also easy to fall into the trap of giving the children the answers – or even worse – the 'right' answers. Children need to know how to find things out for themselves, and make evaluations and judgements for themselves about the reliability of what they have found out. We need to develop children's independence and scaffold their learning but by providing answers, rather than developing the problem-solving approaches, you allow students to avoid the learning process that is needed. This is the part that can be hard work for the children (and the teacher!) but it is necessary to encourage and nurture these creativity skills.

FUSEHILL WORKHOUSE PROJECT

This is an outline of a project I did in conjunction with a class of Year 5/6 children from a local school. Their planned history theme was on the Victorians and in citizenship lessons they were due to consider homelessness, so these ideas were brought together in a project about Fusehill Workhouse (now on the University of Cumbria Carlisle Campus). We used a variety of carefully chosen documentary evidence, in conjunction with a site visit to bring the topic alive for the children.

Maps and plans

First, we used the 1865, 1901 and 1925 Ordnance Survey maps to stimulate interest and curiosity, before the children came onto the site. We enlarged and laminated the maps so that the children could use whiteboard pens on them, to mark places of interest or places we wanted them to find, for example the schools, churches, leisure facilities in the area. The children examined the maps again on their visit, to identify what different buildings had been used for in the past and how they had changed.

We are lucky enough to have copies of the original floor plans for the original workhouse, drawn by the architects, Henry F. Lockwood and William Mawson. It was designed in 1862 for 478 inmates and cost £11,195.15s to build. The plans identify what each room was intended for. They also show the chapel, the workhouse hospital and laundry buildings, and how the entrance has changed. The children could find the trees marked on the main entrance footpath, the site of the laundry – now our sports hall, the morgue, now next to our student accommodation and used by our estates management staff as a base. The original chapel marked on the plan is still in use.

Census data

The census began in 1801 and then it was undertaken again every 10 years, during the spring months. (No census was taken in 1841.) Early census documents are not considered to be as reliable as later census data, as less information was collected – for example no first names were recorded until the 1851 census. From this census onwards a wider variety of information was collected, including health records. It is at this point that phrases such as 'imbecile' or 'lunatic' can be found.

The relationship of each person listed to the head of the household is recorded, their age and marital status. Prior to 1851 ages were often rounded up to the nearest 5 years. The country of birth and occupation was also listed. We do need to examine these with care though, as the address recorded was wherever the person happened to be staying, on that particular day, and so might not have been their main home.

Interrogating the 1881 census

When we first gave the census to the class we asked them to record any questions they might have on post-it notes and we added some questions of our own to deepen their thinking and understanding. Table 4.2 shows the aspects of the census the children researched.

This included a lot of enquiry skills and a lot of interpretation skills – we may never know answers to some of the children's questions but this activity developed children's thinking and questioning skills. They were sometimes disappointed when we could not find the answer to a particular question but this is a life skill; children need to develop the emotional resilience to accept and cope with this kind of 'failure' – which was no one's fault. Sometimes the archive document you really need no longer exists.

■ **Table 4.2** Using the 1881 census, Fusehill Workhouse

Information from the census	Suggested questions/ discussion/issues	Possible solutions/ pointers
7 'indoor' staff plus a porter/ gardener and his wife – one born in the West Indies	How did a person form the West Indies end up as staff here?	Local port of Whitehaven part of the slave trade/ rum triangle – hence Cumbrian Rum Butter!
225 inmates (13 children up to 4 years old)	How big was the workhouse? Why so few and why none over age of 4?	Designed for much larger numbers Another workhouse specifically for children in another part of the city
Range of ages from 1 month old (with his 17-year-old seamstress mother) to 89-year-old Issac Newton, a widower and agricultural labourer from Warwick, Cumberland	Possible reasons/narratives why individuals came into the workhouse?	Some married couples rooms identified on the plans – can they find the people who probably had these rooms?
Range of places of birth – Scotland, Ireland, Isle of Mann, Northumberland, Ceylon, York, London	How did they end up in Carlisle Workhouse?	British Empire?
Wide range of occupations – labourers, domestic servants, cotton related, sailors, navvies	A lot of occupations related to local cotton industry and farming – what was happening in these to lead to these people ending up in a workhouse?	Industrialisation of cotton industry and farming in the area?
Some described as deaf, blind, lunatic and imbecile	Are these terms acceptable now? Beggar/homeless – connotations of language	Discussion of language use and how it has changed – modern terms

Focusing on one person

Focusing on one local person can help to keep a project manageable. As the children were exploring the ideas of homelessness we focused on the well-known character of Jimmy Dyer. There is a statue of Jimmy in our local shopping centre; so many of the children were familiar with this, even if they actually knew nothing about him. Jimmy Dyer was a beggar who travelled around the local markets, festivals and fairs playing his fiddle. He wrote his own music and, according to some of the documents we found, not very well! When Jimmy was too ill to make his living in this way he was admitted to the Fusehill Workhouse. We found him on the 1901 census and we could work out, from the plans, which rooms he was likely to have lived in. Jimmy Dyer died in the workhouse and, like the many others from the workhouse, he was buried in the paupers' section of the cemetery, in an unmarked grave.

Creating a narrative from a painting

In addition to the more local sources we also used the painting (and the original 1869 etching it was based on), *Applicants for Admission to a Causal Ward,* by Luke Fildes. The painting was produced in 1874 (www.workhouses.org.uk/lit/Fildes). This scene, reportedly modelled for him by 'real down-and-outs', depicts applicants queuing for their tickets for entry into the 'casual ward'. Each character deliberately represents a social type: a hungry, cold and seedy adventurer asking for directions from policeman; a mother with black cloak indicating widowhood – or perhaps illegitimate mother, her fine clothes showing a recent decent into poverty; the 'ruffian garrotter' or burglar with the red coat and crutch of professional beggar; the labourer with his sick wife and family – perhaps recently moved from the country to search for a better life; the well-to-do 'toff' who is drunk and has perhaps gambled his fare home; the family who have lost their lodgings through father's illness or idleness. The children were encouraged to choose one of the characters depicted and make up a background narrative about why they were presenting themselves for entry into a workhouse, even if it was only for one night in the casual ward.

Creating a narrative from the census

Once the children had produced their narratives for these characters, with the additional support of the painting, we returned to the census and the children were given one person or a small family to focus on and produce a suitable narrative for them. This really made them consider what they actually knew about each character and the local area at the time.

Photographs and chronology

In order to develop a sense of chronology about the building the children also looked at more recent photographs, showing wounded soldiers and their nurses out in the snow at Fusehill War Hospital in 1918. The building was requisitioned during both World Wars for this purpose.

Oral history

For an oral history project my history trainee teachers had interviewed a range of people related to the Workhouse building during its lifetime. We were able to use an interview of an ex-Royal Air Force airman, who ended up in this hospital after being shot down during the Second World War. He described the routines in the hospital at the time and how he met his wife here. The children were able to link his descriptions to the maps and photographs we had and compare and contrast his experiences with hospitals now.

Role-play

To encourage the children to begin to empathise with homeless people, both now and in the past, the class teacher organised a sleep-over in the school hall. The children were limited to a blanket or sleeping bag but no other home comforts. They were allowed to bring a small amount of money to buy snacks but the snacks available were too expensive for them. The eventually worked out that if they clubbed together they could afford to buy a slice of cake or a sausage roll and share it! This is problem-solving in a real context. At around 2 a.m. the children were woken and told they had to move to a new place as they weren't allowed to stay in this place any longer. The discussion that this experience created was truly amazing and these children clearly were beginning to understand the reality of homelessness for themselves.

■ **Table 4.3** Creativity, history, psychology and examples from the workhouse project

Creativity	Historical knowledge, skills and understanding	Psychology	Examples from the workhouse project
Multi-dimensional thinking Expressing ideas in a variety of media	Creating interpretations through role-play (KSU 3) technologies, displays, paintings, etc. (KSU 5)	Divergent thinking producing a variety of ideas Multi-intelligences	Role-play of homeless and individual narratives
Rational and emotional thinking	Imagination rooted in evidence	Logic and imagination Understanding behaviour and feelings of others Emotional intelligence	Creating narratives for the people on the census – understanding why and how they might have ended up in the workhouse
Playing with ideas and making connections	Causal thinking (KSU 3)	Generating imaginative solutions	Creating narratives for the people on the census
Possibility thinking Transfer knowledge and thinking to new contexts to solve a problem	Making inferences about sources; tolerating what cannot be known (KSU 3&5)	Seeing things from perspective of others through role-play, looking at pictures, conversation	Examining painting, absorbing information from the oral histories, dealing with 'dead ends'

(Continued)

■ **Table 4.3** (Continued)

Creativity	Historical knowledge, skills and understanding	Psychology	Examples from the workhouse project
Integrating subjects	Cross-curricular links within history	A subject is learned through multi-sensory networks	History with Literacy and Geography
Social interaction	Debates, discussions, group work (KSU 5)	Social interaction in problem solving	Finding information about Jimmy Dyer

Based on Cooper (2007).

Evaluating the reliability of the archive documents

Towards the end of the project we asked the children to evaluate the reliability of archive documents they had used, in line with the concept of the '3 R's of archives':

■ Which was the richest? The majority felt the census, as it gave such a variety of information.

■ Which was the most reliable? Most felt the maps and especially the architects plans would be the most reliable.

■ Which was the most relevant? There was a definite split of opinion here with the census, the actual site and maps used on site all being popular choices.

■ If they could only have three documents which would they choose? Did any contradict each other? The children chose a real range for this – clearly demonstrating that different formats and presentations appealed to different children.

This project was so successful that I have used it since with a few small adaptations, with new trainees and also with A-Level students from the local academy.

LADY GILFORD HOUSE PROJECT

This was a collaborative venture between the Carlisle Archive Centre and Petteril Bank Primary School, with support from a professional storyteller. It is a good example of how archives can be used in much more creative ways to develop a range of skills across the curriculum. The outreach officer and a Year 5/6 class from the local school worked on a project, exploring the life and times of a member of the local community. Lady Gilford was chosen, as her home, which has been adapted and extended, houses the new archive building and has been known informally as 'Lady Gilford House' for many years, although few locals would actually know very much about this lady. Lady Gilford lived in the house at the early part of the twentieth century.

The aims of the project

The aims of the project were to:

■ explore how everyday archival records can be interpreted in a creative and accessible way, to bring to life the human lives and times behind the records;

■ widen and develop audiences of people who have no previous experience of archives and to lay the foundations for community participation, in the future development of the Archive Centre.

The project involved twice weekly visits for the children during the Autumn Term. One of the first sessions introduced the children to the archives and the strong room, where they were able to see how the documents were stored and cared for. The original part of the house, where Lady Gilford once resided, was also explored, so the children were able to begin to appreciate the 'upstairs/downstairs' nature of life in a house, which had servants' quarters in the attics, oak-panelled grand rooms and large kitchens on the ground floor. The attic servants' rooms survive to this day, as does one of the grand reception rooms, which is now licensed to hold weddings.

Creating narratives

The professional storyteller was able to find Lady Gilford and her household mentioned in the 1901 census. Based on these details the children were encouraged to create imaginative narratives about the different characters. The storyteller worked with the pupils to develop their voice control and expression, demonstrating how to use movement to illustrate their ideas further. The storyteller also led two twilight Continuing Professional Development sessions with teachers from the school and other Cumbrian archivists and library staff, so it is hoped that this approach will spread further through the county.

Puppets

In addition the outreach officer helped the children to create giant papier-mâché puppets of Lady Gilford, her daughter and various members of the staff, and three of her hounds. Pupils also created a variety of additional items to help to illustrate their stories including, for example, a giant teapot and tea set.

Retelling the stories

Rather than being a part of the children's curriculum this project gradually took over and became the curriculum, with the children working on the project in other subjects, back at school. The children then used all their new skills of projection and expression, along with these very unusual puppets, to present their stories to an audience of parents and local people, including trainee teachers from the University of Cumbria. This was most impressive! Rather than learning set lines, which are often forgotten by children of this age, the children learnt the story and concentrated more on retelling their story to the audience, so specific words were not important. It was a true telling of stories! It was very clear to those of us in the audience that the children were confident and relaxed about their narratives but also about their own abilities as storytellers. They were clearly enjoying themselves, so we in the audience did too! My trainees were amazed at their approaches and they commented on how much they learnt from just watching this performance.

The scope of the project

The project has been hugely successful for all the partners involved. The teachers and support staff have become much more confident in using narrative and storytelling in a variety of ways. Their comments included, 'Personally I've learnt a lot of skills for teaching: tips, activities, exercises that we can use for improving speaking and listening skills, using primary resources: looking at the newspapers went better than I thought, the children loved it. Loads of potential' and, 'It was like a breath of fresh air. It's nice to take learning out of the classroom. The feel of the archives is lovely and we knew we'd get a lot out of it'. The school has built a solid relationship with the archive centre, which will be sustained in the future. It is also hoped that this will develop beyond the school and into the local community, with plans to introduce a library resource area for local residents in one room.

The staff also felt that the children's speaking and listening skills improved enormously. Whilst the performance element was challenging, particularly with a new approach, on the whole they grew in confidence. Pupils commented; 'Now I can stand in front of our class and tell stuff like the story' and 'I've learnt that telling stories is hard work but it is fun as well. It's hard because you've got to think what you're saying and put expression in it'.

This was the first time the archive centre had attempted a collaborative project like this but the outreach officer was thrilled with the outcomes. 'It's been brilliant because we've made a very strong connection with the school that's on our doorstep. This will stand us in good stead for doing further work with the community. Not only do other classes at Petteril Bank want to work with us but other schools are talking about it.'

The professional storyteller has considerable experience in facilitating groups in creating stories using museum objects but with this project he progressed to working with purely written resources. He found it more demanding, though the children were more interested in the written resources than he expected. This clearly demonstrates the potential for this creative approach. The school is already considering how to incorporate archives into future projects, for example how Lady Gilford's House was used as an orphanage during the Second World War.

The project coordinator concluded that, 'A key to the success of the project was using archive records to create storytelling and combining this with the practical making of something visual to support the telling of the story. The project will act as a template for future work at the archives centre'.

CONCLUSIONS AND SUGGESTIONS

These were two very different projects but none the less they were both creative and interesting in their varying approaches. The Fusehill Workhouse project encouraged the children to explore a building they were familiar with and consider how it might be that people ended up being admitted. They were encouraged to compare and contrast this to our attitude to homelessness today. The Lady Gilford Project took an art and storytelling pathway, for the children to consider archival documents with the support of their own creations of stories, giant puppets and objects, to tell their own creative narratives. Both projects lasted a full term with lots of different aspects being incorporated into the children's learning. Most importantly both these classes of children thoroughly enjoyed their experiences.

So in conclusion, consider, and ensure you include:

- The local – real people and real places – develops a sense of place.
- The variety of documents that are available – census, maps, letters, diaries, etc.
- Help the children to tell the story – this can be the hook to capture their interest and curiosity.
- Developing some real historical enquiry skills, thinking skills, life skills.
- Fun and enjoyment – these are real keys to ensuring a successful project.

REFERENCES

Cooper, H. (2007) Creativity in primary history, in A. Wilson (ed.) *Creativity in Primary Education*, p. 181, Exeter: Learning Matters.

Powers, J. (1995) *Pooh's Little Instruction Book*, inspired by A.A. Milne and E.H. Shepherd, New York: Dutton.

CHAPTER 5

USING ARTEFACTS AND WRITTEN SOURCES CREATIVELY

Hugh Moore with Rachel Houghton and Rachel Angus

The chapter first considers the ways in which written sources are generally used in primary classrooms, then considers a variety of innovative ways in which this work could be extended. The next section, which focuses on the Romans, describes case studies investigating the use of artefacts linked to written sources and the question is posed, 'How do we know that?' The third idea is to consider the extent to which looking at writing on an artefact stimulates learning about a larger theme. The chapter includes some exciting written sources and suggests ways in which they could be used in the classroom.

TRADITIONAL USES OF WRITTEN SOURCES

Students often suggest that an effective way of empathising with people from the past is to write a diary entry, imagining it to be from the daily life of a World War Two evacuee for example. This may relate to a misreading of the Knowledge and Understanding of events outlined in the National Curriculum (DfEE/QCA 1999) stating that pupils should be taught about beliefs, attitudes and experiences of men, women and children. Historians, however, know that it is very difficult to understand the motivations of people who lived in the past; why did so many people believe Hitler and why did so many Victorian women believe that their place was in the home, for instance? It is also difficult to have sufficiently deep subject knowledge to be effective at such a task; if we were writing a diary entry for a Roman soldier on Hadrian's Wall would we know what he ate for breakfast, what his children were called, where he came from, what unit he was attached to or what his duties were, for instance? Could we indeed write a diary entry without knowing such things?

Another approach, which is often suggested in a similar manner, is for pupils to write their names in Egyptian hieroglyphics, but again we must consider what are the pupils learning by doing that? They are learning about what hieroglyphics looked like but not the fact that such a script was widely used for sacred purposes and that the Egyptians often used another cursive script for what we might call 'normal' purposes. Nor do we find out about the individual lives of Egyptians, which are sometimes portrayed in their tombs, for example we do not find out about the biography of Seti I (whose tomb is in the Valley of the Kings).

In writing a diary entry or creating hieroglyphics we are inventing a written source but perhaps it is better to reverse this process and ask what was written down in the past and what can we find out from it, because in doing so we are beginning to act as historians ourselves.

The point about this chapter is that, whilst it refers to many written sources, the ideas for working with them are largely enquiry based and are creative and innovative. The sources themselves are sometimes simple, often linked to an object, and easy to get hold of and can be decoded, using resources which are readily available on the internet, via sites such as the British Museum and the Vindolanda Museum. They are also designed to capture the imaginations of children and by being authentic and compelling, to allow for the development of 'the Mantle of the Expert' (www.mantleofthe expert.com).

In terms of teacher knowledge it is hoped that the activities are starting points, which allow for personal interest, whilst at the same time being deeply rooted, to help develop core enquiry skills that lie within the discipline of history.

BECOMING AN 'EXPERT'

Decoding a Roman coin

On the face of it decoding a Roman coin is daunting from many angles and may be perceived as an activity which is probably best left to an expert; it is not only written in abbreviated Latin but the numbers and letters are the same and they are often worn and degraded. Yet to decode a coin is an authentic and satisfying process and is core to that intensely historical question, 'how do we know that?' It is also far simpler than many would believe, as the Romans were a systematic people who used upper-case letters on their coins and the activity is well supported by many internet sites (www. finds.org.uk/romancoins) and reference books (Klawans 1995). The current focus on phonics is also relevant because this task is about systematically blending word elements and sounds (I'd hesitate to call them phonemes but the principle is similar), and associating them with meaning as well as being able to understand (at a higher level) that the roots of English lie within other languages.

Another perceived barrier to this task would be the difficulty of getting hold of a Roman coin but again they are easy to access in museums such as Lancaster, Ribchester, Lancashire Museums Services, Kendal, Tullie House in Carlisle, Senhouse,

Figure 5.1 A sestertius issued during the reign of Caesar Domitianus Augustus, CE 81–96

The British Museum) or by buying replicas (Winter Reproductions, www.ancestors. uk/merchandise.php). Alternatively, for between £5 and £100, you can buy perfectly good originals from places such as Coin Craft (www.coincraft.com) and Timeline Originals (www.time.lines.co.uk).

This activity was based upon a sestertius issued during the reign of Domitian, shown in Figure 5.1. This coin was chosen because it is large and most of the writing (but not all) is legible. The coin was then photographed and enlarged, printed and laminated so that a group was able to work with it. Tip: to photograph a coin success-fully and clearly ensure your camera has a macro setting (often indicated by the image of a flower) as this allows for close-up pictures. It is also best to photograph the coin on a plain but well-lit background using a raking light – this is simply a light shone across the coin to enhance the features by creating contrast between light and shade. (Professionals often use two or three lights shone from different directions.) Photographing the coin is of course an excellent and purposeful cross-curricula chal-lenge for a group of children.

The enquiry

The enquiry challenge for the children was as follows. Could they identify the exact year the coin was made? This is an important tool for archaeologists as they find many coins on Roman sites and these provide great dating evidence.

During the first part of this challenge children were asked to look closely at the coin (illustration) and then make a large sketch of it copying carefully any groups of letters they could see. In this case IMPCAESDOMITAVGGE**COSXVICENSPERPP were relatively easy to see. Once the children had identified these they had to separate the letters into groups that looked as if they belonged to each other thus:

IMP
CAES
DOMIT
AVG = AUG (In the Roman alphabet V = U or W)

GE** = GERM
COS
XVI
CENS
PER
PP

Then the groups were asked to guess what any of the words meant. In this case most correctly thought:

IMP = Emperor (with prompting)
CAES = Caesar
XVI = a Roman number, in this case 16.

It was explained to the groups that many of the abbreviations related to titles given to an emperor so, even though this emperor was not Julius Caesar, they were still given the title Caesar to recall that link. Then they were able to access www.wnccoins. com/0022.htm, www.celatorsart.com/legends1.html, http://dougsmith.ancients.info/ abb.html via tablet computers to see if they could find out what any of the other abbreviations meant:

AVG = Augustus, another title given to most emperors to recall the first emperor Augustus
DOMIT = This emperor's name is Domitian and he ruled from AD 81–96 (CE)
GERM = Indicated that Domitian was also the ruler of the Germans.

Thus we have found out that this coin represents the period of the early Roman occupation of Britain and was made during the first century. The more advanced information was also tackled by some groups:

COS = Indicated that Domitian was Consul, a position in charge of the Roman senate – a bit like our parliament.
XVI = Indicates that Domitian has served as Consul for the sixteenth time so this coin is likely to have been made very late in his reign.
CENS PER = He was censor of the senate in perpetuity (forever); thus he had power to choose who was allowed to be a senator and represent the people.
PP = *Pater Patriae* is Latin for Father of the Country and is a title awarded to emperors later in their reign.

So it is OK for a source to be challenging and often they are seen as an artefact, which can stimulate a sense of awe (Blyth and Hughes 1997). Hoodless (2004: 25) too sees that sources with difficult language can be a 'novelty' and provide opportunities for problem-solving and creativity. Marwick (1989) notes that some documents are difficult for even the skilled historian to decipher because they were written for another purpose.

Blyth and Hughes (1997) believe primary source documents can help children to develop reading comprehension skills, such as selection and organisation of ideas, before voicing them.

Decoding Roman documents

Roman emperors such as Domitian, and kings and queens like Henry VIII and Elizabeth I, are the big people of history, but what about sources relating to the lives of mere mortals? Once again it is possible to look at a Roman example and this one comes from the Vindolanda tablets. These are a group of documents, which were written on wooden tablets and have been found well preserved in the damp clay soil around Vindolanda Roman Fort in Northumberland, which is close to Hadrian's Wall. Some of the documents are official and are requests for supplies or information about the disposition of troops, while others are personal, such as requests for leave or birthday invitations. It is the last two examples which we shall consider here. The first tablet is possibly the most famous. It is Claudia Severa's birthday invitation to 'her Lepidina'.

Enquiry 1: Severa's invitation (Tablet 291)

I download, print, cut out and laminate two examples of Roman wooden tablets and share them with the group (www.vindolanda.ox.ac.uk, tablets online database). These tablets were often written by scribes and then folded, tied and sent to the intended recipient. They are wonderful in that they tell us of the lives and the details of those who lived in a Roman fort and as Robin Birley points out in a video shown in the museum at Vindolanda, sometimes overturn our conceptions of what it was like to be a citizen of the Roman Empire.

We look at the Severa invitation as an authentic document but unfortunately it is almost impossible to read – I have tried many times. However, that almost doesn't matter because when you look at it and consider the language and translation it is possible to see that the text in the bottom right-hand corner is written in a different hand – that of Severa herself. Possibly, according to Birley, this means it is the earliest example of a woman's handwriting in the Roman Empire.

Enquiry 2: Felicio's request for leave (Tablet 168)

However, one of the tablets is far easier to decode and it is a leave request from a soldier in the century of Felicio. (This humble request is written in the same old Roman cursive script as the Severa letter but this time in a clearer hand.) Therefore by looking at a model of the old Roman cursive script (www.guindo.pntic.mec.es) (the Wikipedia site is also very useful) and comparing it with the translation we can quickly see that it is possible to make out the name Felicio and, once we have worked on the 'eria', the name Cerialis.

Historically we learn that by looking at sources we find out about the Romans (Cooper 2000). We learn about the style of writing, that the Romans communicated in Latin (which is related to English), that if we take time we can read these sources (and learn the skills of an expert) then we can make a connection with people's lives in the past and hopefully form the kind of awe and empathy we sought by the writing of a 'diary' entry (Blythe and Hughes 1997).

Historians and archaeologists make inferences and connections, which are key cognitive skills. One way of thinking about this in a primary school setting is to ask, can you make a small clue tell the big story? Here's an example and yet another occasion on which I wish Ridley Scott's film *Gladiator* wasn't a certificate 15.

Enquiry 3: Reading a Roman tile fragment reveals the bigger picture

The Roman tile fragment shown in Figure 5.2 has upon it an official Legionary stamp – these are not uncommon and can be found throughout the Roman Empire. Once again it is an opportunity for sketching or photography with purpose because in order to read such a thing the group needs to record it. You might be doing this while walking beside Hadrian's Wall and looking at a centurial stone or an inscription in any number of local museums in places as far apart as Colchester, Carlisle, Lancaster, London, Newcastle and Northumberland.

The recording will have purpose if the group takes time to try and decode it. On the face of it, once we have worked out what is written on the tile we may find that LEG II ITA does not seem very interesting. How do we make the inferences and connections that an historian uses to tell the 'big story' of history? To do this we need to question the source, find out to whom LEG II ITA refers (Bage 2000; Cooper 2000).

Legion II Italica was founded by Marcus Aurelius during the second century, probably to support him in his campaigns against the Germans. It was originally commanded (alongside the III) by Pertinax, who later went on to become emperor after Commodus died. History is all about making connections, and Marcus Aurelius, as you might recall, is the white-bearded emperor (the nice one) portrayed by Richard Harris in *Gladiator* and Pertinax would be a good model for Maximus (Russell Crowe). Legion II Italica much later went on to support Constantine the Great in his

Figure 5.2 Reference to the second Italian Legion, which throws light on the 'big picture'

campaign to become emperor of the whole empire and fought with him at Milvian Bridge. Constantine was proclaimed emperor in York in 312 and brought Christianity to the empire. In pursuing this we have heard a big story from a small object but we are still partly reliant on interest and subject knowledge about the ancient world.

Reading a Roman account of Boudicca's uprising

Story, of course is the powerful narrative element of history, which is so attractive and sometimes it is quite humbling to find out that the events actually happened. One story, which is often told in school, is about the events surrounding Boudicca's revolt against the Romans. It is perhaps a surprise to find out that these events are some of the best documented in the history of Roman Britain. They were written about by a Roman historian, Tacitus, who was himself related to one of the subsequent governors of Britain, Agricola. For Tacitus these were events within living memory although, in true Roman style, they were told in dramatic fashion. Unfortunately *The Annals XIV* are complex and difficult to read and it has long been my ambition to find a way to work with them in school.

Below, the text is edited to a few paragraphs where the main events are narrated (in Tactitus' words) and to these I have added notes to explain the text still further. The question here is how do we tell the following events as a story?

From *The Annals XIV* (from 29 on) by Cornelius Tacitus (translated by Church and Broadribb):

[Suetonius Paulinus was a Roman General and Governor of Britian and he was busy attacking the Isle of Anglesey (Mona) in Wales to get rid of the Druids when the Boudiccan revolt broke out.]

> *igitur Monam insulam, incolis validam et receptaculum perfugarum, adgredi parat, navesque fabricatur plano alveo adversus breve et incertum. sic pedes; equites vado secuti aut altiores inter undas adnantes equis tramisere.*

He therefore prepared to attack the island of Mona, which had a powerful population and was a refuge for fugitives. He built flat-bottomed vessels to cope with the shallows, and uncertain depths of the sea. Thus the infantry crossed, while the cavalry followed by fording, or, where the water was deep, swam by the side of their horses.

[Paulinus' soldiers were scared by the sight of the Druids.]

On the shore stood the opposing army with its dense array of armed warriors, while between the ranks dashed women, in black attire like the Furies, with hair dishevelled, waving brands. All around, the Druids, lifting up their hands to heaven, and pouring forth dreadful imprecations, scared our soldiers by the unfamiliar sight, so that, as if their limbs were paralysed, they stood motionless, and exposed to wounds.

[Prasutagus, king of the Iceni dies and the Romans take over his kingdom even though, in his will, he had left it jointly to the emperor and his own wife and daughters. Boudicca and her daughters are treated badly and a revolt begins.]

Prasutagus, king of the Iceni, famed for his long prosperity, had made the emperor his heir along with his two daughters. His kingdom was plundered by centurions, his house by slaves, as if they were the spoils of war. First, his wife Boudicca was scourged, and his daughters outraged.

[Another Tribe, the Trinovantes joined in the revolt, as they also hated the Romans, because they had taken their land to found a Roman colony for their retired (veteran) soldiers.]

It was against the veterans that their hatred was most intense. For these new settlers in the colony of Camulodunum drove people out of their houses, ejected them from their farms, called them captives and slaves.

[At the time there were lots of bad omens.]

Their theatre resounded with wailings, and in the estuary of the Tamesa had been seen the appearance of an overthrown town; even the ocean had worn the aspect of blood, and, when the tide ebbed, there had been left the likenesses of human forms, marvels interpreted by the Britons, as hopeful, by the veterans, as alarming.

[Boudicca and her allies attacked and destroyed Colchester (Camulodunum).]

Surprised, as it were, in the midst of peace, they were surrounded by an immense host of the barbarians. All else was plundered or fired in the onslaught; the temple where the soldiers had assembled was stormed after a two days' siege.

[They also attacked the ninth legion.]

The victorious enemy met Petilius Cerialis, commander of the ninth legion, as he was coming to the rescue, routed his troops, and destroyed all his infantry. Cerialis escaped with some cavalry into the camp, and was saved by its fortifications.

[Suetonius left Anglesey and went to London to see if he could protect the city but decided not to.]

Suetonius, however, with wonderful resolution, marched amidst a hostile population to Londinium.

Uncertain whether he should choose it as a seat of war, as he looked round on his scanty force of soldiers, and remembered with what a serious warning the rashness of Petilius had been punished, he resolved to save the province at the cost of a single town. Nor did the tears and weeping of the people, as they implored his aid, deter him from giving the signal of departure and receiving into his army all who would go with him.

[Boudica went on to destroy London and St Albans (Verulamium).]

Like ruin fell on the town of Verulamium.

About seventy thousand citizens and allies, it appeared, fell in the places which I have mentioned.

[Suetonius and his legions chose their place to fight Boudicca carefully.]

Suetonius had the fourteenth legion with the veterans of the twentieth, and auxiliaries from the neighbourhood, to the number of about ten thousand armed men, when he prepared to break off delay and fight a battle. He chose a position approached by a narrow defile, closed in at the rear by a forest, having first ascertained that there was not a soldier of the enemy except in his front, where an open plain extended without any danger from ambushes.

[The Romans fought and defeated Boudicca using their wedge tactic.]

At first, the legion kept its position, clinging to the narrow defile as a defence; when they had exhausted their missiles, which they discharged with unerring aim on the closely approaching foe, they rushed out in a wedge-like column. Similar was the onset of the auxiliaries, while the cavalry, with extended lances, broke through all who offered a strong resistance. The rest turned their back in flight, and flight proved difficult, because the surrounding wagons had blocked retreat. Our soldiers spared not to slay even the women, while the very beasts of burden, transfixed by the missiles, swelled the piles of bodies. Great glory, equal to that of our old victories, was won on that day. Some indeed say that there fell little less than eighty thousand of the Britons, with a loss to our soldiers of about four hundred, and only as many wounded. Boudicca put an end to her life by poison.

My history specialist Year-Four students came up with a number of ideas for under-standing this as a story:

■ Retell the events in freeze-frame with a narrator saying the words of Tacitus.
■ Produce a 'fact book' with photographs of the places in question and associate these with Tacitus' words.

- ■ Present the same information as above, but on PowerPoint, perhaps with some attached video.
- ■ Rewrite the story, practise it and tell it to other classes.
- ■ Produce a 'story board' of the events.
- ■ Rewrite the events on wax tablets or thin sheets of wood.
- ■ Write a play or an assembly based upon the events.

VICTORIAN ENQUIRIES

A Victorian button

The focus of this chapter so far has been on using small written sources and artefacts for enquiry-based learning about the Romans. The following activity is around the Victorians and is about a button (Figure 5.3) and makes interesting use of ICT (information and communications technology).

Once again you can look at the potential this activity has and create your own version of it. It is also about creating a 'big story' from a small artefact and avoids the sort of questions that lead to little learning and a lot of guesswork (often on the part of both the teachers and the learners), when looking at Victorian artefacts, such as 'What is it made from?' and 'Do you think it is made in a factory?'

Figure 5.3 What can we find out about the Victorians from this button?

This is a classic history detective task. The question given to the groups was, 'When and for whom was this button made?' During one version of this activity the group I was working with was lucky enough to be allowed to use smart phones and iPads and so I created Quick Response (QR) codes to serve as clues and teaching prompts. On the back of the button it said: 'The Late J. Hunter Wilkinson 34 Maddox St'. A portable document file (PDF) was downloaded from the London Gazette of 8 January 1869, and whereas this gave a date for the company, groups had to decide whether the button was made before or after this date (www.london-gazette.co.uk/issues/23457/pages/126/page.pdf).

On the front of the button was a crest and since the button is from a livery (servant's uniform) it was the crest of a Victorian family. Recognising crests is a serious challenge particularly as they change over time so, for instance, whilst the central shield (with three diagonal stags) might remain the same the overall crest for the eleventh Duke of Derby will be different to that of the fourteenth.

Once again there was an opportunity for some purposeful photography or drawing which focused attention on a particular aspect of the crest, which, in this case was the wording of the two mottos, *Sans Changer* and *TRIA JUNCTA IN UNO*. A QR code was created (by visiting http://qrcode.kaywa.com, pasting the web address into the URL slot, asking it to generate a code and then clicking on the code and saving as an image) which led to the page on the Stanley family (the Earls of Derby) on Wikipedia http://en.wikipedia.org/wiki/Earl_of_Derby. The final part of the puzzle was solved again when another QR code linked the Latin phrase to the Order of the Bath and the group had to find out which of the Earls of Derby have been awarded the Order of Bath. In this case it was the sixteenth and seventeenth Earls and the dates of the sixteenth century coincide most closely with those on the reverse of the button. Thus mystery of the button was solved and the group have learned about cross-referencing, family crests, servants' liveries and the Earls of Derby.

Victorian written sources

Queen Victoria's diary

So far I have (mainly) confined my discussion to artefacts which contain written sources, but what about purely written sources?

In looking at later written sources it is important that we recognise their beautiful breadth and variety, especially when associated with the Victorians. I have a few favourites and these range from Mr Wackford Squeers introducing *Nicholas Nickelby* to the pupils at Dotheboys Hall to the BBC's adaptation of Elizabeth Gaskell's *North and South*. Films like *The Young Victoria* (www.iwannawatch.net/2011/02/the_young_victoria-2009) also have clear potential and this time the advantage of being certificate 'U'. They also relate nicely to some of Victoria's letters highlighted by Heather Palmer (www.victoriana.com/doors/queenvictoria.

htm), although you may have to choose your examples more carefully than you might imagine. The best for our purposes are where she describes her own children and grandchildren:

> Leopold ... is the ugliest. I think he is uglier than he ever was. I hope, dear, he won't be like the ugliest and least pleasing of the whole family. He walks shockingly – and is dreadfully awkward – holds himself as badly as ever and his manners are despairing, as well as his speech – which is quite dreadful. It is so provoking as he learns so well and reads quite fluently; but his French is more like Chinese than anything else; poor child, he is really very unfortunate.

When reading such a source we have as always to spot and exploit its potential in the learning environment. We might use it to ask questions about what it tells us of Queen Victoria's relationships with other people and who she liked and didn't like. What did she think about: her uncle William IV, her mother, the comptroller Sir John Conroy, the Prime Minister Lord Melbourne, Lady Flora Hastings, Prince Albert, her eldest daughter Vicky, her eldest son, the Crown Prince Bertie, John Brown and 'The Munshi' for example? There may also be some room for delicate debate around what happened between her and her mother and how Queen Victoria felt when she read her mother's diaries and letters after she died.

Victorian fiction

One of my history specialist final-year students, Rachel Houghton, has a passionate interest in Victorian literature and has been researching its use in school. In doing this work she found that Victorian novels were often available but seldom used because teachers feel nervous about them. Rachel then did a lot of work to choose passages from novels which could be used in school and tried them out with children.

Prior to her teaching she had introduced the notion of how historians use sources to construct an idea of history. She had also talked about what contemporary literature is and why it can be used as an historical source. \Finally she had asked the pupils what they already knew about the Victorian workhouse.

Extracting information from the text

Rachel's extract was from *Oliver Twist*, Chapter Two:

> The members of this board were very sage, deep, philosophical men; and when they came to turn their attention to the workhouse, they found out at once, what ordinary folks would never have discovered – the poor people liked it! It was a regular place of public entertainment for the poorer classes; a tavern where there was nothing to pay; a public breakfast, dinner, tea, and supper all the year round; a brick and mortar elysium, where it was all play and no work.

They established the rule, that all poor people should have the alternative (for they would compel nobody, not they), of being starved by a gradual process in the house, or by a quick one out of it. With this view, they contracted with the water-works to lay on an unlimited supply of water; and with a corn-factor to supply periodically small quantities of oatmeal; and issued three meals of thin gruel a day, with an onion twice a week, and half a roll on Sundays . . . The relief was inseparable from the workhouse and the gruel; and that frightened people.

Rachel deliberately chose a challenging extract from *Oliver Twist* where it describes the living conditions of an early Victorian workhouse. The aim of the task was for the children to extract information from the text and use historical skills to construct a picture of what it was like to live and work in a workhouse, for a Victorian child. She read and scanned the text with the group, to allow the text to become more familiar. Pupils also selected unfamiliar words and tried to understand their meanings by highlighting them and entering into a discussion with the rest of the group to see if they could define them. Should they not have been able to agree a meaning through discussion or if they have any other difficulty they could then use a dictionary.

Using a whiteboard, children worked in pairs to construct their own questions (such as: who, where, how and why?), about the source and then came together as a whole group to answer each other's questions, with the extract as a focus point. If there was a question they were having difficulty answering, Rachel asked the children what they could do to find out the answer.

In carrying out a task such as this, careful thought might be given to resourcing the work and providing a context for the children's thinking. The book extract can be pasted into a leather-covered notebook and placed in a 'Victorian' bag perhaps along with good-quality Victorian photographs and other artefacts. Additional information could also be placed inside such as a set of workhouse rules and a menu printed on browned paper and a census return for that workhouse. In addition, an enlarged A3 version of the Dickens text and a set of highlighters would be effective in helping the children to analyse the source.

Once they had read through the passage and worked out its meaning the group then prepared their questions. Next, the group worked to see if they could answer the questions through using their own historical knowledge and the supporting materials. Finally, where they did not know the answer to a question, they considered where they may be able to locate the answers.

Later there was also a consideration of how Dickens' description of the workhouse matched the reality of life in the workhouse.

Questions pupils asked about the source

▪ Who were the members of the board?
▪ Why was it not ok for the people to like it in the poor house?

■ Why did the workhouse frighten people when they changed it?
■ When did this happen?
■ Why did people have to go into the workhouse?
■ Why did they want people to starve in the workhouse?
■ Was the water dirty?

The pupils' views on a Victorian workhouse:

> The workhouse was a place where you went if you were poor and had nowhere to live. At first, in the story people liked the workhouse and didn't mind going in because it was nice and they got fed. The men who gave money to run the workhouse didn't like this because the more people who went in the more money they had to spend.
>
> They came up with a plan to make the workhouse a horrible place so no one would go in unless they had to. They fed them horrible food like watery porridge called gruel because they had an unlimited supply of water. They also got to eat bread and onions. They fed people horrible food to frighten them so they would not go to the work house.
>
> When we looked at other documents from the workhouse, we learnt that not all workhouses were like this. Some workhouses fed people bread, cheese, vegetable and broth. But there were some strict rules and if you didn't follow them you would lose a meal or could be fined 4d.

Conclusions from the research

Through a well structured and guided session pupils were able to take on the role of a historian and create good questions that interrogated the source and extracted key information about Victorian society.

Through reading a story the children were able to relate emotionally and empathically to their child counterparts from the past. One child commented, 'It wasn't very nice living in a workhouse when they change it to make it more horrible. I'm glad we don't have workhouses nowadays, I wouldn't like to go in one . . . I think you would be sad if you were a child in the Victorian times and you had to go into the workhouse.'

Children understood that fiction still had value as an historical source and they knew that Dickens had witnessed first-hand what it was like to live in Victorian times. The children were also able to cross reference with other sources to make their own conclusions of what it was like to live in a workhouse. Rachel Houghton came up with an analysis of how pupils interpreted the text, shown in Figures 5.4 and 5.5.

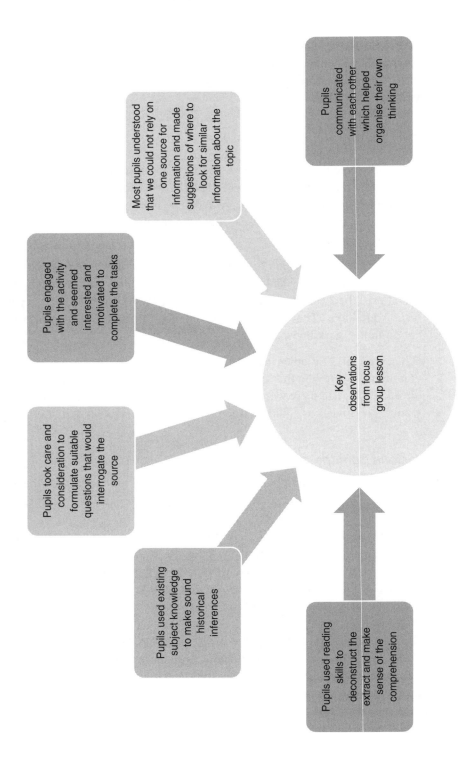

Figure 5.4 An analysis of how pupils interpreted the text from *Oliver Twist*

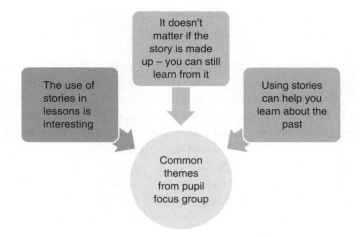

Figure 5.5 Analysis of pupils' views about using fictional texts in history

CONCLUSION: AN ANALYSIS OF THE USE OF WRITTEN SOURCES IN PRIMARY SCHOOLS

Rachel Angus, another fourth-year initial teacher-training student specialising in history, was also involved in conducting research into the use of sources in school. This was based on a case study in which she filmed a group during two lessons in which sources were used. I shall let her excellent analysis of what was happening during the lessons she observed be the last word in this chapter:

> The first lesson was with Years 5 and 6 children of mixed ability and gender. The group was chosen to give a snap-shot view of probable child responses to the activity and further responses from this group of children were gathered directly after the lesson. The responses from that interview and the data from the lesson observation were then compared to another pre-written lesson checklist, which aimed to determine motivation, engagement with the sources, use of historical skills and overall lesson success. This then formed a starting point from which to design a second session, which had only 6 participants, a focus group of six children ranging from Years 3–5 (mixed ability and gender), in order that I might concentrate on the responses of those children during filming. Following this lesson, a short interview was conducted with those same children.
>
> During the initial lesson the teacher used a large number of sources and added in pictures in order to find something she thought would appeal to the class. This may have indicated a lack of confidence with using sources and some inexperience in their use. I concluded that using one or two sources would have been more appropriate and could be made 'interesting' to the children, through the process of source analysis and historical interpretation. It was noted

that the children, motivated prior to the lesson, lost motivation during the task, because they were given the documents to look at 'without any clues as to how to do it or what it might be for' (Fines and Nichol 1997: 82) and so failed to engage with any of the sources on a meaningful level, although they did take an interest in several.

A lack of understanding about the process of source analysis can lead some practitioners to lose sight of the usefulness or appeal of primary written sources, and can have a negative impact upon their view of source lessons (Eamon 2006; Noakes 2010). In turn, this can lead to tedious and superficial source tasks which have a detrimental effect on the quality of history teaching, because they are irrelevant and based mainly of fact acquisition. This was true in the observation of Lesson 1, where the children were left to read and understand all the sources without any assistance, with the task of 'extracting facts' for a task, the aims of which had no clear objective.

During the second session I used a more critical approach that drew upon and further developed what I had seen in the first lesson. The approach this time was through encouraging group discussion (Bage 2000; Cooper 2000) and questioning of the source (Bage 2000; Card 2010; Cooper 2000), whilst considering the source context, reliability, author's motives and intentions (Eamon 2006; Blyth and Hughes 1997). It also employed a more analytical approach, by considering the inferred meaning of the text (Marwick 1989; Bage 2000), and encouraging historical interpretation (Bickford 2010; Droysen cited in Ziemann and Dobson 2009), backing up assertions with evidence from the text (Cooper 2000). Additionally, using a scanned copy of an original document proved to be successful in terms of developing a sense of awe for historical documents, which can be artefacts in their own right (Blyth and Hughes 1997; Hoodless 2004), and with careful adaptation, it was possible to successfully use an original document (containing complicated language, sentence structure, handwriting and themes) with children at the lower end of key stage 2: More than this, it succeeded in maintaining the motivation of pupils during the lesson, captured their interest (one child commenting that they found it fun to read, and another saying they enjoyed the story it told), and began (or continued) to generate an appreciation of original source documents, with one child remarking '... it's proper evidence'.

REFERENCES

Bage, G. (2000) *Thinking History 4–14*, London: Routledge Falmer.

Bickford III, J.H. (2010) Complicating students' historical thinking through primary source reinvention, *Social Studies Research & Practice* 5(2): 47–60. Education Research Complete, EBSCOhost [Online]. Available at: www.ebscohost.com (accessed 9 November 2011).

Blyth, J. and Hughes, P. (1997) *Using Written Sources in Primary History*, London: Hodder and Stoughton Educational.

Card, J. (2010) Printed pictures with text: Using cartoons as historical evidence, *Primary History* 56(10): 10–11 [Online]. Available at: www.history.org.uk (accessed 15 November 2011).

Church, A.J. and Broadribb, W. (trans.) *The Annals by Publius Cornelius Tacitus*, Internet ASCII text source: gopher://gopher.vt.edu:10010/10/33

Cooper, H. (2000) *The Teaching of History in Primary Schools: Implementing the Revised National Curriculum* (3rd edn), London: David Fulton Publishers.

DfEE/QCA (Department for Education and Employment/Qualifications and Curriculum Authority) *National Curriculum for England and Wales: handbook for primary teachers in England*, London: DfEE/QCA.

Eamon, M. (2006) A 'genuine relationship with the actual': New perspectives on primary sources, history and the internet in the classroom, *History Teacher* 39(3): 297–314. ERIC, EBSCOhost [Online]. Available at: www.ebscohost.com (accessed 9 November 2011).

Fines, J. and Nichol, J. (1997) *Teaching Primary History*, Oxford: Heinemann Educational.

Hoodless, P. (2004) History and written sources, *Primary History* 26: 25–26 [Online]. Available from: www.history.org.uk/resources/resource_277.html (accessed 2 November 2011).

Klawans, Z.H. (1995) *Handbook of Greek and Roman Coins. An Official Whitman Guidebook*, London: Golden Books, Random House.

Marwick, A. (1989) *The Nature of History*, Hampshire: Macmillan Education.

Noakes, J.D. (2010) Observing literacy practices in history classrooms, *Theory and Research in Social Education* 38(4): 515–544. ERIC, EBSCOhost [Online]. Available at: www.ebscohost.com.

Ziemann, B. and Dobson, M. (2009) *Reading Primary Sources: the interpretation of texts from nineteenth- and twentieth-century history*, London: Routledge.

CHAPTER 6

CREATIVE APPROACHES TO TIME AND CHRONOLOGY

Hugh Moore with Rachel Angus, Caitlin Brady, Caitlin Bates and Caron Murgatroyd

THE CONCEPT OF CHRONOLOGY

Developing children's chronological understanding is, rightly, considered very important. But understanding the passing of time is more complex than reciting the names and dates of monarchs. First, this chapter considers innovative and engaging ways of learning about time and sequence, and similarities and differences within and between periods, which encourage us as practitioners to allow the children to build up their own mental maps in active ways. Then it considers, through working with children, how to help them make sense of a timeline and to develop children's historical imagination by linking evidence, understanding and imagination to chronological questions.

It is important at this point to begin to understand what we might mean by the concept of chronology; are we thinking purely about time, the passing of time, the way in which events relate to each other and whether we have a vision of the past? Or is it something simpler? Is it a question of whether we have a mental map of the past? Or even more simply, is it a question of a child's ability to understand which of the 'Invaders and Settlers' came first, the Romans, the Vikings or the Saxons?

Dawson (2004: 1) proposes that 'Chronology is not simply an ability to place events in order . . . . It is also a sense of scale, a sense of period and a sense of 'the framework of the past'. Whereas Haydn has suggested a four-part classification for teaching and learning about time (labelled T1–T4), summarised as follows (cited in Dawson, 2004: 2):

T1   Time-dating systems and conventions and vocabulary

T2   A framework or map of the past over the time-span laid down in the National Curriculum

T3   Knowledge of a number of short-term frameworks, e.g. key events and chronology of the Norman Conquest or World War Two

T4   Deep Time: an understanding of the true scale of the past from the formation of the earth onwards.

Chronology is of course all of the above, because it represents the passing of time and our conception of the passing of time. Therefore, in conceiving this chapter I am aware of all aspects of chronology from the simple order of events to, to borrow a phrase from Douglas Adams (1987), 'the interconnectedness of all things' or in other words how the past has unfolded to make the present.

As an historian I fear being asked about the past because I don't fully understand it and the more I know about the past the more I understand that I know hardly anything. The past is simply too complex, it is after-all the history of everything that has happened in the whole world and so, therefore, when I teach about the past it is about allowing students and pupils to make their own connections with the past and then begin to order those connections.

A few days ago I was walking with my three boys on Great Carr in the Lake District when I came across a small memorial to seven Canadian aircrew and one member of the Royal Air Force Volunteer Reserve, who died when their Halifax bomber aircraft LL505 crashed on the 22 October 1944. Scattered around and down into Broad Slack lay the remains of the bomber and that coupled with the beautiful position on the hilltop, with views as far as Snowdonia, The Isle of Man and South West Scotland, meant it was a very poignant place. Other special factors made it an even more powerful moment; as a boy I had been fascinated by World War II aircraft and latterly I'd often climbed in this area with my wife, who had since died. An excellent overview of the site, as well as a photograph of the men who were lost, is provided at www.yorkshire-aircraft.co.uk/aircraft/ll505.html.

This was a piece of history that I could crouch down and touch, here it was still in the place where it had happened and whilst being there I was able to visualise the aircraft and imagine the events that led to its loss. It was a place where the past really happened. I often feel that the important moments in teaching chronology are when students and pupils realise that the events they are studying really happened and that they are not simply stories.

Herein lies the contradiction of history – some history is more real (because we can visualise and connect to it) than other history and the past that is less real is the past that is beyond our experience. Yet many writers, such as Hoodless (2010), Arthur and Phillips (2000), Husbands (1996) and Philpot (2008), tell us that understanding chronology is vital. So the question is how do we, as teachers, pupils, student teachers and learners of history begin to work with and develop an understanding of chronology?

Sequence, dating, classifying and enquiry-based learning

There are of course many simple ways of doing this and remembering to attach an area of study to the class timeline is one of the most effective. It is also tempting to look at change and continuity and one of the simplest activities I have used with students is to create a timeline of old domestic irons.

Irons timeline

These irons are often cheap to buy and their beauty lies in the fact that in outline and shape they are all remarkably similar (Figure 6.1), whether they are powered by charcoal, heated by the fire (sad irons), connected to the gas supply or electric, and they are part of most people's everyday experience, so we can easily understand them. Another beauty of the historic irons (if we are looking for opportunities for enquiry-based learning), is that in the past some people were still using sad irons while others already had electric ones, the simplest iron (sad) is not the earliest and they are well documented in reference books (Sambrook 2004).

The 'irons task' is to use books and the internet to try and arrange them in the correct order. It is a fine enquiry task, because, while many gas irons were used during the 1930s, mine dates from the 1950s/60s, and it is only through observation and asking good questions like, 'why does this one have a plastic handle while that electric one has a wooden handle?' that this 'problem' can be sorted out.

Figure 6.1 A selection of irons

This activity, therefore, allows us to use enquiry skills to order, date and classify a series of objects. It also helps us to consider the nature of technical progress and the evolution of ideas.

This short activity is a lot of fun and it allows for many further teaching opportunities. I tend to award group points for doing this task; the maximum score is nine (for my irons) and on two or three occasions during the task I'll give the groups interim scores but no other clues. This way it becomes a competition, which means I always have to be careful to clear the irons back into the boxes before giving the scores. This task also means you will have to be very confident of your own dating of the irons and you need to aware that the boxes of irons can be quite heavy.

Personal chronologies

Another and in some ways even simpler activity given to students which has clear potential in school is where I ask them to think about, collect and record their own personal chronologies. This is done by asking them to bring in evidence to tell the stories of their own lives, which they weave into a 'Scrap Book' story. I help them with the process by showing them my own, complete with photographs, copies of documents and anecdotes and as you can imagine they really enjoy this. Part of the point of this exercise is to encourage the students to behave like historians in that they would not only tell their own story but provide the photographs and evidence to prove it. They enjoy the presentations where they get to share their own lives. A note of caution: I once showed the students a picture of my wife, Ginny and told them what had happened to her and some of the students cried but begged me to keep the slide in my story. I was uncomfortable about doing this. So we had a debate about people who didn't want to share their lives and thus the activity became a group task, where one person would bring in their evidence and then the others would interview them and create a 'Scrap Book' that became a sort of 'This is Your Life, XXXX'.

Longer timelines

This next activity is more challenging and deliberately features a collection of objects about which we might know far less. They included; a mammoth vertebra (Figure 6.2), an Egyptian necklace, a Palaeolithic axe, a bronze spearhead, a Greek salt bowl and a Roman tile. The artefacts could as easily be from within the last 200 years: sugar cutter, ringlet tongs, a fish-oil lamp, a hot-water bottle and a Codds bottle. (The Codds bottle was patented by Hiram Codds in 1875, for carbonated drinks. It has a marble and a rubber washer in the neck. The bottles are filled upside down and pressure of the gas on the marble sealed it against the washer.)

However, the objects I used are difficult for many reasons. We need to be an expert to know what they are. They are from time periods about which we may know less and the vocabulary relating to the objects is obscure and complicated. This time the chronology embedded in the task is far deeper and requires more from the participant who needs: developed enquiry skills, deeper subject knowledge, the

Figure 6.2 A 60,000-year-old vertebra

understanding of a more complex vocabulary and the ability to work with a set of larger numbers.

I ask groups to use the internet to arrange the timeline and this means they will have to try a variety of hypotheses and ways to describe the objects in order to be able to identify them. Thus the vertebra is a bone and groups recognise that quickly, but many of them think it looks like a skull or a pelvis; it is only through asking good questions and being prepared to try out different theories that the group recognise it first as a vertebra and then as a very large vertebra. Once the object is identified it can be placed against a timeline and with such an old object (*c.* 60,000 years old) a new set of questions arises: who or what used these objects, what were their lives like, when did they live and what do we call them?

Obviously as the students/pupils identify what they are looking at they acquire information that they have (this time) to keep and use:

■ First human arrivals – early arrivals at Happisburgh in Norfolk, 700,000–800,000 years ago.
■ At Boxgrove, Sussex, flint knapping was used to produce bi-face hand axes, *c.* 500,000 years ago.
■ Neanderthals/Mousterian culture: Lynford Quarry in Norfolk has the remains of about nine butchered woolly mammoths and Mousterian butchering tools, *c.* 60,000 years ago.
■ Africa – first humans, 2,500,000 years ago.
■ Neanderthals, Neander Valley, Germany, 130–30,000 years ago.
■ Very cold. Northern Europe abandoned for long periods, up to 11,000 years ago.

The students/pupils then apply all the statements they have collected to the objects and are asked to classify them in terms of what was happening in Britain, at this time, and in the rest of the world. They have also been asked to apply dates (in years ago) and finally to include events that they have found out about, which they regard as significant, such as the development of writing.

As I said before, this activity was designed to be challenging, although it has the potential to be far simpler (see the work of Rachel, Caitlin and Caron below), and it was aimed at developing the cognitive skills of those undertaking it as they (like an historian) have to sew different strands of evidence together.

This activity was, in part, to raise awareness that while the Babylonians and Mesopotamians were developing writing and later mathematics and the Egyptians were building the Pyramids and the world's largest ritual buildings at Karnack the experience of those living in Britain was different. Tables 6.1 and 6.2 allow us, for example, to compare the magnificent and enigmatic Silbury Hill (in Wiltshire) with the Great Pyramid of Khufu, which was built around the same time. It also allows us to see that while the Greeks were expanding their knowledge and understanding of the world in the magnificent city of Athens we in Britain were constructing breathtaking monuments such as Badbury Rings. Table 6.2 was also designed to provide the reader with a list of useful places to visit or investigate when studying such topics.

Researching the use of timelines with different age groups

These ideas have all been tested in school by a group of fourth-year history specialist Initial Teacher Training Students (Rachel Angus, Caitlin Brady and Caron Murgatroyd), who spent some time trying out these approaches. As a group they discussed which types of activities would be most successful in evaluating how chronology is understood by children. They were to try them with each year group, within a primary setting and this resulted in a combination of three short activities, which were differentiated for each year. These activities comprised:

1   Ordering a selection of time-related vocabulary by duration, i.e. which is the shortest amount of time (second) to the longest amount of time (millennium). This was to glean whether the children understood the basics in chronology.
2   Using time periods, children were to discuss and order images, artefacts and words, all chosen to appeal to a variety of learners, from the furthest period in the past to the most recent, on a timeline. The timeline was blank except for BC/BCE '0' and AD/CE. This was to allow the students to assess whether children had a good understanding of what those terms meant.
3   Using artefacts (irons). The children were to order these from the oldest to newest and discuss their decision-making process.

They found that all three chronology activities undertaken within the school provided a valuable insight into how children process historical information. The most successful of the activities as a whole was the artefacts activity. Having the objects there to physically touch and investigate enabled enhanced learning for many of the children who took

▪ **Table 6.1** Timeline1: How do we as adults and teachers make sense of time?

5,000 years ago

Bronze spreads to Old World around the Mediterranean

Civilization in Indus Valley begins around 4,500

Structures of standing stones begin in Europe 5,200

Literary compositions occur Mesopotamia by 4,400 of which the best known example is the Epic of Gilgamesh

Pyramid age in Egypt is from 4,650–4,400

Chinese practice silk weaving, 4,700

Troy (Anatolia) is an important city from 5,000 to 3,000

Shang dynasty in China from 5,000 to 3,000

European Bronze Age begins *c.* 4,300

Minoan Crete and the palace of Knossos from 4,500 to 3,400

The wheel is found in Denmark and Holland by 4,800

4,000 years ago

Iron working develops in Western Asia by 3,500

Mycenaean Greece, 3,550–3,150; Agamemnon lived there at time of the Trojan War

Egypt Imperial Age (Valley of Kings etc.) from 4,000 to 3,000

Large mining complexes at Mitterberg in the Austrian Alps produce 10,000 tonnes of copper

3,000 years ago

Large burial mounds are built in Brittany and Wessex where there were sources of tin

Phoenicians develop 'Greek' alphabet around 3,000

Knowledge of iron spreads through Europe between 3,500 and 2,500

Persian Empire, 2,550–2,330

Classical Greece, 2,950–2,350

Celtic Europe, 2,800–2050

Rome conquers Gaul and Egypt, 30

Roman incursion to Britain, 55/54

part. However, it was clear that some groups struggled with the time vocabulary, particularly the larger the amounts of time; millennium, century, etc., and in addition, in the longer timeline task children struggled to put the time periods in the correct order.

The following is a transcript which was made from a recording of the discussion as Year 3 pupils undertook task 2: The children knew what a timeline was and had heard of all the time periods they had to order, although they were unfamiliar with the terms AD/CE and BC/BCE.

■ **Table 6.2** Timeline2: Does Stonehenge make sense on its own?

5,000 years ago

The Circle at Stonehenge; the main phases date from 5,500 to 4,000 years ago with some evidence of much earlier work. The stone monument was erected around 4,300 years ago

Other Circles: Avebury (Wiltshire), Long Meg and Castlerigg (Cumbria), Stones of Stenness and Ring of Brodgar (Orkney).

Other monuments: The Village of Skara Brae (Orkney); the amazing 130-foot-high Silbury Hill (Wiltshire) (4,400 years ago). No less mysterious are chambered cairns and portal dolmens, many examples of which can be found in places like Bant's Carn and Chûn Quoit in Cornwall and Carnholy in Dumfriesshire

3,000 years ago

Earliest metal use in Britain is copper

Hambledon Hill (Dorset) is a large earthwork of over 100 ha which was occupied from the Neolithic in various phases into the Iron Age and may have been abandoned about 2,300 years ago (Pryor 2003)

Flag Fen (Cambridgeshire); Bronze Age farm – with walkways and reconstructed roundhouses

Mining of tin occurs in Cornwall and bronze is produced on the Great Orme in Wales

First use of iron occurs *c*. 2,750 years ago

Early hilltops are fortified such as Norton Fitzwarren (Somerset) and Rams Hill (Berkshire) and later much larger contour forts such as Old Sarum and Badbury Rings (Dorset)

Tribal kingdoms are known throughout Britain as well as wheel-made pottery. Coins issued by tribes in the south and Lincolnshire

Foreign trade centres become powerful like Hengistbury Head (Dorset)

Year 3 pupils and task 2 (sequencing images, artefacts and words)

They're extinct [Dinosaurs].

What about the Egyptians, are they extinct?

No.

So how come they're here?

Because they got killed.

What all of them?

Yes.

So the Romans, do you think they are before Jesus was born?

Yes.

The Romans and the Normans we think they were before Jesus was born?

Yes.

And then so after Jesus was born we have the Egyptians, the Greeks.

Look at the clothes they're wearing – are they like the clothes we wear today?

· No, that one's a statue.

I think you should swap WW2 and the Victorians.

No they're today.

So the final running order is: Dinosaurs, Egyptians, Greeks, Normans, Romans, Victorians, WW2.

I think you should swap the Victorians with WW2.

Year 1 children and task 3 (sequencing artefacts)

The next extract comes from the Year 1 children, as they were working on task three. In doing this task it was important to think carefully about the characteristics of the irons that we are asking the children to examine. Some of the irons look old and it is clear that they have iron bodies and wooden handles but what about the newer ones? Are we aware of those that have plastic not wooden handles and which electric irons have thermostats and which do not? Children notice things and particularly when the Year 5s are carrying out this task are we prepared for them to notice not only that the newest iron has an aluminium sole plate but that the pre-war irons have a nickel-plated shine whereas the later ones are chromium? What would our response be if they did notice this (even if we hadn't) and how would we allow it to develop into a chance for further enquiry?

Interviewer: Do you know what these are? [*Points at the irons*]
Children: All the olden days stuff.
             It's to do with your ironing.

Interviewer: Why do you recognise this one?
Children: It looks like one we have today.

Interviewer: So is this going to be a new one or an old one?
Children: A new one.
That one looks old.

Interviewer: Why do you think this one looks old?
Children: Cos it's really big.

Interviewer: Is that one older than this one?
Children: Yes.

Interviewer: Why do you think that?
Children: Cos this one's really rusty. And it's dirty.

Interviewer: What do you think this does? [*Points to the plug*]
Children: You plug it in and it makes it all real. And you put some water in it and it makes it all hot.

Interviewer: How do you think this one gets hot?
Children: You plug it in and it makes all the things warm.
[*Children sorted irons into two piles – old and new*]

What the students found out

Having interviewed both staff and children the student group reflected on what they had learned, drawn from their reading, in particular Hoodless (2010) and Cooper (2007) and formulated the following proposals:

■ Place a topic or enquiry in its wider historical framework before and after it has been studied.
■ Have a permanent timeline in classrooms.
■ Keep a whole school timeline – perhaps in the hall. This could be referred to in assemblies, prior to topic or following topic, and children could have the opportunity to feed back their topic 'expertise' to the whole school during assembly time.

Learning dates:

■ Children could memorise a small number of key dates, which they can use as markers for reference.
■ We should be careful not to put children off history by overloading them with fact learning.

Pupils making their own timelines:

- Children watch videos/film relating to the period and reference what they have watched on the timeline.
- Children place photographs of work they have done, visits they have made, costume events and feasts on the timeline.
- Children create ICT fact books and presentations and reference them on the timeline.
- Indicate links to other online resources. Note the BBC Interactive Timeline.
- Children create personal timelines of their life or another person chosen by them.
- Add photographs of object they have seen from the periods.
- Find significant documents and sources relating to each period and add them to the timeline.
- Create a timeline through the use of a 'circular booklet, three-dimensional line, or as a vertical or horizontal two-dimensional wall display' (Foreman *et al.* 2008: 156).

Use class timeline as a reminder of key dates. Be aware that time has been measured differently in the past:

- Where do the names of our days and months come from?
  - January – Janus the god of the beginning and the end.
  - July – named after Julius Caesar.
  - August – named after Augustus Caesar.
  - September – the seventh month (it became the ninth because of the two Caesars).
  - October – the eighth month.
  - November – the ninth month.
  - December – the tenth month.

- Historical versions (Aztec calendars/sun dials/movement of the planets or stars/obelisks/Stonehenge etc).
- Versions of measuring time that developed historically but that are still important today (farming calendar/the seasons).

Sequencing activities:

- Ordering and dating photographs, buildings, paintings and artefacts such as irons or clothing using skills such as observation, enquiry and deduction.
- Ordering/sorting/sequencing assorted evidence to build a story.

Writing:

- Writing biographies (perhaps famous people in history). Children could then select key paragraph headings, which can be developed as labels for a timeline – this could be developed into a class 'sorting' exercise to order their famous people chronologically.

■   Writing up an historical (or real time) event into a story. This will require chron-
    ological and subject knowledge as well as sequencing skills. Can they turn
    Tacitus' account of Boudicca into a story?

For younger children:

■   Writing events they have experienced as a story. This will require chronological
    knowledge and understanding, and a certain amount of sequencing.
■   Mathematical ability is crucial for understanding and interpreting historical data
    such as timelines, census returns, statistics, Roman numerals, etc.
■   For using timelines effectively – applying scales and numbers is an excellent
    task and remember that we can list time in different ways – both in years ago
    and by date.

Using positive and negative numbers:

■   For using the CE/AD/BC/BCE scale on timelines. (Further ideas can be found in
    Cooper (2007: 94–96, Chronology and Literacy connections) and in Cooper
    (2012: 41–52).)

In terms of thinking once again about the case of the bomber on the hill there are
several ways in which we might classify its position in history. The first is in terms
of its place in a longitudinal history; that is, as part of the timeline of events which
have happened to our country – in very much the same way as we might measure
our history by kings and queens. Thus it would sit nicely on one of those long paper
lines where we can measure (by the use of dates) the order of events. By doing this
it would allow us to see (if we didn't know already) that 22 October 1944 was getting towards the end of WWII. The other ways are in terms of events, WWII; or
period, the twentieth century; or even by place, the history of Britain. But there is
also the idea of learning by concept or using ideas or an engagement we have
about a period of time. As a young boy I found the idea of WWII fascinating and I
probably knew quite a lot about the aircraft of the period (to the extent that, as my
boys and I were watching a programme on the Arctic, I excitedly identified that the
seaplane they were using was a de Havilland Beaver), but as so often happens, by
the time I got into the sixth form and later to university I found that the idea of
knowing such things was no longer cool. I asked male colleagues of the same age if
they had a similar experience and readily found two who had been 'into' the tanks
of the period. It is not hard to find examples of children who are similarly engaged.
During her research Rachel Angus was interviewing a group of Year 5 children, to
find out what they knew about castles, when she came across 'William' who knew
about the Middle Ages without having been taught about it in school and from
memory he told her the following about the Viking invasions and 'King Arthur' and
gave them dates between 500 and 800 (Figure 6.3):

- Kings Alfred, Harold and William and about the Bayeux tapestry
- Richard the Lionheart who was killed in 1199
- The Battle of Agincourt and the Hundred Years War
- What the symbol of two fingers meant and how it related to the English longbow.

This was a far from isolated example, and I have come across a similar example of a Year 5 pupil who knew a great deal about the Ancient Egyptians and many others who know about Henry VIII and his wives or were really passionate about ancient history and especially the Greeks.

Such knowledge is born out of a passion for a subject and can come about at a remarkably young age (see Robson 2004). Such knowledge of course can be disconcerting, especially if we, as teachers, develop the uncomfortable feeling that one of the children may know more about a subject than we do but as good teachers we know that such knowledge is also worth celebrating. It is also interesting to consider what may lie at the root of this enthusiasm and exploiting its potential to inspire others.

I was talking to my 5-year-old nephew Aidan about his Playmobil castle and knights when I was surprised to find that he had a good deal of knowledge and conceptual understanding on the subject of castles. Children are gaining this interest through play (Dixon and Day 2004), through story (Farmer and Heeley 2004) and through film, games and toys. Enthusiastic children do not leave it at that. They want more, more toys, more books, more visits to castles, more films and more games and this leads not only to an increase in their subject knowledge but also in their ability to make connections and inferences between the subject areas.

Figure 6.3 William, a Year 5 pupil's knowledge about the Middle Ages, learned from out-of-school sources

Throughout this chapter I have alluded to subject knowledge and we must recognise it is this element which lies at the heart of chronological understanding, because without the imaginative tools to engage with the story of the past any timeline is meaningless.

WHAT IS SIGNIFICANT TO RECORD AND INVESTIGATE?

The bombing of the Twin Towers or World War II?

A group of Post Graduate Certificate in Education (PGCE) students (Moore and Ashcroft 2010) once told me with some confidence that 9/11 was the most important event in World history. This led me to create a lecture on World War II in which we handled a deactivated 1942 machinegun and then looked at the shocking 60 plus million lives, which were lost country by country – ending of course with the USSR. We also considered some of the subsequent effects of the conflict by looking at the Iron Curtain, nuclear proliferation, the establishment of the state of Israel and the formation of the National Health Service in Britain. Many of the students, subsequently, considered that WWII was the biggest event in history, but was it?

Invention of writing?

At the end of the first lecture one of the PGCE students asked me how important I thought the invention of writing had been. He was right of course, because without a huge range of developments in human technology and thought nobody would have been able to make a Halifax bomber, gas chambers, machineguns, let alone the atom bomb.

Ancient history?

Ancient history has a unique position in the curriculum and those who love it will understand its role in motivating and interesting learners. Most people cover the Greeks or the Egyptians, whilst a few also look at the Indus Valley or Sumeria, Babylon and Mesopotamia. Why, given what I've already said about making connections with the past, do these early civilisations continue to inspire?

An example of the significance of Ancient Egypt

Using Egypt as an example we can see that the remains of the civilisation are exciting, iconic, mysterious, very big and utterly compelling. This is a big society, which speaks to us from the deep past and tells us of a completely different world. Egyptian paintings, for example, provide us with pictures of a people whose lives are utterly different from ours; they dress differently, the pictures are highly stylised and the associated writing has an air of magic and ritual. This then is the stuff of films and legends. So what place does it have in our understanding of chronology?

A third-year initial teacher-training student, Caitlin Bates, has created some of the most interesting and original approaches to studying the Egyptians that I have seen. Here is her plan for teaching a lesson on the Egyptians, which is both immensely practical and allows us to make connections with the past by modern experimentation.

Caitlin's plan

The main activities will be split into four stations; two of these activities will be done before break and other two after, as children need to have looked at the Book of the Dead (Faulkner 2008) before they can understand some of the example hieroglyphics. (The Book of the Dead is a collection of Ancient Egyptian spells for gaining access to the after life). Class teacher (CT) will explain at the start what each station is about and the tasks to be carried out there. The stations will each have a sheet with the task written on it as well, so that CT does not need to re-explain after each move. CT and support staff to supervise but not be constantly at one station.

Children will have 30 minutes at each table, allowing for 5 minutes between moves to pack up their work and make the table ready for the next group. Each group will have the opportunity to work at 1 station before break and 1 after.

At each station the children will be asked to think about:

■ What do these things tell us about Ancient Egyptian beliefs?
■ What do these things tell us about Ancient Egyptian life?

These questions will be written on prompt cards on each table to remind the children to think about it. CT and support staff will ask children these questions as part of their assessment.

Before break: Both these activities require relatively low input from CT or support staff in terms of direct teaching – children will be investigating for themselves and CT will observe and question. CT's main role will be to explain the tasks and give further insight into the artefacts and resources if children struggle to interpret them.

Afterlife station

Resources:

■ Images from Book of the Dead
■ Example map.

The task sheet will read: 'Create a map of a journey to the afterlife'.

Children will interrogate these sources to create an understanding of what the Egyptians believed about the afterlife. Individually, in their topic books, children will create their own maps, mapping the journey from death, to burial, to the spirit leaving the body and then through the kind of trials they might encounter on their journey to paradise. Children can interpret this task in a variety of ways, but an example beginning will be given to those who may struggle.

Language: Book of the Dead, Map of the afterlife, paradise, the devourer, Thoth, Osiris, Amun-Ra.

Artefacts station

Resources:

- Shabti figure
- Figure of a baboon
- Small heart amulet
- Pictures of artefacts.

The task sheet will read: 'Investigate these artefacts. Can you find out what they were for? What objects would you choose to go in your tomb?' Children should then place the objects in order of importance, giving reasons for this.

Language: scarab, amulet, shabti.

After break: Both these activities require more hands-on involvement from CT and support staff as there is a more practical element. CT will initially be at the hieroglyphic station to explain the task and show the group the papyrus and explain how it is made. This group can then get on with the task whilst supervised by support staff. The mummy station will initially be looking at the resources, supervised by support staff, to answer any queries and then the CT will work with them to create their mummified fruit. Whilst doing this CT and support staff will monitor the whole class and observe and question children as they work.

Mummy station

Resources:

- Pictures of mummies
- Picture cards of the process of embalming (see www.ancientegypt.co.uk/mummies/story/main.html)
- Small apples
- Knife (for cutting apples)
- Baking powder
- Table salt
- Plastic drinking cups
- Measuring cup.

The task sheet will read: 'Why did the Ancient Egyptians mummify the dead?'

Children to investigate the resources and discuss why they think the ancient Egyptians mummified their dead. Children have looked at the Book of the Dead and may have some ideas about Egyptian beliefs regarding this. Children will order the picture cards to show the process of embalming. Children will explain to CT what they think and CT will expand on this and give them more information about the purpose of mummification – to keep the body intact through embalming and the use of Natron, a desiccant to dry out the moisture.

CT to explain that we will be using a mixture of baking powder and salt to form a desiccant to dry out a piece of fruit and see if this process really works.

CT to lead the children in a mummifying experiment. Each child will have two quarters of apple (of equal size if possible – children can weigh both pieces before hand and note this on the results sheet) and a control piece will be kept aside. CT will demonstrate the experiment. Put a quarter of the apple in one cup and the other quarter in another. Fill the measuring cup with baking powder up to one-third mark. Then add salt until the cup is filled up to the two-thirds mark. Mix the salt and baking powder together in the cup. Pour the mixture into one of the cups containing an apple slice. Make sure the entire apple slice is completely covered. The children will each do their own and then leave on the side until next week where this will be followed up in a science lesson. Children should think about how to make it a fair test – CT will ask the children why they might leave one piece of each type of fruit (the control) un-mummified. Children should understand that this is to see the difference between the mummified fruit and the normal fruit after a week. Children will make predictions as to what they think may happen.

Mummified fruit will be placed to the side of the classroom alongside the control fruit.

Children will wash up and clear their table ready for the next group.

Language: canopic jars, embalming, mummification, fair test, control.

Hieroglyphics station

Resources:

- Examples of hieroglyphic texts
- Decoder www.jimloy.com/hiero/alpha.htm
- Charcoal
- Water
- Soot
- Drawing paper
- Reed pens.

The task sheet will read: 'Create your own holy texts using hieroglyphics. You could pray or do a spell or even a description of a god – but remember it, it's a sacred text!'

Looking at hieroglyphics and creating their own individually: CT will show the group some papyrus brought back from Egypt. CT to explain how this was made (thin strips from the papyrus stems, laid in rows and pressed down tight to squeeze out all the water, then left to dry. They had to be rubbed down with a stone to smooth the surface for writing.)

The group will use thick paper instead but will create their own ink, as the Egyptians would have, by mixing soot or charcoal with water and using reed brushes with pointed ends. Children will have decoder to help them copy the symbols. CT will explain how hieroglyphics work – can be written left to right, right to left, or top to bottom (can be determined according to the direction of animals' heads), scribes often made up other symbols for groups of letters, vowel sounds not usually used, etc.

CT will explain that as these are holy texts the children must only write something holy – for example a spell or a prayer or a description of a god. They can be as imaginative as they want.

The group will look at some examples of hieroglyphics. They will also have seen some examples of spells at the afterlife station before break.

Children will create their own hieroglyphics which can be stuck into their topic books once dry. Those who finish quickly can use pencil crayons to add colour or they can create another.

Language: hieroglyphic, papyrus, script, decipher, decode.

Plenary

Talk about interpretation – bias.

CT will then ask the children whether or not these things can be trusted to give us a true picture.

CT will show and read 'The Cannibal hymn' from King Unas's tomb (www. maat.sofiatopia.org/cannibal) on the smart board and discuss how the purpose of pyramid texts was to present life at its best and often the people would make statements such as, "I am the son of Osiris" as they thought this made them look better in the afterlife and helped them get through the trials and judgements.

CT to ask children if they can think of any more examples of this that they found in their investigations today.

Reflection on Caitlin's lesson

What Caitlin has set out here is a series of activities, which allow an intelligent understanding of the Egyptians to develop. This is full of subtlety. She does use hieroglyphics but she stresses their role as a sacred script, she demonstrates the process of desiccation with common kitchen chemicals and allows the children to see how the rituals associated with mummification are recorded in the Book of the Dead. Such lessons are a vital tool in building chronological awareness and enable us to begin making an important link with the past. If we are aware of how and why things were done in the past then we can begin to build links with how the same things are done now.

CONCLUSION

Most of us who teach history with passion do so because we love the subject. We love its complexity, we love its drama and stories and we love that idea of hidden mysteries, which are waiting to be solved. For some of us there is also passion in the evidence, the artefacts, the archaeology, the documents and the paintings and photographs of long-dead characters. We order this by applying timescales and labels as they best fit and we celebrate the differences and similarities with the past with school trips and views of tantalising evidence. We also know that if we teach history by its labels and numbers we will risk the subject becoming boring and mundane. So as careful teachers we build opportunities to look at change, continuity, numbers and dates into our teaching but we simply allow these chronological insights to support our teaching of this wonderful subject and make it a little less obscure.

REFERENCES

Adams, D. (1987) *Dirk Gently's Holistic Detective Agency*, London: Heinemann.

Arthur, J. and Phillips, R. (2000) *Issues in History Teaching*, London: Routledge.

Cooper, H. (2007) *History 3–11*, London: David Fulton.

Cooper, H. (2012) *History 5–11*, London: Routledge.

Cunliffe, B. (2008) *Europe Between the Oceans, 9000 BC–AD 1000*, London: Yale University Press.

Dawson, I. (2004) *Time for Chronology? Ideas for developing chronological understanding*. Available at: www.history.org.uk/resources/secondary_resource_102_8.html.

Dixon, J. and Day, S. (2004) Secret places: 'You're too big to come in here!' In H. Cooper (ed.) *Exploring Time and Place Through Play*, pp. 92–108, London: David Fulton.

Farmer, A. and Heeley, A. (2004) Moving between fantasy and reality: sustained, shared thinking about the past, in H. Cooper (ed.) *Exploring Time and Place Through Play*, pp. 52–64, London: David Fulton.

Faulkner, R.O. (trans.) (2008) *The Egyptian Book of the Dead*, San Francisco: Chronicle Books.

Foreman, N., Boyd-Davis, S., Moar, M., Korallo, L. and Chappell, E. (2008) *Can virtual environments enhance the learning of historical chronology?* Available at: http://ehis.ebscohost.com/eds/pdfviewer/pdfviewer?sid=d34c1de1-664f-405b-b2cc-c48f29077e5f%40sessionmgr115&vid=1&hid=101

Hoodless, P. (2010) *Chronology*. E-CPD (On line Continuing Professional Development units) www.history.org.uk

Husbands, C. (1996) *What is History Teaching?* Buckingham: Open University Press.

Moore, H. and Ashcroft, S. (2010) Teaching WWI and professional development, *Primary History* (54).

Philpot, J. (2008) *Chronological Understanding*. Available at: www.history.org.uk/file_download.php?ts=1206543408&id=912 (accessed 24 October 2011).

Robson, W. (2004) Kings, queens and castles, in H. Cooper (ed.) *Exploring Time and Place Through Play*, pp. 40–51, London: David Fulton.

Sambrook, P. (2004) *Laundry Bygones*, Haverfordwest: Shire Books.

CHAPTER 7

CREATIVITY AND HISTORICAL INVESTIGATION: PUPILS IN ROLE AS HISTORY DETECTIVES (PROTO-HISTORIANS) AND AS HISTORICAL AGENTS

Jon Nichol

PREFACE – TWO HISTORY MYSTERIES

The first section of the chapter, *The Mystery of the Saracens' Receipt* examines the initial phase of identifying and working on a single historical source, the receipt, to introduce a topic. *The Mystery of the Empty Grave* incorporates a Harry Potter genre magic history novelette to illuminate how creative thinking can be turned into creative teaching.

The two mysteries are vehicles to explore teacher creativity in developing effective pedagogy for 'little c' pupil creativity (Craft 2001). The *Mystery of the Saracens' Receipt* is a new creative experience that began in March 2012. *The Mystery of the Empty Grave* has had a creative teaching life since 1970, going through numerous permutations and developments to reflect changes in our own cultures and the rapid technological changes that have moved us from the era of Caxton to the era of Berners-Lee.

INTRODUCTION

Creativity and connectivity

Teacher creativity can help develop the sophisticated, complex and challenging pedagogy that produces outstanding history teaching and learning. Such creativity has a common factor: making connections between apparently unconnected elements to create something that is new, vibrant, striking and effective. Creativity is often spontaneous – a eureka moment – the solution arrives unheralded, unannounced at any time, often soon after a period of intense cogitation. This chapter examines two such cases of creative connectivity: *The Mystery of the Saracens' Receipt* and *The Mystery of the Empty Grave*.

Creativity empowers the teacher to produce lessons that excite, intrigue, challenge and develop in pupils a wide range of thinking, social, organisational and communication skills. Creativity is rooted in the ability to make connections, – connectivity – drawing upon the knowledge, understanding and imagination of the creator that can be wide-ranging, eclectic and apparently unrelated. Indeed the highest forms of historical creativity involve making connections between apparently unconnected elements to produce a completely new view of the subject. Creative connectivity reveals and illuminates what was previously hidden and unconsidered. Sir Tim Berners-Lee tells us how his creative connectivity produced the World Wide Web:

> Creating the web was really an act of desperation, because the situation without it was very difficult when I was working at CERN (European Organisation for Nuclear Research) later. Most of the technology involved in the web, like the hypertext, like the Internet, multifont text objects, had all been designed already. I just had to put them together. It was a step of generalising, going to a higher level of abstraction, thinking about all the documentation systems out there as being possibly part of a larger imaginary documentation system.
>
> (Berners-Lee 2007)

The Saracens' Receipt's connectivity linked it to the *English National Curriculum for History*'s (DfE 2012) wider world context at the end of the Roman Empire. *The Saracens' Receipt* mystery is an entrée to the major Islamic historical dimension for pupils as members of a multi-ethnic, multi-faith and multi-cultural English society in which Islam plays a huge part.

British History

8 In their study of British history, pupils should be taught about:

a the Romans, Anglo-Saxons and Vikings …

b aspects of the histories of England, Ireland, Scotland and Wales, where appropriate and about the history of Britain in its European and wider world context, in these periods.

(DfE 2012)

The Mystery of the Empty Grave's connectivity was to make the link between Harry Potter and history when Harry Potter novels were omnipresent as personal readers in the bags of pupils we were teaching. If we could combine Harry Potter and history we would be able to draw upon and sustain pupil interest, enthusiasm and involvement. The eureka moment was when the teacher I work with was discussing a possible local history programme for her pupils; she said that there was a mysterious death in the 1820s in the woods where the school now stands. The woods surrounded a local gothic mansion, Warley Abbey. A man was tried, the defence said he had been thrown from his horse and died because a ghost, The Grey Lady, had frightened it. Eureka – the Grey Lady lived in Warley Abbey, she was a friend of Hogwarts' ghost, Headless Nick – so Warley Abbey was the Hogwarts field centre where Harry, Hermione and other Hogwarts' pupils did field work.

Creativity and history teaching

Creativity, micro-history and macro-history

History mysteries involve discovering and working upon evidence: the initial clue can be a single source such as a tax receipt or a burial mound that contained an apparently empty grave. In investigating historical mysteries as proto-historians history detectives, or in role as historical characters, pupils learn both historical content (fact – propositional or substantive knowledge) and how to develop history's disciplinary skills, processes and concepts (procedural or syntactic knowledge), i.e. history as enquiry. Investigating the tax receipt and the burial mound has two dimensions: the unique historical situation at a specific point in time and place, micro-history, and learning about each mystery's overall historical context and the period in which it occurred, macro-history.

Our two history mysteries have contrasting micro-history and macro-historical settings. Their micro-history contexts were the funeral of an Anglo-Saxon king in *c*. AD 625, in a burial mound on an Anglo-Saxon headland overlooking the estuary of the river Deben in East Anglia and a village in Egypt on 25 April AD 642, when the tax collector arrived to claim delivery of 65 sheep in part payment of tax owed. Both mysteries share the same macro-history big picture: the Decline and Fall of the Roman Empire civilisation from *c*. AD 500 to 700 in an age of conquest, migration, settlement, colonisation, evangelism and imperialism that shaped Western European, Mediterranean and Middle East history, including Christianity and Islam. (Maps of the Roman Empire in AD 600 can be found on Google Images.)

Fascinatingly, two silver spoons in the treasure found in the Sutton Hoo empty grave directly link the two mysteries. The spoons may have reached East Anglia as a gift or as trade goods before being buried in the grave. They are engraved with the words Paulos and Saulos, written in Greek (a photograph of the spoons can also be found on Google Images).

What is involved in teacher creativity?

Teaching creativity and teaching and learning principles

Teaching creativity does not occur in a vacuum: it draws upon the extensive and sophisticated professional pedagogic knowledge of the teacher. Such pedagogic knowledge is multi-faceted, shaping the teachers' values and beliefs which shape how they teach. It includes:

■ *detailed academic knowledge of the historical topic*; both *what* is known – 'know that' knowledge (facts) and *how* it is known – 'know how' knowledge (history as an enquiry – processes, procedures, skills, disciplinary concepts and protocols);

■ *an understanding of children's cognitive development*, how they think and what they are capable of thinking when studying history;

■ *knowledge of the school:* its ethos, orientation, staff, curriculum, assessment, teaching and learning styles;

■ *a pedagogic repertoire (praxis)* that provides the building material for creating an outstanding teaching and learning;

■ *a willingness to explore, experiment, imagine, speculate and take risks.*

Two major creative factors are the assimilation of principles for teaching and for pupil learning. The *Nuffield Primary History Project*'s teaching principles (Table 7.1) and *Cognitive Acceleration in History Education*'s (CACHE) framework for learning (Table 7.2) permeate the shaping and development of our teaching programmes.

Learning principles mirror teaching principles. We based CACHE upon the six axioms of Cognitive Acceleration in Science Education (CASE) adding to them a seventh, Bloom's (1974) concept of *Mastery Learning*. CACHE takes fully into account that classrooms are highly complex, social environments in which learning involves pupils working individually and cooperatively with their peers in a structured, organised and progressive way (Shayer and Adey 2002).

■ **Table 7.1** Nuffield Primary History principles for teaching

---

1 Questioning

2 Study in depth

3 Authenticity

4 Economy of resources

5 Accessibility

6 Communication

■ **Table 7.2** Cognitive acceleration principles for supporting pupils' learning in history combined with Bloom's principle of mastery of learning in order to promote cognitive acceleration

1 Cognitive development

2 Concrete preparation

3 Cognitive conflict: problem-solving

4 Social learning

5 Metacognition

6 Bridging

7 Mastery learning

THE MYSTERY OF THE SARACENS' RECEIPT: PERF 558

PERF 558 enables pupils as history detectives to investigate a specific document at a specific point in time in order to develop an understanding of the macro-history of the end of the Roman Empire in the Eastern Mediterranean and the rise of Islam as a world religion and as ruler of the Middle East and North Africa. PERF 558 is the Saracens' tax receipt, the oldest surviving, dated Islamic document – AH 22 (Anno Hegirae) (AD 642) from Heracleopolis, in Egypt. (A photograph of PERF 558 can be found on Google Images.)

PERF 558 is a manuscript (a hand-written document). It is a single piece of papyrus written on both sides. Apparently of no importance, PERF 558 spent 1,300 years unnoticed, ending up in a bundle of documents in an archive in Vienna.

I spotted PERF 558 in a newspaper article an historian, Tom Holland (2012a), had written. The article was an exciting account of solving the history mystery locked in PERF 558. Connectivity involves making links – I realised that PERF 558 is a marvellous starting point for teaching about the Roman Empire, Western Europe and the Rise of Islam from *c.* AD 500 to 700. It stirred my creative teaching juices because:

■ it was a single source, perfect for use with teachers and children;
■ it contained a range of clues that the teacher and pupils could use to solve the mystery;
■ it would require pupils to research the clues' meaning and significance to create their understanding of its micro- and macro-historical contexts, i.e. the fall of the Roman Empire and the rise of Islam (Holland 2012a, b).

Unlocking the mystery

How can we use our historical expertise to unlock the mystery of PERF 558 for teaching? To make sense of PERF 558 I used my historian's training. The first step was to find the original receipt in full. Tom Holland's (2012a) article includes a photograph of the document, with a couple of sentences about it and its library reference number – PERF

558. So, the Internet came to the rescue. I typed PERF 558 into Google. Up popped a long list of references. I chose Wikipedia because it not only gave an academic summary of PERF 558 but also listed the academic sources Wikipedia had used to write about it. One of these was a highly detailed contemporary academic paper about PERF 558 that included a full translation (Jones 1998).

Stage 1. Making the document readable for pupils

In order to challenge pupils, the first Nuffield Primary History Project principle, they must be able to read their sources – both primary and secondary. The article included a full translation of PERF 558 in several relatively unconnected sections, like pieces in a jigsaw puzzle. While each was clear, they needed extensive collating to produce a single, coherent document. The receipt was written on two sides: only after editing it did the penny drop that it was *two receipts*: one in Arabic for the Saracens (Arabs) and one in Greek for the Egyptian administrators who were collecting the tax for their new Arab rulers. A local priest and clerk wrote the receipt in Greek. An Arab, Ibn Habid, then summarised the document in Arabic – perhaps at the same time, but probably later. Figure 7.1 shows the full text, in a form teachers and their pupils can interrogate.

Stage 2. Meeting the challenge of unlocking the mystery: Processes, procedures and teaching principles

Understanding the meaning of the receipt was a prelude to thinking creatively about how to use it for teaching: the teaching activity should mirror the processes historians use to understand it and its significance. They:

■   *read it* – the first step; then
■   *ask questions* about it, identifying clues it contains;

God! In the name of God! I, Emir 'Abdallah, to you, Christophoros and Theodorakios, Intendants of Herakleopolis!

For the maintenance of the Sarasins who are with me, I took from you at Heracleopolis 65 sheep, I repeat: sixty-five and no more, and as an acknowledgement of this fact, we have made the present confirmation.

Written by me, Jean, notary and deacon. On the 30th of the month of Pharmouthi of the 1st indiction.

In the name of Allah, the Compassionate, the Merciful! This is what Abdallāh, Son of Jabir, and his companions-in-arms, have taken for slaughter sheep at Heracleopolis. They have taken from a representative of Theodorakios, second son of Apa Kyros, and from a representatives of Christophoros, eldest son of Apa Kyros, fifty sheep as slaughter sheep and fifteen other sheep. They gave them, for slaughter, for the crew of his vessels, as well as his cavalry and his breastplated infantry in the month of Jumādā the first in the year twenty-two. Written by Ibn Hadid.

Figure 7.1 Translations of the Greek and Arabic (*italics*) texts of PERF 558

- *research answers* (information) to the questions and the clues;
- *organise and analyse the factual information and evidence* (knowledge) into a preliminary account, including a chronological framework – what Hexter (1971) called the first record of the past;
- *use their own wider knowledge*, their second records, to infer, to deduce, to use informed imagination, to hypothesise, to explore, to speculate, to hypothesise, to test theories so as to reach conclusions to solve the mystery. The second record 'is everything he [the historian] can bring to bear on the record of the past in order to elicit from that record the best account he can render of what he believes actually happened in the past' (Hexter 1971: 80);
- *communicate understanding.*

Stage 3. Questions and questioning

To unlock the meaning of *The Saracens' Receipt* involves questioning. Academic historians, teachers and pupils use the same trigger question words (Figure 7.2) to generate questions to solve history mysteries.

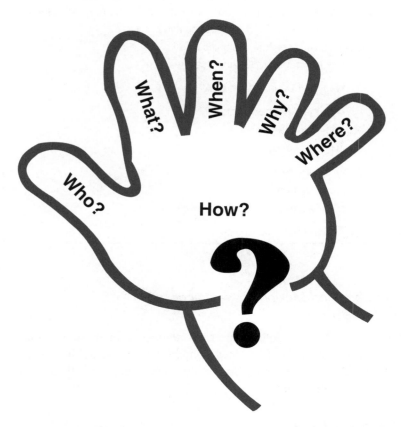

Figure 7.2 Trigger words (question heads) used to generate questions, which help to solve historical problems

I used the trigger words shown in Figure 7.2 (*question heads*), to generate *question tails*. Question heads and tails about PERF 558 are shown in Table 7.3.

■ **Table 7.3** Question heads and tails used to examine PERF 588

Question heads	Tails
How	was the receipt written?
	did the historical situation that the document was written in come about?
What	what does it say?
	what is it?
	is it for?
	what language is it written in?
	is it about?
	does it tell us about the society at the time?
	do historical sources [books/articles/other sources] tell us about it?
	is the overall historical situation it is from?
	is its wider historical significance?
	has happened to it since it was written?
When	was the document written?
Where	was the document written?
	has it been since?
	is it taken from?
Who	wrote the receipt?
	was it written for?
	are the people in the document?
Why	was the document written?

Stage 4. Textbreaker: Making the text accessible – reading it for meaning

Pupils and teachers have to interrogate their sources – interrogation that requires detailed extraction and of the clues they contain before researching their meaning. This involves breaking into sources from multiple perspectives. All such sources are genres. A genre consists of its:

1   cultural context (culture)
2   content (field)

3   overall structure (mode) with its specific conventions, layout, linguistic features, framework form)
4   source's purpose (tenor), i.e. its creator's intention in relation to its intended audience.

These elements combine to give the genre its voice or *register*. We used genre theory to create a tool, *Textbreaker,* to break into any text or source, decode its element, read and understand its content (Nichol, 2010). Table 7.4 shows how Textbreaker unlocked the *Mystery of The Saracens' Receipt* drawing on the categories in Textbreaker to squeeze out information.

■ **Table 7.4** How the mystery of PERF 558 was solved using Textbreaker

Tenor	The purpose of the document – author and recipient
Author	The tax collector
Recipient	The Arab rulers in charge of the Egyptian tax gatherers and the Egyptian tax gatherers
Purpose	To record the requisitioning of 65 sheep for the Arab (Saracen) army of occupation of Egypt in AD 642 (AH 22). The receipt's two versions were for the Egyptian tax collectors and for the Arab rulers of Egypt whom the tax collectors worked for. The receipt was for part payment of taxes.

Mode	The channel of communication
A receipt	Elements that all receipts have in common and enable us to understand them
Conventions or form of the genre	The form/structure of the receipt: Date; place; amount paid; signature/statement of giver and receiver; who from; who too; nature of payment (logical structure and pattern of receipt genre)
Layout	How the receipt was laid out – order/pattern

Field – content

Nouns	Role	Ethnicity	Notes
People:			
Jean	Notary and deacon – working for the Egyptian government	Egyptian	A clerk, an official – a member of the Coptic church. He wrote the document in Arabic and Greek

(Continued)

■ **Table 7.4** (Continued)

Field – content

Nouns	Role	Ethnicity	Notes
Emir Abdallah	Commander	Arab	Commander of the Arabs requisitioning sheep for the Arab (Saracen) army at Heracleopolis
Theodorakios Christophoros	Government officials for the Herakleopolis region	Greek/ Egyptian	Egyptian officials of Greek origin from the city of Herakleopolis. Heakleopolis governed the area the village the sheep were taken from
Apa Kyros	Father of Theodorakios and Christophoros	Greek/ Egyptian	Father of the officials Theodorakios and Christophoros: to identify who they are
Representatives	Men in charge of the sheep	Egyptian	The men who were in charge of the sheep: probably farmers
Crew	Crews of ships	Arab	The ships would have been those of the Arab fleet that supported the invasion of Egypt
Cavalry	Mounted soldiers	Arab	Members of the Arab army that had invaded and conquered Egypt from 639
Infantry	Foot soldiers	Arab	Members of the Arab army

Animals

Sheep	65: 50 to be taken and slaughtered	Egyptian	The 65 sheep were supplies for the Arab army and fleet, see Culture below for context

Objects

Vessels	Arab warships and transports	Arab	The Arab invasion fleet

Places

Heracleopolis	An Egyptian City – administrative centre	Egyptian/ Greek	A Greek city Alexander the Great founded 80 miles from Cairo

Historical concepts

Chronology	Purpose	Ethnicity	Notes
30th of the month of Pharmouthi	To date the receipt	Greek	The Christian calendar 25 April 643

(Continued)

Historical concepts

Chronology	Purpose	Ethnicity	Notes
Year AH 22	To date the receipt	Arab	The Arab calendar AH 22 AH *Anno Hegirae* (in the year of the Hijra). It is the first recorded document using the Islamic system of dating – after Muhammed's flight from Mecca The Arab calendar was introduced in AD 639

Evidence

The document	A receipt	Arab	The nature, form, reliability of the document: a papyrus document, internal clues indicate that it is genuine

Culture

The Islamic expansion in the period after Muhammed's death, resulting in the conquest of the Easter Roman Empire, including its heartland of Egypt from 639 to 641. Tom Holland's article (2012) says that we can now see that the document marks a seismic shift; the Magariyai would implant themselves in Egypt far more securely than the Greeks or the Romans ever did. With them they brought Arabic, which is a novelty on PERF 558, but is now so native to Egypt that Egypt is now seen as a powerhouse of Arabic culture. Yet even this transformation does not convey the full extent of the changes. The tax receipt issued in Herakleopols in 'the year 22', the oldest surviving datable document had brought a new age into being. To a quarter of the people alive today this is of more than historical interest, for it touches, in their view, on the nature of the Devine. What brought Magaritai to Herakleopolis, and many other cities, has long been at the heart of a global religion, Islam. It has been too readily forgotten that the Arab conquests were part of the decline of the Roman Empire. As Gibbon said in the eighteenth century, the barbarian invasions of Europe and the victories of the Saracens, opens up dramas not hinted at by traditional Muslim narratives. In the west, provinces had also witnessed the collapse of the superpower, foreign invaders and the struggle of locals to establish for themselves a new security

Teaching creativity

The next phase is for you to turn *The Saracens' Receipt* into a teaching programme in which pupils solve its mystery and in so doing develop an understanding of the end of the Roman Empire in both Western Europe, the Mediterranean and the Middle East from *c*. AD 500 to 700/AH 82. To help, you might like to consult the following available from The Historical Association and its website, www.history.org.uk:

■ *Primary History Journal*, which contains a wealth of ideas, approaches, cases and case studies in its themed editions (the volumes on Reading and Writing might be of particular interest);

■   *Nuffield Primary History Project* guidance and exemplar lessons;
■   *History in Initial Teacher Training* (HITT) teacher-training packs;
■   podcasts, newsletters and other information.

The second section of this chapter, *The Mystery of the Empty Grave*, is a case study of the creative teaching process in action, again starting with a single source, a grave in a burial mound that apparently did not contain a body.

THE MYSTERY OF THE EMPTY GRAVE: A CASE STUDY OF CREATIVE HISTORY TEACHING

Introduction

Since the Schools Council History Project in the early 1970s made excavation a central element in its *What Is History* teaching programme we have been simulating the excavation of the Anglo-Saxon Sutton Hoo burial mound of *c*. AD 625/AH 3, on the banks of the River Deben at Woodbridge, Suffolk. Our teaching creativity has involved pupils as history detectives in the visceral excitement of excavating and discovering the mystery objects in the burial mound's grave, interpreting them and reconstructing the burial ceremony and its significance.

The new creative teaching element in the Sutton Hoo Case Study was applying the Harry Potter genre (see p. 103 above), through the medium of a Magic History Mystery novelette, *The Mystery Of The Empty Grave*. The main characters in each Magic History Mystery novelette are two children, Sam and Jane (aka Harry and Hermione), who travel back in time to solve a history mystery with the help of magic and their Uncle John (aka John Fines). We first used the Harry Potter idea with a 10- to 11-year-old mixed ability, but highly literate class of multi-ethnic pupils at a school in Sandwell, Birmingham. The novelette's teaching programme incorporated our existing Sutton Hoo Scheme of Work (SoW). The Sutton Hoo SoW includes a wide range of stimulating and lively teaching and learning activities (see *Primary History* 51: 22–25) including writing a poem describing the burial (a funeral poem for Raedwald) based upon the Anglo-Saxon poetic genre in Seamus Heaney's translation of *Beowulf*. All the teaching resources referred to can be downloaded from www.history.org.uk. In Primary Articles and Resources search for Sutton Hoo – classroom archaeology in the digital age.

Setting the scene

The introduction to the History Mystery novelette explains how we linked Harry Potter and history teaching:

> *The Magic History of Britain: the Mystery of the Empty Grave*
>
> Two children, Jane and Sam, travel back in time to solve a history mystery. Jane is a young witch whose family has come to live in England from the West

Indies. Sam is her best friend. Sam's mum and dad come from Norway. Jane has many hobbies – writing, reading, writing stories and archery. Sam is a wonderful swimmer, ice skater, judo champion and kick-boxer, who loves computers, making models and mending machines. Jane lives at 2, Aelfred Road, Axchester, a small, English country town. Jane and Sam go to the local school, where they suffer from an old fashioned and deadly boring history teacher, Miss Woodhead.

The novelette's narrative served as our core text for a set of teaching activities. Pupils in teams of three or four work as archaeologists to excavate the burial mound. Each team's members have one or more complementary roles; manager/team leader, observer, organiser of resources, recorder and reporter. They work *as* a group as opposed to *in* a group – otherwise it is impossible for them to complete the task.

Outline of activities

Among the teaching activities were:

1   *Asking questions* to drive on the investigation, using a letter Jane and Sam had received about an archaeological discovery in a burial mound, with a photograph of the burial mound. They were going to stay in a house and become involved in the excavation.
2   *Doing a jigsaw puzzle* of what might have been buried in the burial mound, the outline of a Saxon ship that Jane's naughty sister had cut up into small pieces.
3   *Helping Jane and Sam solve the problem of how to organise the burial of an Anglo-Saxon king.*
4   *Participating as a team in excavating the burial mound* and working out from the clues they had discovered what the mound's burial chamber contained.
5   *Creating a classroom museum exhibition of the objects in the grave.*

Resources (downloadable from www.history.org.uk)

1   The Sutton Hoo photo of Mrs Pretty, and the outline of the burial boat, the marks its rotting wood and rivets left in the sandy soil;
2   proforma for planning a king's burial chamber;
3   the grid rectangle for recording what the pupils found when excavating the burial chamber;
4   pictures of the downloadable objects – two copies of each in a wallet/envelope for each grid rectangle;
5   glue sticks, magnifying glasses, scissors, A3 and A4 paper and card;
6   the museum exhibit template.

The teaching

It is September 1939 – Sam and Jane are visiting the house of Mrs Pretty, of Woodbridge, Suffolk, to help her with the excavation.

■   Tell the class that Sam and Jane's Uncle John has given Jane an envelope containing a letter. The letter is from an archaeologist, Gerhard, who tells them about a history mystery that they can help to solve. The letter reads:

21st July 1939

Dear Sam and Jane,

The enclosed photograph is of Mrs Pretty, Mr Brown and two other archaeologists. The picture shows the large mound that we are going to excavate. When you arrive, in five weeks time, I hope you can help us in finding out what the large mound might contain.

Best wishes

Gerhard

■   The class helps Jane and Sam to solve the mystery.

Activity 1. Asking questions

■   In pairs, the pupils are asked to come up with three questions they would like to ask the archaeologists about the burial mound, using the key trigger words to help – who, where, when, why, how and what.
■   We pool their answers on the board and discuss them.

For the following activities we make the pupils work as groups of three or four, with a common goal, separate complementary roles and tasks that force them to work co-operatively (N.B. each group must have a good reader or writer). Split the class into eight or nine groups of three or four pupils: not friendship groups. Number the groups 1–8/9: pick out 8/9 good readers before you start numbering, then place one with each numbered group.

Give the group members separate, complementary roles: reporter, recorder, monitor of activities, manager of resources.

Activity 2. The jigsaw puzzle: making sense of the cut-up photograph

Prepare eight or nine envelopes of the grave ship outline cut into pieces. Differentiate, if necessary, between higher and lower ability groups – the higher ability group can have lots of oddly shaped pieces to fit together.

- *Hand out the envelopes* with the pieces, the card for sticking down the finished jigsaw, glue sticks.
- *Explain the task* – set a time limit for jigsaw, ask children how long they think is appropriate.
- *Feedback*: each of the groups feeds back on what the picture shows.
- *Ask them where they would dig* to find any buried treasure.
- *Ask them to guess what* it might be.

Activity 3. Imaginative reconstruction: the burial chamber

Introduction: Jane thought hard about what might be buried at the bottom of the burial mound. She knew that the Oseberg Viking boat had contained the treasures of a queen. If there was a king and queen buried in the Sutton Hoo burial chamber, what might the grave contain? How might it be laid out?

The grave goods: Jane looked in her magic seeing mirror. It had searched through the Internet and books and also looked at Saxon poetry, in particular *Beowulf*. This was the list of things that it came up with what such a grave might contain (Table 7.5).

- Can you, in pairs, and then pooling your ideas in fours, plan out how the queen of the Saxon king might have planned out the burial chamber of her husband, putting in it the goods listed in Table 7.5?
- Discuss your plans as a class, drawing up on the whiteboard or blackboard / flip chart, a plan that you can all agree upon.

■ **Table 7.5** Proforma for planning a king's burial chamber

THE KING OR QUEEN'S BURIAL

Plan out what the king's burial chamber might have been like. It is 6 metres long by 3 metres wide. Make sure that you put all of these things on your plan:

Object	Size	Tick
The body: it is fully clothed	2 metres long	
Bowls, silver – three	25 cms across	
Buckle of belt – solid gold	10 cms long	
Cauldron, huge, for cooking	50 cms across	
Chain mail	Same as a very long woolly jumper	
Cloak	2 metres long	
Coffin of wood (WAS there a coffin???)	2.2 metres × 50 cms	

(Continued)

■ **Table 7.5** (Continued)

Object	Size	Tick
Dagger	20 cms long	
Drinking horn	30 cms long	
Helmet	Size of crash helmet	
Iron chain to hang cauldron from	3 metres long	
Lamp	Bedside lamp, small	
Purse lid with money	15 cms across	
Sceptre	30 cms long	
Shield	1 metre across	
Silver dish, huge	50 cms wide	
Spears	Each 2 metres long	
Spoons	10 cms long	
Standard made of iron	2 metres high	
Sword belt, leather – over shoulder	1.5 metres long	
Sword	1.5 metres long	
Wooden bottle	Milk bottle size	
Wooden bucket, large	70 cms high, 50 cms across	
Wooden burial chamber	3 metres by 2 metres	

Activity 4. The classroom dig: digging up the burial chamber and making sense of the clues

The archaeologists decide to excavate the middle of the ship. The classroom is organised with eight spaced-out tables. Each table represents one rectangle on the archaeological grid.

One group will sit at each table. They will excavate by moving from table to table; how will they record what they find? (I.e. lead on to the concept of a grid of the excavation.) The grid we use has eight rectangles. Each square will be numbered, e.g. A1–4, B1–4.

■ *We use eight tables*, one for each rectangle, for the purpose of digging. Each pupil has a grid sheet with the eight rectangles.
■ *Children have to fill in the relevant rectangle for the object on the table* that they find the most interesting. Each rectangle can contain more than one object. Each rectangle has to have a title, a brief sketch of the object/s and one or more labels.
■ *On the command: 'Change!'* each group moves to the next table and repeats the task of recording an object.

■   *Feedback*: one person from each group tells of the object that they have chosen for their own grid square and why.

Activity 5. The museum exhibit

This forces the pupils to think about the nature and purpose of the objects they can present as a classroom display. This leads to discussion of what the nature and purpose of the grave might have been and follow-up work on clues, involving drama and writing/ presentation in different genres.

■   *Tell the class that we are going to produce an exhibition* of the goods that we found in the grave.

■   *Each pupil will prepare an exhibition sheet* for one of the objects in the grave. The teacher will ensure that all objects are presented in the exhibition.

■   *The class puts up the classroom museum exhibition* of the Sutton Hoo grave finds. In order to write the captions for the objects on display children recorded their inferences on archaeologist's record sheets, stating the grid reference for the object, its name, what they thought it was, who might have owned it, what it might have been used for, who might have made it, what it was made of and what might have happened to it since, together with a drawing of the object.

CONCLUSION

The Mystery of the Saracens' Receipt and *The Mystery of the Empty Grave* combine in suggesting a creative approach to the curricular problem of teaching about Christianity and Islam, Jihad and Crusade, Imperialism, the rise and fall of civilization, migration and settlement, multi-culturality, multi-ethnicity, toleration and extremism. All are present in the shared macro-history of these two mysteries, geographically posed at opposite ends of the Roman Empire that had straddled the European, Mediterranean and Middle Eastern World from the time of Christ until AD 650 or AH 28.

REFERENCES

Berners-Lee, T. (2007) The academy of achievement (interview), Washington, D.C. 22 May 2007, www.achievement.org/autodoc/page/ber1int-1 (accessed October 2012).

Bloom, B.S. (1974) An introduction to mastery learning theory, in J.H. Block (ed.) *Schools, Society and Mastery Learning*, New York: Holt Rinehart and Winston.

Craft, A. (2001) Little c creativity, in A. Craft, R. Jeffrey and M. Leibling (eds) *Creativity in Education Creativity in education*, pp. 45-46, London and New York: Continuum.

Department for Education (DfE) (2012) *English National Curriculum for History* (ENCH) KS2, www.education.gov.uk/schools/teachingandlearning/curriculum/primary/b00199012/history/ks2 (accessed October 2012).

Hexter, J. H. (1971) *The History Primer*, New York: Basic Books.

Holland, T. (2012a) The fall of the Roman empire and the rise of Islam, *The Guardian*, 30 March.

Holland, T. (2012b) *In the Shadow of the Sword: the Battle for Global Empire and the end of the Ancient World*, London: Little, Brown Book Group.

Jones, A. (1998) The dotting of a script and the dating of an era: the strange neglect of PERF 558, *Islamic Culture* 72(4): 95-103.

Nichol, J. (2010) Difficult and challenging reading: genre, text and multi-modal sources – Textbreaker, *Primary History 56, 'Doing History With Written and Printed Sources'*, The Historical Association, www.history.org.uk/resources/primary_resource_3718_3.html (accessed October 2012).

Shayer, M. and Adey, P.S. (2002) (eds) *Learning Intelligence: cognitive acceleration across the curriculum from 5 to 15 years*, Milton Keynes: Open University Press.

CHAPTER 8

USING CREATIVE DRAMA APPROACHES FOR THE TEACHING OF HISTORY

Cherry Dodwell

This chapter considers the role of drama in developing historical understanding. A case study shows how creative drama was developed from a local legend to enhance historical understanding. It is intended that this can be used as a model, which can be translated into other local contexts.

DEVELOPING HISTORICAL THINKING THROUGH DRAMA: FROM LOCAL TO UNIVERSAL

Where children live and their surroundings are important to them; they have a natural curiosity about their landscape, the people and past events and want to delve into them. Drama can help develop stories, myths, legends and investigations of past events and this involves discussion and debate and the exploration of new ideas. What in a local story or myth is 'real' and what is imagined can be very important considerations.

A legend from Widecombe-in-the-Moor

This project can connect many subject areas and asks children to look back at the past in a particular setting and try to understand differences in place and culture over time. There is a defined area to investigate hinged on a particular spectacular event in a Devon village.

> On the 21st of October 1638 an exceptionally violent storm occurred. It struck on a Sunday afternoon during a church service. A huge thunderbolt hit the church roof and sent masonry and debris flying down into the congregation, resulting in six people being killed and sixty two injured.
>
> (www.legendarydartmoor.co.uk/jan_reynolds.htm)

The folk tale which arose is similar to the story of Faust, who sells his soul to the Devil, in return for money and women, the 'Luck of the Devil'. A folk tale is a generic term for different narratives. Often they involve a local ghost. There are folk tales where a moment of definable (or indefinable) historical actuality is embedded, within any amount of fantastic invention.

The art of storytelling

A local professional storyteller could become involved; the Society for Storytelling provides a list of storytellers (www.sfs.org.uk), who will come into school if you want to work with a professional. The site gives a range of resources, local groups and provides support for teachers.

TRANSLATING STORY INTO DRAMA

Importantly most of the play should not be scripted but should evolve naturally from the drama activities with the class. A written script is best avoided, so that language is natural and spoken by the children in 'their own words'. There can be a traditional narrator who talks to the audience to tell particular sections of the story. A 'running order' plan of the scenes to view on a chart, as they are constructed, can be helpful. This should be a working document which can change as the project develops.

Will there be an audience?

The class can work towards devising a play to enjoy for their own delight (and learning), or for a particular 'audience' – to show to another class or to invited family and friends. The decision on 'audience' can be made at a particular point during the development of the piece. How do the class feel about the work? It depends on their age, confidence, previous drama experience and what the agreed aim is for all involved. It can be just about the process and there need not necessarily be a product (a play). If there is a performance it should be a celebration of achievement, not an embarrassing stilted recitation lacking confidence.

Getting started

This project can include a class visit, in this instance to the church at Widecombe-in-the-Moor and exploration of the village where the legend is set. A guided tour can be arranged, perhaps by a local historian.

The class can explore the incident through drama, as villagers who lived and worked in Widecombe at that time:

- Finding out about the village in the 1600s: home life, village life, schooling, social events, travel.
- Industrial archaeology of Dartmoor: working life, tin-mining.

■ Aspects of English heritage: folk songs, folk music, country dance.
■ Church building of the period, church and belief.
■ Importance of storytelling (little printed material available, no other media).
■ Information from parish records, burial records, the churchyard.

The story raises questions about changes over time, moral judgements, social behaviour and religious ideas. The teaching ideas suggested below can be modified to fit time available. Some may prefer to do the project intensively and combine it with a residential or a day trip, so how the suggestions are used can be flexible.

The use of drama here is a key feature as children learn to think 'as if' they were the characters who inhabit the story but they are also learning about differences between past and present. These may be in subtle ways and it is useful that these differences are opened up for discussion, in the hope that new understandings emerge.

The opening promenade: opening up the story

The promenade allows children time to see each other's ideas and then discuss and redraft their own. It allows pooling of ideas collectively and is a way of demonstrating how a community of learners can develop their ideas to support learning for all involved. In this 'promenade' the children 'visit a gallery' set up around a room or hall, where key sources, relevant to the story, are displayed: maps, pictures, photographs, artefacts, information about people who lived in the village in the period. These may be found on line or loaned from a local museum.

In the Widecombe legend pictures of a local tin-miners and mines as well as information about the great storm in October 1638 are essential. Let the class 'promenade' and spend time looking at the display items. Events surrounding the great storm at Widecombe in 1638 are recorded on four wall plaques on the inside walls of the church tower. The events of the great storm at Widecombe were recorded in the form of a poem, which was written on wooden panels and is understood to be the work of the village schoolmaster, Richard Hill, son of Roger Hill who was one of the villagers killed in the incident. The Rev. George Lyde also recorded the events in a long verse poem which can be seen in Dymond's (1876) book. Pupils can try and translate this; it is in old English. Photographs of the panels and copies of the poem can be displayed for the promenade.

The register of burials lists fifteen names up until 13 October 1638 which are then followed by:

Hill, Roger, Gent – 23 October
Meade, Robertt – 23 October
Milward, Sibella – 23 October

Hamlyn, Susan (wife of James) – 23 October
Sheere, Walter – 1 November
Beard, Bridgett Wid. – 6 November

Ask children to make a note of any interesting names on the maps, or anything that is of special interest to them.

Then and now

Following the promenade, children work in mixed groups of five or six. Sheets of A2 paper, felt pens, blue tack or pins for hanging charts are needed. Each group has a sheet of A2 paper, folded in half lengthwise. Children list, in one column, things most have in their houses today and in the other what they think would have been in a 'normal' village house 400 years ago.

Display the charts around the room/hall and 'promenade' again to look at class ideas. Groups then take down their own charts, and revise them with any new ideas discovered. In the final feedback allow time for discussion of any misconceptions or uncertainties that arise. It quite shocks children to realise that life has not always been so comfortable.

■   *Extension/homework task.* In pairs, one is to have a shoe box and make a model of their own bedroom and all the things in it and their partner a model of a room of a young person 400 years ago. Stack these boxes against a wall to make an interesting display.

■   *Extension task.* Have a map of Great Britain and a map of the world on the interactive white board. Ask children where they have visited in the UK and draw lines from the place they live to where they travelled to. On a local map show where local children might have travelled 400 years ago. Most would never have left their village. Again the contrast in the 'world' view of children now and then can be raised for discussion.

Physical warm-up, sounds to movement

Dartmoor in winter can be a cold and windy place. Recorded sound effects can be useful here. Sit in a circle. In groups of three, everyone makes sounds of the wind and a thunderstorm, quietly and steadily. Conduct the sounds building as a crescendo. Linking arms the class sway gently when the sound is quiet, then rock and move more energetically as the storm and sound build. The same exercise can be undertaken with free movement, beginning to move slowly with the sound of the wind and thunderstorm, building to more energetic movements. Then back to a circle.

After the physical activity ask the class to sit in the circle very quietly and concentrate. If the lights can go out and a candle put in the centre of the circle this creates a special atmosphere.

During the following narration, pre-recorded sound effects can be played in the background to help maintain the atmosphere. The teacher relates the opening narrative of the story, first describing the village, how 400 years ago on winter nights it would be a dark and lonely. Try to create the effect of 'another place and time'.

Tell the story

Just imagine 400 years ago in the village of Widecombe-in-the-Moor, a beautiful village, still there today, with its quaint little houses and great church – the same church that was there 400 years ago, but the church has something very different about it today. It has a different steeple now, because one day, 400 years ago, the steeple fell down into the church in a great thunderstorm. Imagine how frightening that must have been for the villagers. There was only a candle to huddle around in the dark at home. Imagine trying to sleep, hearing a great storm outside – and so on …

The class can make the sounds and physical movement above, while this section of the narrative is spoken. Later they can write their own opening to the story and set the scene or use the above.

Characters for the story

In groups of 5/6, on A3 paper, the class makes a list of who might have lived in the village and their likely occupations. There was a small village school. Invent names for the schoolmaster and children who might have been pupils. Explain that they are going to hear a story about a tin-miner who lived in the village, named Jan Reynolds. Add his name to the character list.

Drama strategy: spontaneous improvisation

This is a method of exploring character, issues or events. It is important to establish a 'safe' way into improvisation. Some children are natural performers, but it is best to work with all the class, until everyone feels comfortable with the work. You are aiming to ask them to perform but it is essential to have the right atmosphere in the group before you ask them to demonstrate their ideas, even to each other.

Allow just three to four minutes for each improvisation. Circle improvisation is a very useful starting technique for a class not used to drama. They work with a variety of people on a set of ideas to practise spontaneous improvisation. This is good for confidence building as nobody is 'on show'. The teacher is outside the circle and can move in on any pair who are not on task, but children enjoy this technique as they tend to see it as a game. Children work in pairs, and begin with a partner of their choice, not realising they will (because of the sequence) work with a variety of others they have not chosen to work with, as it is part of the game. Working with a partner you only have to think of one set of interactions, which is manageable for beginners.

Set up instructions for circle improvisation

Ask everyone to find a partner and choose who is A and who is B. All the 'B's are to stand in a large circle in the middle of the hall facing outwards to the walls. Then ask their partners to go and face them, so the class are standing in two circles, everyone facing their partner.

■ *Improvisation 1: Description*

A and B are characters on the village green. Children decide on names from the suggested list of village characters and tell each other who they are and what their job is. Then, on the count of 3, children go into role and discuss the terrible storm that had taken place the night before ... explain where they were and what happened during the storm. (Widecombe is famous for storms.)

'A's move on one place to the left (clockwise): that is, the outer circle moves once clockwise to the next person on the inner circle. At each turn of the circle each new pair tries a different short improvisation. Once you have set this up give at least four turns to the circle. This will allow children to role-play and try things out with a range of partners. You can use all the following, or select a few. Each 'turn' will take approximately 4-5 minutes, with the description, plus the 'rehearsal' time for the improvisation.

■ *Improvisation 2: Using persuasive language*

A and B are two school children on their way to the village school. (Decide on names.) B is what A's mother would describe as a 'bad influence'. B tries to persuade A to take the day off school and go on the moors where they could watch the tin-miners at work, 'for a laugh'. B's brother Jan is a tin-miner and he says he knows the way to the mine. 'A's try to resist as they know it will lead to trouble.

'A's move on one place to the left (clockwise).

■ *Improvisation 3: Gossip*

A is the vicar, B is a villager. (Decide on name from the chart.) The vicar complains to the villager about the way some of the young men in the village are behaving, getting drunk at night and fooling around loudly on the village green, when they should be at home, especially a young man called Jan Reynolds. Children invent reason why. 'A's move on one place to the left (clockwise).

■ *Improvisation 4: Discussion-complaining!*

Two tin-miners (male) are in the inn having a drink. (Decide on names.) You are talking about a young man called Jan Reynolds. You both agree that working in the tin mine is hard and exhausting work, underground and dangerous. Jan has become a bit of a liability as he is often late for work and doesn't do what you consider to be his fair share of work. He is sometimes half asleep after a heavy night's drinking and not as fit as he should be. You discuss whether you should talk to him and tell him to pull himself together, but he has a bit of a temper so you discuss the approach you might take, to try and get him to be a better work mate. 'A's move one place to the left (clockwise).

■ *Improvisation 5*

You are two young girls (decide on names), who work in the local farm as dairymaids. You see Jan regularly as you all leave the village early in the morning to go to work outside the village. You know him well and he used to be good fun but you both find him a 'pain in the neck' now as he is always flirting and neither of you is interested in him, as he is known to be unreliable, a heavy drinker and always gambling. You plan to avoid him as he is getting on your nerves!

The above scenarios give the children the chance to work 'in role' as different characters in the village, exploring particular aspects of the story through their own ideas, making it up for themselves. This allows them to enter the story in a very particular way, inventing and imagining what was taking place for different characters at the time the story was set. Their ideas are based on information about the event, added to what they have learnt from observation in the promenade and from discussion of the past and present in group work, plus any reading or research that has been undertaken in class. Next we move on to develop their drama skills.

Drama strategy: polished improvisation

Children choose a partner to work with. Each pair selects one of the above scenarios from the circle improvisation to work on and improve. They can be inventive and work away from original outlines. Remind them to use the names of their characters. Allow five minutes to work together, as they are in effect inventing a new scene. Then stop and explain you want them to repeat the improvisation 'to polish it and improve it'. They now need to work out and write down clearly, on an A5 sheet of paper, the names of their chosen characters, where in the village they are, what time of day it is and the opening lines they both speak. They must also invent a title and write that on the other side of the sheet. Then they must plan an opening freeze-frame (still picture) for their characters … and an end freeze-frame. You now have a complete list of short scenes that can be woven together to create the opening of the play, which will be short glimpses of what may have been going on in the village in October 1638. Pin these 'snippet scenes' on the wall.

Introducing the story

■ *Storyline 1.* You now have a number of short snippets of gossip from different characters, which can make an opening scene in the village, where you 'hear' what is going on. It does not matter if two pairs chose the same characters, as this can be easily adapted later.

Now put the pairs into groups of four. Each pair performs their 'snippet' scene to the other pair. This allows them to try out their scene in a safe way with just two others watching, so they are not on show to the whole class. This builds confidence. The watching pair have to give the performance 'Two Stars and a Wish', that is say two positive things about the work and give one realistic suggestion (the wish) for improvement. This is a first basic step for encouraging peer evaluation of performance work. This can be written on the 'snippet' cards in a different colour.

■ *Storyline 2: Teacher as narrator.* Now you have heard me speak of Jan Reynolds – a young man who lived in the village of Widecombe-in-the-Moor on Dartmoor. He was a fit strong young man and he worked as a tin-miner. Being a tin-miner was very hard work. He came from a good, honest, hard-working family but he was one of those characters who always seemed to fall into trouble, without even trying! Continue to describe Jan in this vein as he was described previously: cards, gabling, betting borrowing, being seen as trouble; the villagers said no good would come of him, but Jan took no notice. In a classroom session it might be useful before this practical work to look at tin-mining on Dartmoor.

Role-on-the-wall group work: How do we imagine Jan?

Cut a role of wall-lining paper into six lengths the height of the tallest person in the class, one sheet per group. One person in each group lies down on the sheet and another draws the outline of their body onto the paper. The charts will be hung on the wall later.

Divide the class into six mixed-gender groups.

Using the outline drawing, write down the following on to the chart after group discussion.

Decide how old you think Jan is at the stage you have been given and write this on the chart by his name at the top. Each group describes Jan in a different situation:

■ as a young boy;
■ what Jan wears when he goes to work as a tin-miner;
■ what he wears to go out in the evening;
■ what he might wear to go to church for a wedding;
■ what he wears when he goes to bed.

On post-it notes each group prints clearly:

■ words that might describe his character at that age;
■ words that describe what he looks like at that age;
■ what the character they role played might say about Jan.

Stick the notes around the edge of the chart. The class needs to build a joint picture of Jan. Display the charts and promenade. Discuss the invented character, drawing out essential points. Next the class invent Jan's family, friends and acquaintances. First, as a class, they decide:

■ How many brothers or sisters, their ages and names.
■ Look back to the list of invented characters in the village. Who would he know in the village?
■ Then in groups write clearly, on post-it notes, suggestions for his school, work and leisure friends. Invent their names and write the suggested age.

This exercise is to give time to think about who might have lived in the village 400 years ago, by looking at Jan and his connections.

Feedback: teacher takes ideas from groups and collates on a chart.

Groups contribute one idea at a time. The teacher has a large spider diagram with Jan in the centre. Put the post-it notes into 'groups' of those who know Jan, inside different bubbles: family; childhood friends; tin-miner friends from work; young men he drinks or gambles with (some overlap as work mates?); village characters: inn-keeper, vicar, teacher, farmers, farm labourers, local merchants.

Improvisation

In pairs, A plays Jan and B someone he knows. Pupils select a character from the devised lists. This way there will be a good selection of scenes with Jan talking to a range of different invented characters. Ask pairs to develop a short scene from Jan's life, setting the place or situation, which they need to decide on together first. Check the ideas and stress they should fit with the period and place: home, local inn, church, village green, tin mine. If there are any unsuitable scenes historically speaking this needs to be discussed and the scene adapted to be in keeping. Remind the class to look back at the pictures in the gallery. Allow time to approach the improvisation spontaneously, and then time to develop and polish. Encourage children to use a local accent and any local words they know.

Match pairs and let them view each other's scenes, to begin to build a picture of Jan's life.

In the matched pairs develop two scenes from the life of Jan Reynolds, one pair are the 'leads' for a scene and the other pair the lead for the other, but all four involved in both scenes. The teacher needs to watch ideas and draw a class plan of how scenes could be connected logically, possibly a scene at home, one at work, one out with his friends. Roll the scene so that each is performed in turn. Back in class, research can help children develop more authenticity.

■ *Storyline 3: Teacher as narrator.* Many years ago, when night fell and winds howled around the cottages and inns on Dartmoor, people huddled round their fires for warmth and often told each other stories, like this one. Jan is said to have met the Devil and made a contract with him. Both get something from the contract. Jan is said to have sold his soul to the Devil and in return got 'the luck of the Devil'. For Jan this meant his luck would change. He would win money with his gambling and he would be popular with the girls. He would have everything he wanted – but the Devil has the right to claim Jan's soul – at any time he chooses …

Stylised performance

This scene lends itself to a 'stylised' performance, as something unreal and unworldly happens. It is a good opportunity to raise discussion about why the legend developed.

Basic movement work

Put the class in a straight line in order of height, then paired with a partner of similar height.

■ *Exercise 1: The mirror.* A faces B: then A leads and B has to follow the movement, exactly as in a mirror. Stand in the same place a few feet apart. B leads. The teacher has to look at pairs as they walk around try to see who is 'the leader'. This can also be tried in teams of four.

■ *Exercise 2: Follow my leader – the mirror.* B leads. B can move anywhere in the room, and A has to follow movements exactly, 'working in unison' (basic dance term). Then A leads. (This exercise can be worked in trios and then in teams of four.)

■ *Exercise 3: The power of the hand.* This exercise is taken from the work of Augusto Boal (2002). His work concerns power and the dynamics of power in a society. A puts a hand half a metre away from B's face and then slowly moves the hand. B has to follow the hand and stay the same distance away. This gives A 'power', as they can make the exercise easy or very difficult for B.

Explain how A has 'the power' and how this was a random choice. How did they use their 'power'? Were they reasonable? Did they make it incredibly difficult?

Then give B the power. They can get their own back!

The pair (then in groups) form a 'statue', in which it is clear who has 'the power'. Look at those which are visually strong. How can we achieve visual images of power on the stage?

Class discussion: When the Devil is a character in a story it creates problems for showing in performance work. Where might the Devil approach Jan? When? Where might he approach Jan? What form do you think he might take? When? How does he manage to persuade Jan? How is the contract made? How willing is Jan? What state is Jan in? In groups develop the temptation of Jan as a scene for showing.

This particular scene could be stylised. How might you convey the idea that the Devil is a voice in Jan's head? The 'Devil' could be played by a group, who approach

Jan as 'temptations'. Or several people can 'be' the Devil, working in unison as in the above exercise.

How do they seal the contract between them? Ask class for suggestions for music for this scene, or develop a percussion 'soundscape'. The use of sound, lighting, music and movement is an obvious bonus. Masks can be made, in art for the spirits and the Devil Jan sees.

Dance and song

Market scene: Widecombe Fair. 'All along, down along, out along lee'.

It is really good if work can be undertaken on local dance and song to support research about the fair/markets. It is great fun to open this market scene with country dancing, Morris dancing or a local 'traditional' dance and the singing of a local song, in this case 'Widecombe Fair', which has its own amusing song, 'Uncle Tom Cobley'. The song has probably been around for hundreds of years. Explain that these customs and traditions performed the very important task of bringing the village together and preserved the sense of community that was indispensable to the villages.

■ *Storyline 4: Narrator (teacher or class members)*. The class can write an introductory narrative to the Widecombe Fair scene, now they understand how the narrative is used, before the practical drama.

Lesson following Storyline 4

If you have any pictures of villagers in this period it would be helpful to display them now. Sitting in a circle, mixed-gender groups (three or four) choose a group of characters who know Jan and might go to the fair. Spend a few minutes deciding on their roles, names and a little about the characters they are inventing.

From circle centre, teacher asks questions at random, to be answered in role: 'How do you know Jan? What's your occupation? What's your opinion of Jan? Have you noticed a change in him recently? What have you noticed? What have you seen? How do you account for his recent change of fortune?'

Set up the market place in the hall with tables and chairs. Groups decide on where they are in the space in freeze-frame starting position. Bring the market alive:

■ In mime only, tell the class they have to act as in the market place, in the above chosen roles. What task are they doing as the picture opens?
■ Re-run, this time with speech. It may be useful to repeat the above narrative as a starter. (NB: Nobody plays Jan at this stage.)

Freeze. Isolate one or two conversations for 20 seconds each. Discuss how Jan will come in – how will characters in the group react? Choose a confident performer in the class to be Jan, who enters into the market. Do this first as a freeze-frame.

Thought tracking

Group writing in role

Give everyone a piece of card on which to write their name, then the name of their character. In role, everyone writes down the feelings and thoughts they have about Jan (five or six lines), as he walks into the market. Give an example. His sister Mary: 'Our Jan, there he is, I don't know what's got into him He seems to be a different person. He seems to have had such amazing good luck when he plays cards at the inn.' Discuss what they are going to say with others in their group, so that the comments link. This will help to produce a variety of comments. But it must be their characters' recent private thoughts about Jan.

Everyone sits in a circle, facing out with Jan in the middle. The cards are scattered face up. Light on this would heighten the effect. In character each person (not necessarily methodically around the circle), leaves their place, walks to their card, picks it up and addresses their comment directly to 'Jan', then puts the card down and goes back to their place in the circle.

Go back to the market freeze-frame, then as Jan moves near each group they say their thoughts about him from their card (which they can quickly learn). The idea is that Jan can 'read their thoughts' so he knows what they are thinking. The rest of the class can hold the freeze-frame or work in silent mime. Small groups come 'alive' and say their lines as he approaches. Jan can do this 'walk' differently each time, so everyone has to be prepared to do their lines without quite knowing which way he will turn! If the scene is for showing then you might need to make a selection of the comments. Give the cards back. Ask the class to write one question on the other side, which they would like to ask Jan and explain how they are going to use them in 'Conscience Alley'.

Conscience Alley

Class in pairs, A and B.

The class stand in two rows, A and B, the length of the hall/space, facing each other. Jan walks slowly down the alley. This can be done to a drumbeat for dramatic effect. He stops by each pair who, in turn, ask their questions. Jan doesn't reply. He just listens, then walks slowly to the next pair.

This develops the children's questioning skills, but it also shows how everyone is thinking about Jan since his meeting with the Devil. In groups revise the stylised scene where the Devil claims Jan's soul. Some music/lighting/mask making/scenery/costumes/props all of these could be added. Teacher reads out the final narrative. Play thunder-storm effects at suitable level to heighten atmosphere.

■ *Storyline 5.* Describe how, the following Sunday, Jan went to Widecombe Church as usual, and took a pack of cards to play at the back during the sermon. But he was tired after a hard week of physical labour in the mine and he had had a few drinks, so he soon fell asleep. Describe the terrible storm. Describe how the church tower started to collapse, how some were buried in the masonry, how the Devil descended from the roof, seized Jan and carried his dead body up to the church tower, where his horse was tied to the pinnacle, and how, when the horse broke loose into the storm, it sent the pinnacle crashing down into the church. Conclude that, 'The last anyone ever saw of Jan Reynolds was when the Devil's horse passed over the Birch Tor mine, the Devil was holding Jan tightly as his horse climbed the sky. Four of Jan's playing cards fell from his pocket and fluttered down to earth. When the cards hit the ground they left four imprints, which serve as a warning to all potential "soul sellers" and anyone who dared to play cards in church'.

Explain that four acres can still be dimly seen to this day – in the shapes of the stone enclosures on the slopes of the Ace Fields (Grid Ref. SX6881). On that same day in an inn at Postbridge, some miles from Widecombe, the landlady served a stranger in a black cloak. As he drank his ale, the liquid sizzled and steam was seen to come from the tankard – or perhaps it was smoke. Later, when the landlady looked at the money the stranger had paid her, she saw that it had turned to dead leaves.

Six people from the village died in the church because of what happened that day, and it is recorded that sixty people were also injured.

RESEARCH EXPERTS: THE FINAL SCENE

Children (in suitable working groups) can act as researchers on the internet to learn more about Jan's story, and report back on what they have learnt (e.g. on the Book of Common Prayer).

In a final practical session the class has to work out how to dramatise the final scene. It can be organised as a section of a church service (as in the Book of Common Prayer) and the questions and answers can be sung (or chanted), to give the scene the feel of an oratorio, as a religious feel is appropriate. The actual arrival of the Devil and the ensuing consternation in the storm and the falling church steeple can be performed with a giant mask for the Devil and the storm represented by sound effects and movement work, with a chorus of spirits making discordant noises against the end strains of the sung or chanted 'oratorio'. The litany of the names of the dead parishioners (pp. 121–2) can end the scene.

It is important that the emerging story designed by pupils is treated with equal status to the story that already exists. Legends change over time. Children should understand that they have created one version of a legend but that it is also important to include valid evidence for events surrounding the legend and other information they have researched about the period. They will learn to understand that often historians have to 'best guess' what really happened. They have to look at what is recorded, to look at artefacts available of the time and place, or look at other items available or written about the event nearer the time and place, that might be based on oral evidence, and do their best to understand where the truth might really be. Table 8.1 gives a synopsis of the drama strategies used in the case study. They should help you to design a drama based on your own local legend.

■ **Table 8.1** A synopsis of the drama strategies used

Improvisation – spontaneous	Where you 'make believe' in a spontaneous manner
	Where you take the ideas from a spontaneous improvisation
Improvisation – polished	and work on them to improve and develop a scene for showing
Freeze-frame	A still or 'frozen' moment of significance within the drama
Still image	People take up a pose to construct a picture describing what they want to say
Narration	Part of the story is spoken to the audience, by a narrator (outside voice), or by a character within the drama (inside voice) who tells the audience what is going to happen next – or the story from a particular perspective
Thought-tracking	Actors within the drama speak aloud their private thoughts or reactions to events
Hot-seating	Teacher or pupil(s) can be 'in the hot seat' and the class can question them 'in role' about their character or about their feelings on events in the drama
Role-on-the-wall	Draw an outline of a life-size figure and use the outline to collect information, design costume/dress/appearance. Can also add comments about the character (post-it notes useful) and the character's own thoughts as 'thought bubbles'
Conscience alley	Group form two lines to make an 'alley'. A character walks through the alley and everyone in the line gives advice or says how they feel about the situation, how their conscience would tell them to act; or the children in the lines just ask the character a different question each. The character walks along the alley listening to the questions but does not respond
Collective role-play	Several people play the same part simultaneously to provide mutual support and present a range of ideas
Meetings	Ask the group to come together in role to present information, plan action, solve problems
Mantle of the expert	Individuals are asked to take on a role with specialist knowledge that is relevant to the situation in the drama (see Heathcote 1991)
Teacher in role	Teacher takes on a role of a character within the drama to develop ideas, ask questions, or to set up tension

REFERENCES

Boal, A. (2002) *Games for Actors and Non-Actors*, London: Routledge.

Dymond, R. (ed.) (1876) *Widecombe in the Moor*, Torquay: Torquay Directory Company.

Heathcote, D. (1991) *Collected Writings on Education and Drama*, edited by L. Johnson and C. O'Neill, Evanston, IL: Northwestern University Press.

Sandles, T. (2007) *Jan Reynolds and the Devil*, www.legendarydartmoor.co.uk/jan_reynolds (accessed October 2012).

Useful websites

- Talking books: www.bbcaudiobooks.com
- Stories from the web: www.storiesfromtheweb.org/sfwhomepage.htm
- Internet public library: www.ipl.org/div/kidspace
- Inspirational reading spaces: www.booktrusted.com

CHAPTER 9

CREATIVITY, CONNECTIVITY AND INTERPRETATION

Jon Nichol

INTRODUCTION

The British government includes Interpretation as one of the six dimensions of the *English National Curriculum for History* (ENCH):

1   Chronological understanding
2   Cultural, ethnic and religious diversity
3   Change and continuity
4   Cause and consequence
5   Significance
6   Interpretation
    a   Understanding how historians and others form interpretations.
    b   Understanding why historians and others have interpreted events, people and situations in different ways through a range of media.
    c   Evaluating a range of interpretations of the past to assess their validity (Department for Education 2011).

These dimensions underpin the study of history as a process of enquiry, i.e. procedural or syntactic knowledge (disciplinary concepts, skills, processes, protocols and procedures) that produces factual, i.e. propositional or substantive knowledge (Rogers 1979). Teachers need to understand the six ENCH dimensions to develop pupil knowledge and understanding of them. Accordingly, Interpretation is one strand in the ENCH's eight-level attainment target for pupils – it states that the average 9–10 year old pupil should: 'Begin to know about and suggest different interpretations of events, people, situations and related changes, causes and consequences (ENCH Attainment Target).'

This chapter focuses upon the development of pupils' understanding of Interpretation as a concept both through them studying interpretations and creating their own. An interpretation is a conscious reflection on the past with the aim to present an understanding of it to others.

Pupil interpretations draw upon interpretations of contemporaries and others such as artists, reporters, film-makers and novelists, as well as historians. Each interpretation is a genre with its authorial voice or register that consists of:

■ the author or authors' view of their intended audience (*tenor*)
■ the nature of the genre (*mode*) and the mode's specific structure, organisation, pattern, presentation, conventions, style (*form*)
■ its content (*field*)
■ its cultural context (*culture*).

Interpretations' genres have infinite modes, for example, audio recordings, collages, comics, drawings, expressive movement, fiction, films, folk songs, folk tales, models, paintings, plays, portraits, sculpture, theme parks, vernacular memory, video, virtual reality, wall displays and websites, as well as more conventional forms: academic textbooks, biographies, academic monographs, lectures, museum and art gallery guide books, newspaper and magazine articles, research-based reports, school history textbooks, topic books, Wikipedia entries (McAleavy 2000: 74).

While Interpretation is a central feature of the ENCH, it has received limited attention (McAleavy: 78). Hilary Cooper's *History 3–11* (Cooper 2007: 25–32) contains a comprehensive review of the teaching of Interpretation to 3–11-year-olds and related research (also in Cooper 2012: 33–40). The Historical Association's creative, imaginative and valuable Transitions Project (Historical Association) focused on the development of pupil understanding of Interpretation. Pupil knowledge develops from them studying a range of interpretations in order to create their own. The Transitions Project's schemes of work are shown in Table 9.1.

■ **Table 9.1** Historical Association transition projects

---

1 Films, History and Alexander the Great

2 Was Boudicca Britain's First Hero?

3 Joan of Arc – Saint, Witch or Warrior?

4 The New Elizabethans

5 How Cruel Were the Victorians?

6 Interpretation and Poor Victorian Children

7 Living Museums and Victorian Britain

8 Myths and War Evacuees

9 How Do We Remember John Lennon?

In 1991/92, to introduce teachers to the new ENCH concept of Interpretation John Fines and Tony Hopkins carried out valuable research into older pupils learning about Richard III and the disappearance of *The Princes in the Tower* through studying a full range of historians, playwrights and others interpretations of Richard III and what happened to *The Princes in The Tower*. They gave the sources in their original, full form. The pupils studied, analysed, compared and contrasted different interpretations before creating, comparing and debating their own interpretations. *Learning to Teach History in the Secondary School* (Haydn *et al.* 1997) has a clear and valuable chapter on the subject. Interpretation is not mentioned in the index of Levstik and Barton's (2008) North American comprehensive review of research into history education.

If we widen the concept of Interpretation to include historical explanation, the field expands considerably; both in terms of academic historians' (Hexter 1971; Evans 1997) and history educationalists' analysis of its meaning (Cooper and Chapman 2009: 92–93).

An explanation of the relative absence of literature on historical interpretation arises from Interpretation being one element in the process of pupils working on historical sources. Questions on sources when treated as Interpretations can include those shown in Table 9.2.

Because Interpretation is subsumed in the holistic procedural/syntactic knowledge of history as enquiry – 'Doing History' – we teach it as one element in pupils working on their sources. As with all disciplinary concepts, it is integral to the long-term, incremental, implicit and tacit development of pupil's historical skills and related understanding of the evidential basis of histories, all of whom are interpretations that students both study and create (Table 9.3).

■ **Table 9.2** Questions about sources treated as interpretation

1 Who created the source?

2 On what evidence is the source based?

3 Why was the source created?

4 How reliable is the source?

5 What does the source tell us about the subject?

6 What ideas does the creator of the source want to convey?

7 What ideas about X does the source give?

8 Why did the source's creator base the interpretation upon these ideas?

■ **Table 9.3** How pupils can both construct their own interpretations and compare those of others

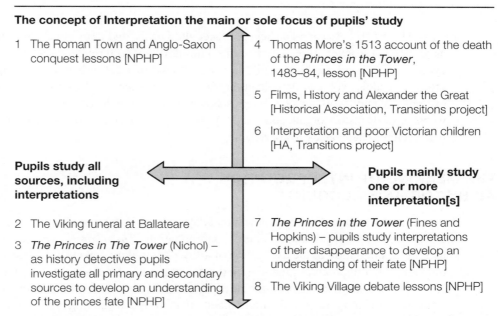

The concept of Interpretation the main or sole focus of pupils' study

1 The Roman Town and Anglo-Saxon conquest lessons [NPHP]

4 Thomas More's 1513 account of the death of the *Princes in the Tower*, 1483–84, lesson [NPHP]

5 Films, History and Alexander the Great [Historical Association, Transitions project]

6 Interpretation and poor Victorian children [HA, Transitions project]

Pupils study all sources, including interpretations

Pupils mainly study one or more interpretation[s]

2 The Viking funeral at Ballateare

3 *The Princes in The Tower* (Nichol) – as history detectives pupils investigate all primary and secondary sources to develop an understanding of the princes fate [NPHP]

7 *The Princes in the Tower* (Fines and Hopkins) – pupils study interpretations of their disappearance to develop an understanding of their fate [NPHP]

8 The Viking Village debate lessons [NPHP]

'Doing History' – focus on the construction of history using primary and secondary sources and history's disciplinary concepts, including Intepretation

The Nuffield Primary History Project's (NPHP) schemes of work integrated pupil study of interpretations as one aspect of their pedagogy, for example, a lesson in which pupils drew on their knowledge of two interpretations of the impact of Anglo-Saxon invaders upon a Roman town. The pupils annotated their copies of an Alan Sorrel picture of a Roman forum in *c.* AD 410 with how it might have appeared 200 years later, following the Anglo-Saxon invasion, using evidence extracted from an Anglo-Saxon poem, *The Ruin* (The Historical Association, The End of Roman Britain, www.history.org.uk).

In this chapter we draw upon two other NPHP schemes of work that involve pupils in studying and creating interpretations:

■ *The Vikings*: *c.* AD 800-1100 as invaders, settlers and traders: a scheme of work. The Vikings scheme of work's twelve topics involve pupils studying a wide range of interpretations, their genres and creating their own.

■ *The Princes in the Tower – The Mystery of the Missing Children*: a scheme of work. The disappearance of the Princes in the Tower from 1483–1485 is the classic history-teaching 'who dunnit?'. Pupil interpretations, as history detectives, of what happened to the princes, requires close examination of both historians' and contemporaries' interpretations of their fate and other contemporary evidence.

The NPHP team and teachers produced the *Vikings* and *Princes* schemes of work as participant teachers-researchers (curriculum developers) through an action research cycle that involved teaching pupils in a wide range of rural, urban and metropolitan primary schools. You can download the final version exemplar lessons, resources and examples of pupil work for *The Vikings* scheme of work from the Historical Association's website, www.history.org.uk and *The Princes in the Tower* clues in a digital form from http://centres.exeter.ac.uk/historyresource.

THE MEANING OF INTERPRETATION: AN HISTORIAN'S ACCOUNT

We turn to an academic historian, an archaeologist, for insight into and understanding of the historical disciplinary concept Interpretation. *The Vikings* scheme of work includes a simulation of the excavation of a Viking burial mound at Ballateare, the Isle of Man, based upon an academic archaeological report of the excavation (Bersu and Wilson 1966). Gerhard Bersu concluded his report with a detailed interpretation that brings the funerary rites and interment to life through recreating the burial. Bersu based his report on the evidence the burial mound contained, his knowledge of Viking and European history from *c.* AD 800 to 1100 and his wider understanding of the historical significance of ritual, ceremony, culture and social structures. The burial mound clues included jewellery, weapons and a man's body buried in the burial pits below the mound, the blocks of turf used to build the burial mound, a woman's skeleton half way down the mound and a pile of large stones near its summit. Bersu uses this archaeological evidence, his knowledge of similar funeral ceremonies and his wider knowledge to create an interpretation that dates and identifies the society and culture of the man and woman in the grave.

Deconstruction of Bersu's interpretation of the Ballateare excavation reveals that it has a chronological structure, and uses inference, deduction and his informed imagination to reach conclusions. It also contains subsidiary explanations (interpretations) of different aspects of what his excavation discovered. Bersu's interpretation combines both his historical knowledge – its substantive or propositional dimension and how he had created his interpretation – its syntactic or procedural knowledge: i.e. history as enquiry.

The Ballateare funeral mound interpretation includes the following.

Imaginative reconstruction, based upon evidence

We can now visualise the sequence of events involved in the interment and the ritual connected with it.

Chronology/sequencing

In chronological order:

■   the digging of a grave pit;
■   the dressing of the man's body and putting it in its coffin;
■   the burying of the coffin with artefacts and weapons in the grave pit;
■   the building of the burial mound from blocks of turf;
■   the placing of cremated remains of animals and a female human body on a platform near the mound's top and covering them with turves;
■   digging of a post hole at the top of the mound;
■   placing of the post in the hole.

Reconstruction of an historical situation: the funeral ritual (inference, historical imagination)

The funeral ritual consisted of:

■   digging the coffin pit, preparing the burial mound, organising the funeral;
■   the destruction of his weapons and shield, with two possible interpretations:

1   possibly the arms and armour of the dead man may have been destroyed either to prevent grave robbery, or
2   in the belief that a man's weapons had to be made useless to prevent his haunting the living;

■   dressing the man's body in a woollen cloak and placing it, his dagger and destroyed sword, spears and shield in and around the coffin;
■   filling the pit with sand;
■   building the burial mound as a symbol that signified the man's role and status.

The informed imagination

The mound was made from turfs from elsewhere, not local soil (significance):

> I feel inclined to suggest that this also had a symbolic meaning ... . The sods may represent the fields of the dead man, so that more of his property, in addition to the grave-goods in the coffin, might be represented in his burial.
>
> (Bersu and Wilson 1966)

A sacrifice of a woman (cause and consequence):

> the dead woman was laid ... as a sacrifice. The woman may not have been killed where she lay, for rigor mortis had already set in, as is indicated by the raised arms of the skeleton.
>
> (Ibid.)

Sacrificing and cremating animals (laid on the burial mound's platform with the woman's body) – sacrificed and burned elsewhere (interpretation):

> a solid layer of cremated bones, bones of animals mixed bones… They apparently represent an offering of the livestock of the dead man and suggest that he was a farmer.
>
> (Ibid.)

A post – flagstaff (inference):

> In the centre of the platform, just above the middle of the burial pit, a hole had been left for the insertion of a substantial post, which must have been kept in a vertical position by packing stones.
>
> (Ibid.)

Typology (inference)

Bersu related the evidence in the grave to similar finds in other excavations and knowledge of the development of Viking jewellery, decoration and design – typology. The artefacts similar to those at Ballateare are both identifiable as Viking and datable – hence both identifying the burial as Viking and dating it.

A narrative – an account

Bersu's recreation of the burial, in the report (account) genre, reveals that the man in the grave pit was a ninth- or tenth-century Viking Isle of Man warrior and farmer of high social status. He was buried with a sacrificial victim who may have been a slave girl, a thrall.

TEACHER CREATIVE CONNECTIVITY, PUPIL CREATIVITY AND INTERPRETATIONS: *THE VIKINGS* AND *THE PRINCES IN THE TOWER*

The Vikings and *The Princes in the Tower* schemes of work illuminate the transformation of academic historical subject knowledge into pedagogic (teaching/curricular/ learning) knowledge that enables pupils to understand existing historical interpretations, interpretations' genres and how to create their own.

Teacher *creative connectivity* links academic subject knowledge to a key, over-arching pedagogic idea to create a teaching activity with its detailed teaching script, associated resources and materials. Pupil creation of their own interpretations depends upon teacher pedagogic inputs, support and guidance – guided performance.

THE *VIKINGS* SCHEME OF WORK

The Vikings scheme of work involved twelve separate topics (shown in Table 9.4), each lasting from one to five 1–1.5 hour lessons. Interpretations played a part in the teaching of all topics: we will examine three based upon Gerhard Bersu's

■ **Table 9.4** The Vikings: source material, teacher connectivity, pedagogy and pupil interpretations

1 Viking sea-going ships	Using a ship's outline to plan what a family would take with it when emigrating	Annotating the picture of the Viking ship to show an emigrant family's possessions
2 Viking markets and trade	• A market game that creates a Viking market • A trading board game of the Viking world	A market held in a Viking town Trading in the Viking world, from Greenland to Central Asia
3 Academic knowledge of Viking 'thing' or council and Viking emigration	Social decision-making game in which groups discuss, debate and decide upon whether to fight, emigrate or negotiate with Harold Finehair	Accounts that report the debate from the perspective of a Viking family participating in the debate of whether to fight, surrender or emigrate
4 Viking emigration	Storytelling – using a saga	Pupil writing of their own sagas
5 The Viking settlement	Settlement simulation	Pupils create a Viking community that has settled a valley in the Lake District
6 Viking place names	Translation of names to recreate Viking landscape	Map of Viking valley pupils can use to recreate the settlement pattern
7 The Viking warfare – attack on Exeter	Using the Anglo-Saxon chronicle to develop expressive movement to tell the story of the Viking raid	Drama – expressive movement, based upon pupils reading the text and bringing its scenes to life

archaeological report of the Ballateare burial, a contemporary' account of a Viking funeral in Russia in the tenth century (topics 3 and 4) and an academic historian's interpretation of the factors that led to tenth-century Viking migration from Scandinavia (topic 8).

The creative teaching connectivity of topics 2–4 linked the historical record to classroom teaching through:

■ taking the *original excavation report* and linking it to the overarching pedagogic idea of *a pupil simulation of the excavation of the Viking burial mound*;

■ a *contemporary account of a similar Viking burial in Russia* (Foote and Wilson 1970: 408–411) and linking it to the overarching pedagogic idea of *transformation of that interpretation from a symbolic, (written) into an iconic (pictorial) form* using the comic genre.

Topic 8's creative teaching connectivity linked *an academic interpretation* of factors that led to Viking emigration from Norway with *a class role-play* in which pupils took the role of Viking villagers faced with the decision to flee, surrender or fight when faced with the threat of King Harald Finehair conquering their isolated fjord village.

Topics 2 and 3: Simulation of the Ballateare excavation

Viking Burial Mound introduces teachers to the excavation simulation, Figure 9.2.

Viking Burial Mound

In this simulation of an excavation, the children investigate a past event and imaginatively reconstruct what happened, on the basis of the evidence uncovered. The lesson is based on a real archaeological dig by Gerhard Bersu in 1946.

Two items in the resources are supplied as separate downloads. One is a PowerPoint presentation. The other is an account of Viking funeral customs by Ibn Fadlan, an Arab Muslim trader who witnessed a Viking burial in Russia in AD 922. Read this through before sharing it with children – you may want to cut out some of the sex and violence. It is supplied as a Word document for easy editing.

You can download the burial mound simulation's exemplar lessons and resources from www.history.org.uk. In Primary Resources search for Viking burial mound.

The Ballateare simulation involves the pupils in marking their finds with annotations on a cross-section outline of the mound and an eight-rectangle archaeological grid of the grave pit's contents. They discuss, in groups and as a whole class, their interpretation of the finds and their significance. A transcript of feedback from a Year 5/6 class indicates how their interpretations both draw upon Gerhard Bersu's excavation report and cover a range of the key concepts in this chapter's opening paragraph. Pupil interpretations of what, as archaeologists, they had discovered included:

- *It's the burial of a warrior [asked to justify this claim] – because he's been buried with weapons of war and they're placed as he would have worn them.*
- *It's a man who has murdered the woman near the top of the mound; he has then been murdered in turn, and the murder weapons have been put into the grave with him.*
- *The woman skeleton could be his wife.*
- *Yes, they've buried all his things with him, and her too.*
- *She might have been alive when she was buried, because she's got her arms stretching up, and the soil would be falling on her.*
- *She's been killed, her head's been bashed in with a heavy implement, it says here.*
- *His skeleton has rotted and hers hasn't because she's near the top, and he's at the bottom, and it's wetter lower down in the ground, so his body has rotted away.*
- *The man in the grave is a farmer and they've buried his animals with him.*

Topic 4: Transformation of the Ibn Fadlan account of the Viking funeral into eight scenes using the comic genre

The teacher prepared an edited version of the Viking account suitable for a mixed Year 3/4 class. The class copied the account into their books from the board, were then given comics for us to jointly work out the nature of the comic genre they would use in their interpretation of the Viking account. They then used the account to produce their own eight scene interpretation of the burial.

Topic 8: Viking migration

For Topic 8, Migration, we wanted to enable pupils to understand an academic historian's interpretation of Viking migration from Norway in the mid-ninth century, Figure 9.1.

The key questions the class investigated were: Why did the Vikings migrate? What form did their migration take? We knew that the west coast Vikings lived in communities at the head of long inlets, fjords and that they had local assemblies, things, where they took collective decisions. Teacher creative connectivity linked *the highlighted short passage in the Foote and Wilson account* above with a pedagogic activity: *an interactive role-play simulation* that cast pupils in role as Viking villagers. The simulation aimed to actively develop pupil understanding of the historian's interpretation of the factors that led to migration. Our planning notes are given below.

On the west coast [of Norway] there was a population who farmed and fished, but among them were also a comparatively large number of sea-borne warrior chieftains. They were not in a good position to maintain themselves by trade, because they had nothing much to sell (no demand for Norway's fish existed at this time), but they were in a position to take a toll of other people's commerce and able by foreign raiding both to enrich themselves with plunder and to take a share in international trafficking, especially perhaps in slaves.

They applied themselves to piracy and sometimes to conquest in the British Isles, particularly in Scotland and Ireland, but also held a commanding position in Norway because they sat on the coastal waters through which the traffic to and from Trondelag and Halogaland passed. The need to solve the problems posed by these gentlemen partly explains the enforced unification of Norway, against the geographical odds, at an early stage in the period we are considering.

Towards 900 the young king of Vestfold, encouraged by his advisers, took it into his head to become sole ruler of Norway. His name was Harald, son of Halfdan, generally called Harald Finehair. Community of commercial interest dictated alliance with the earls of Lade, and when this combination was effected, the allies moved steadily southward from Trondheimsfjord against the chieftains of the west coast. **Some of these joined them, others fought or fled,** but Harald's success was constant and he finally won a decisive victory sometime in the 890s, in a naval battle fought in Hafrsfjord, just by Stavanager. Henceforward it was accepted in principle that there should be a king over all the Norwegians, and Harald Finehair's right to rule was so firmly established that the same right was freely accorded to men of his blood for centuries thereafter.

Figure 9.1 An academic interpretation of tenth-century Viking migration (Foote and Wilson, 1970: 41)

The Viking migrant and settler

Introduction

We have finished the dig and burial. The children have some idea of Viking life and society. We will now face them with the problems of migration and settlement. This needs to be located both in time and space, i.e. dates and maps.

We will focus in on a Viking community, working backwards from the Isle of Man dig.

Aims

1   To develop an understanding of why and how the Vikings left home and settled abroad
2   To understand the nature of Viking settlement and society
3   To develop language skills and understanding in the context of the shared reading of the information text.

Key questions

■   Why did the Vikings leave their homes to settle abroad?
■   What form did their migration take?
■   What did they take with them?
■   How did they settle when they arrived?

Resources

1   The text – the instructions of the game, including a map…

The teaching

We need to allocate the pupils to Viking families, give them names and read through the information sheet and labels so that each pupil knows its family members and situation.

- There are eight families in the valley.
- They are freemen who agree to obey their leader, Earl.
- Each family owns slaves or thralls.
- The families live on farms scattered around the valley.

1   *Jarl Knut and Astrid:* He is the Viking chief of the valley. He and Astrid have a large farm. Harald Finehair is an old enemy.
2   *Eric and Inga:* They have a farm at the head of the valley. Eric is the valley's priest. He is in charge of the temple where there is an altar to Thor. Inga's best friend is married to one of Harald's jarls.
3   *Thorsten and Freya:* Thorsten is the valley smith. His family has a blood feud with a relative of Harald Finehair. Harald has promised to put Thorsten on trial when he conquers the valley.

4 *Karl and Ingrid:* Karl is a farmer who is also a skilled stone carver. Karl is a fierce fighter who refuses to take orders but is willing to go on Viking raids with Knut. Karl is an enemy of Thorsten as they are rowing over who owns a farm.

5 *Olaf and Brondie:* Brondie's sister is married to one of Harald's warriors. Brondie is jealous of the long legs and beauty of Astrid.

6 *Rollo and Helga:* Rollo is married to Ingrid's sister, but they have fallen out over who owned their father's prize cow when he died.

7 *Bjorn and Karen:* Bjorn killed Eric's favourite slave in a drunken quarrel. Bjorn has refused to pay the fine or blood money to Eric.

8 *Swein and Gerda:* Gerda is from the Isle of Man and is a Christian. She and Eric the priest are fierce enemies. Harald has said that he could become a Christian.

Figure 9.2 Pupils' roles in Viking families

It's 1 March AD 890:

You live in Sunn Fjord on the West coast of Norway.

A messenger has just arrived from the King of Norway, Harald Finehair.

The Jarl or chief of the valley calls a meeting of its people – its Thing. The chief speaks:

> 'Harald Finehair has ordered me to go to court with all fighting men to serve in the King's army. Harald says that we must stop our raids on trading ships.
>
> The King also says that from now on he will rule our village.
>
> One of the king's jarls says that he owns our land.'

Figure 9.3 The king's messenger arrives

What shall the Thing decide to do?

1 Surrender?
2 Fight?
3 Flee abroad with all your families and animals, tools, household goods? How might you flee?

1 You have just come back from a raid on Britain.
2 You sailed to the port of Dublin and then to relatives on a rich island, the Isle of Man.
3 From there you sailed to West Cumbria and looted a monastery in a rich valley full of fish and timber.

All the families of our village had a meeting because we were going to have the King of Norway take over our village.

We decided to have a meeting of the Thing to vote as to whether we surrender, fight or flee to another land.

The families who wanted to fight said they wouldn't flee because they would be going down the fjord and the soldiers would be going up the fjord and the people would get hurt.

The families who wanted surrender said they wouldn't flee or fight because if they would flee then they would go to one country and the King of Norway would send all his men out to different countries and in the end they will find you.

The families who wanted to flee said if they fled they would be much safer.

I wanted to surrender because if you fled they would catch and you would die and if you fought you would die so you might as well surrender.

Figure 9.4 The Thing: our Viking council, Melanie

Tied up in the harbour is your raiding boat, ready to sail.
There are also three trading boats.
You can take all of the valley's eight families with you.
The village chieftain, Jarl Knut, calls a meeting of the village assembly, the Thing. At the Thing the families discuss among themselves and with other families what they will do. The Thing is called to order, each family reports back its view.
A second message then. The process is repeated. The final phase of the teaching ends with each Viking producing his or her own interpretation; Figure 9.4 is an example. It indicates that Melanie had assimilated an understanding of the academic view of factors leading to migration in producing her own interpretative account.

THE PRINCES IN THE TOWER

Viking Migration was grounded in a single academic interpretation of the factors that led to tenth-century Viking migration from Norway. We use an historian's interpretation, written some 30 years after the event, to introduce a scheme or work in which Interpretation plays a major role. *The Princes in the Tower* scheme of work's creative teacher connectivity links the *historical record, the sources,* about their disappearance, with *casting pupils in the role of history detectives* (Nichol 1992). To investigate the princes' disappearance, we divide the pupils into teams of 2–4 history detectives. As detectives, each team has to:

■ ask questions;
■ plan out the enquiry;

- discover the clues that might contain answers to a question or questions they have asked (these take the form of clue cards or a database on the computer), downloadable from http://centres.exeter.ac.uk/historyresource.
- read, process, extract information, sort it out and organise it chronologically and as a concept map/web, hypothesise, speculate, discuss, argue and agree upon a solution;
- communicate their interpretation of the princes' disappearance to the rest of the class;
- discuss and debate the different interpretations they produce to see if they can agree on a solution.

In the form of a clue card (Figure 9.5) we introduce pupils to an interpretation of their disappearance – Sir Thomas More's account of their murder in his 1513 *History of Richard III*, written some 30 years after they vanished.

The lesson plan, Table 9.5, details how the pupils are able to:

- read the difficult and challenging full Sir Thomas More text (we give this out with or instead of the clue card) – we use the full account to maximise the number of clues that pupils can investigate;
- plan out their enquiry.

Processing the Sir Thomas More interpretation deepens pupil understanding. The pupils then investigated and worked on a full range of sources about the disappearance of the princes, including contemporary and other historian accounts. They used the background information and evidence they extracted and assimilated to create their own interpretations/explanations of the mystery such as Allanah, aged 11. The beginning of Allanah's interpretation is shown in Figure 9.6.

Sir Thomas *More* sharpened his quill pen and dipped it in the ink. It was a spring morning in 1515. As he gazed from his window, Sir Thomas thought of how he should tell of the death of the two young *princes* who had vanished between 1583–85 when living in The *Tower of London*.

'I shall rehearse you the dolorous end of those babes [not as gossip and rumour say, but as I know to be true]. King *Richard* after his coronation, taking his way to Gloucester, devised as he rode, to fulfil the thing which he before had intended. That his nephews living, men would not reckon that he could have right to the realm, he thought therefore without delay to get rid of them, as though the killing of his kinsmen, could amend his cause, and make him a kindly king [A].

[King Richard asked one of his men to kill the princes. The first man refused. Richard then asked Sir James *Tyrell* to murder the children. Tyrell gets the *keys* to The Tower.] Sir James Tyrell devised that they should be murdered in their beds. To the execution whereof, he appointed Miles *Forest* one of the four that kept them, a fellow fleshed in murder before time. To him he joined one John *Dighton* his own horsekeeper, a big, broad, square strong knave [B].

Figure 9.5 Sir Thomas More clue card

■ **Table 9.5** Bringing the text to life

1 Title

Having listened to the story, give it a one-word or phrase title.

2 Scenes

As the story is read, draw pictures of its scenes on A4 paper folded into four. Give each scene:

(a) a title
(b) a caption.

3 Dictionary

Skim-read the piece, highlighting or underlining any words you do not know. Use the word list to write in or work out the meaning of words that you do not understand.

4 Word hunt

Under each point below write down words from the text about them:
Places:

People:

Objects:

5 Argument

What words and phrases did Thomas More use to build up ideas about the people in the story?

6 Author and audience

Brainstorm what thoughts and feelings Sir Thomas More might have had when he was writing his story about the Princes.

- Who do you think he was writing his story for?
- How might this affect how he wrote it?

7 Dramatic re-enactment

- Working in groups. Take any one scene from any of the paragraphs. Decide in detail what was going on in the scenes, who was there, what they were doing.
- Work out a freeze frame for the scene, and present it as a tableau.
- The rest of the class have to guess what scene you are showing.

8 History detectives

You are a history detective called in to investigate the crime outlined in Thomas More's story.

- You have to set up an incident room.
- Draw up a list of questions that you would ask.
- Decide upon the steps you would take in investigating the mystery.

The Princes in The Tower by Allanah

One of the greatest real mysteries of all time is the princes in the tower. There are many speculations on what really happened. Were they killed by Richard III? Or were they secretly hidden forever?

There are many ideas, the most common one being that Richard III ordered them dead, therefore making himself king of England. This does have some evidence towards it …

Figure 9.6 The beginning of Allanah's interpretation

The class then discussed and debated a number of their interpretations, vigorously disagreeing upon what they considered happened, with full reference to the evidence they had studied.

CONCLUSION

This chapter has explored the meaning of Interpretation and creativity in the teaching of history to 5–11-year-olds. A common factor has been teacher *creativity connectivity* – the making of the link between the historical knowledge to be taught and a key teaching activity, i.e. how it can be taught – its pedagogy. Conversely, pupil creativity depends upon teacher management of their learning with the guidance and support that enables pupils to create their own historical interpretations. Such creativity brings the past to life in a stimulating and rewarding way that holistically develops the full range of disciplinary concepts and the skills, processes, protocols and high-level skills, including literacy that outstanding history teaching and learning entail.

REFERENCES

Bersu, G. and Wilson, D.M. (1966) *Three Viking Graves in the Isle of Man*, The Society for Medieval Archaeology Monograph Series, No. 1.

Cooper, H. (2007) *History 3–11*, London: David Fulton.

Cooper, H. (2012) *History 5–11*, London: Routledge.

Cooper, H. and Chapman, A. (2009) *Constructing History 11–19*, Sage.

Department for Education (2011) *History: key concepts,* www.education.gov.uk/schools/teaching andlearning/curriculum/secondary/b00199545/history/programme/concepts.

ENCH Attainment Target, *Primary curriculum subjects,* www.education.gov.uk/schools/ teachingandlearning/curriculum/primary.

Evans, R.J. (1997) *In Defence of History*, Cambridge: Granta.

Foote, P.G. and Wilson, D.M. (1970) *The Viking Achievement*, London: Book Club Associates.

Haydn, T., Arthur, J. and Hunt, M. (1997) *Learning to Teach History in the Secondary School*, London: Routledge.

Hexter, J.H. (1971) *The History Primer*, New York: Basic Books.

The Historical Association, The End of Roman Britain, www.history.org.uk.

The Historical Association, Transitions Project, www.history.org.uk.

Levstik, L.S. and Barton, K.C. (2008) *Researching History Education*, London: Routledge.

McAleavy, T. (2000) Teaching about interpretations, in J. Arthur and R. Phillips (eds), *Issues in History Teaching*, London: RoutledgeFalmer, pp. 72–82.

More, T. (1513) *The History of King Richard III.* www.r3.org/bookcase/more/moretext.html

Nichol, J. (1992) *The Mystery of the Princes in the Tower.* The clue cards can be downloaded from www.history.org.uk/resources.

Rogers, P.J. (1979) *The New History, theory into practice*, The Historical Association. Reprinted (2010) in *International Journal of Historical Learning, Teaching and Research* 9(1). www. history.org.uk/resources/primary_resource_3220_150.html.

PART III

A BROADER PERSPECTIVE OF CREATIVITY AND HISTORY

CHAPTER 10

CREATIVE EXPLORATION OF LOCAL, NATIONAL AND GLOBAL LINKS

*Penelope Harnett and
Sarah Whitehouse*

This chapter draws attention to the importance of studying a range of histories at local, national and global levels. It begins by considering the potential of the locality for developing creative opportunities for learning history. Creative approaches to learning about families are discussed, together with ways in which children can learn about each others' histories. The chapter examines how local, national and global links may be developed through studying personal stories and the push and pull factors, which have influenced people's movements to and from places. It looks at the British dimension and European dimension in learning history and concludes with some suggestions for planning local, national and global links.

STARTING POINTS IN STUDYING THE LOCALITY

The locality offers a rich resource for children to develop their historical understanding. A creative starting point may be to take children on a walk around their locality, inviting them to record different features, which they have observed as photographs, drawings, notes or video clips. Once back in the classroom, children may use these recordings to develop their own enquiries; to ask questions about the different features which they have observed and begin to think how they may be able to answer their questions.

Prompts about different places they have visited within the locality may include questions such as:

■ What is this place like?
■ Why is it like it is?
■ What was it like in the past?
■ Who visits this place now and who used to visit this place in the past?
■ Do I like this place? How do I feel in this place?
■ How may this place be improved?

Such questions are good starting points for enquiries, and involve children in a range of investigations across different subject areas, to extend their understanding of their locality. Catling (2006: 27) notes the strong connections between geography and history, which can be developed through locality studies. He outlines key questions which interconnect the two subjects and concludes that, 'Their natural interconnectedness in human affairs needs to be drawn clearly to children's attention, enhancing their learning and enlarging their sense of the world'. Figure 10.1 shows an example of ways in which learning in different subject areas was developed from a local walk around the centre of Bristol.

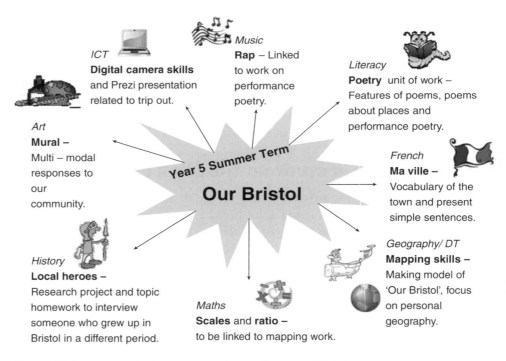

ICT
Digital camera skills and Prezi presentation related to trip out.

Music
Rap – Linked to work on performance poetry.

Literacy
Poetry unit of work – Features of poems, poems about places and performance poetry.

Art
Mural – Multi – modal responses to our community.

Year 5 Summer Term
Our Bristol

French
Ma ville – Vocabulary of the town and present simple sentences.

History
Local heroes – Research project and topic homework to interview someone who grew up in Bristol in a different period.

Maths
Scales and **ratio –** to be linked to mapping work.

Geography/ DT
Mapping skills – Making model of 'Our Bristol', focus on personal geography.

Figure 10.1 Cross-curricular responses to a walk around Bristol

The diagram indicates the creative ways in which trainee teachers at the University of the West of England encouraged children to record their learning about the locality. They used poetry to communicate their emotional responses to Millennium Square in Bristol. Trainees reflected on what they could see all around them and what changes and events might have occurred in that place, using the device 'Not Yet ...' to structure their poetry.

Not Yet ...

A man stares into the past

With his golden magnifying glass

'Not yet' he sighs, 'not yet' ...

From nothing Bristol began

A river, a spring

Along with time people came,

Brought along their dreams and chains

Not yet have Indian ships come into harbour

Or has Rajah Roy set foot on British soils

Not yet have the dulcet tones of the Bristolian choir boys been heard

Nor have they been sent off to war,

Some never to return

Not yet has Field Marshall Smith been issued

With his bayonet and Bible

Not yet has Archibald Leach left Bristol for Hollywood

Nor his body been frozen in time in Millennium Square

Not yet do we know the distance to the Sun,

Nor do the voices of the BBC

Resonate in Millennium Square like a humming bee.

Not yet can science and seas

Be explored in Bristol's cobbled streets.

Or do people walk on the reflections of a giant metal sun.

It's getting hot in here,

Somewhere over the rainbow ...

Not yet do iguanas walk the Bristol streets

Nor do strange two-wheeled vehicles speed to and fro

Not yet do giant eyes blink at us from café windows

Nor do electrical eyes watch our every move

Not yet is man forbidden from swimming in the sea,

Or basking in the sun, freely.

Not yet was access so restricted

Thieves lurking on every corner.

Not yet is Andy the banker smiling down from the billboards

Shaping the soul of Bristol

With his million dollar grin

Not yet is the horizon made of glass

Not yet does the forest look like this

Nor does water conceal sharp objects

For now it simply flows freely,

Through you, untouched, Bristol city
(Megan Isaac, Julie Ricard and Robert Beardwell)

LINKING LOCAL TO GLOBAL AND GLOBAL TO LOCAL

The locality offers starting points for children to understand more about where they live. It is important for children to foster an identity with their locality and to engage in learning about their communities. Such learning also helps to develop children's understanding of their place in the wider world. This is paramount in today's globalised world, where we are inextricably linked together in all aspects of our daily lives, from the clothes we wear, to the food we buy, to the news we hear about. How can children begin to make sense of this if they do not understand their own locality?

One way of making links with the wider world is through school partnerships. Much can be gained from this approach; reciprocal partnerships enable schools to learn from one another. However, Fran Martin is quoted (Maddern 2010) as saying that this is not always the case and warns of partnerships between schools which often reinforce stereotypes and foster neo-colonialism. Schools may be partnered with schools elsewhere in the world, but there are also creative opportunities for linking schools situated more closely together.

Case study

The following case study describes learning which occurred when two schools (Shield Road Primary School and Bannerman Road Primary School) in different areas of Bristol (Filton and Easton) chose to link up and explore their locality together.

As part of their project on their locality Year 3 children developed a range of historical and geographical enquiries and also began to explore some of their own family histories. At Shield Road Primary School most of the children in the class were white British, although a few children came from African Caribbean backgrounds. Children mapped where their families came from around the world and also from within Britain. They were encouraged to ask questions, including investigating how long their families had lived in Bristol, why they had moved to the city and the different occupations of their parents and carers. Such questions provided opportunities for the children to discuss their ideas and to develop further historical enquiries. It also led the children to consider who else lived in Bristol and who might have moved to Bristol in the past.

The class teacher, Philipa Statter decided to use the interest which children showed in other people living in Bristol, to link with another school within the city. Bristol, like most cities in the UK, is very culturally diverse and Philipa decided to forge links with Bannerman Road Primary School in Bristol, which educates children from a wide range of cultural and ethnic backgrounds, so that children could learn about each others' histories and also the history of their different localities.

It was agreed that the children from Shield Road Primary School would visit Bannerman Road Primary School and interview the children about their families and their experiences of living in Easton. For both groups of children it was an opportunity to share and talk about living in Bristol and to discuss similarities and differences in their experiences.

The children from Shield Road visited their local high street in Filton, prior to their visit to Bannerman Road and were able to use this experience to compare their high street with Bannerman Road's high street, which they visited in Easton. The children were encouraged to look first at similarities between the two high streets and to explore features which they shared in common, before they began to identify differences. Children were asked to take a 360 degree view of one area, noting everything which they could see in all directions from one spot. This encouraged them to take some ownership of their learning and provided them with the 'freedom' to record their own thoughts and ideas, not necessarily the ideas of the teacher. Different ways were provided for children to record their thoughts and ideas, including sketching, taking digital images, poetry such as a Haiku, and using a digital microphone or a talking postcard or by creating a wordle. (A wordle is a fun tool that creates 'word clouds' from text; the largest words are those used most in the text and the smallest words are used least.)

The High Street in Easton had many similarities with that near Shield Road, including the range of shops and amenities (chemist, cafe, church, newsagent). One distinctive difference, however, was the local supermarket; the colours, smells and contrasts here were amazing. For example, there were over 40 varieties of rice and a range of fruit and vegetables that the children had never seen before! The children were shown around the supermarket and told about the different foods on sale. They learned about the shop's history and how it had started as a small corner shop before growing into a supermarket, which imports food from all around the world. Children had many questions about how the High Street had developed and were able to find out more about the history of Easton, using the contributions of community members, which were invaluable.

The variety of foods available in the supermarket fascinated many of the children from Shield Road and led to informal conversations concerning food at lunch time and what children ate at home. Children were immersed in exploring similarities and differences between their life styles; key features in helping them come to an awareness and understanding of their own unique identities, as well as some of the experiences which they share with all children of their own age.

This was also evident in some of the questions compiled into a questionnaire by children from Shield Road Primary School. They were interested in asking:

■　What languages do you speak?
■　How long have you lived in Easton?
■　Do you go to a church, mosque or temple?
■　Where are your family from?

Such questions related directly to children's personal identities, but there were also other questions concerning the school and the locality:

■　Do you have fun in your school?
■　How many children are in your class?
■　Do you think the drawings in Easton are graffiti or art?

This interesting mix of questions enabled the children to collate a variety of data, which looked at similarities and differences between their own experiences and also between the localities where they lived.

The above case study illustrates how interacting with children from other schools heightens children's awareness of both themselves and of their shared identities. It also provided starting points for children to explore potential global connections with the locality through first-hand experiences.

Making wider connections through personal stories

Children have many and varied connections with the wider world. Figure 10.2 was drawn by seven-year-old Henry, who lives near Cardiff. He has recorded some of the different connections he has. He has included members of his own family, who live in different places and listed places that he has visited. Henry has also thought about his own daily life and included foods that he has eaten and football players he enjoys watching.

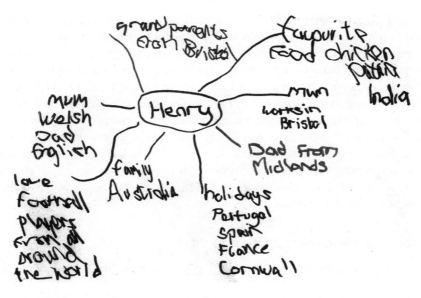

Figure 10.2 Seven-year-old Henry's connections with the wider world

Such experiences provide rich opportunities for developing creative enquiries. Hilary Claire (1996) reminds us of the powerful connections which can be made with the wider world through personal stories. Her work with children alerts us to the many hidden stories which abound and the sensitivity which needs to be employed in both listening to and sharing these stories. She emphasises that 'such work must be grounded in a classroom ethos in which trust and mutual respect are well established' (Claire 1996: 29).

Establishing connections through studying the movements of people in the past

This theme provides opportunities for exploration at local, national and global levels and engages children in thinking of people's different motivations for moving; the extent of 'push or pull' factors. Children might have their own experiences of moving to recount and it is also useful to consider both movements of people within the UK as well as further afield. For example, in the nineteenth century industrial towns grew up, as people moved from the countryside to find employment; the Highland clearances depopulated large areas of northern Scotland and Ireland for England and also further afield for the USA and Canada. Following the Second World War, new industries developed, including the car industry, which attracted people to work in the Midlands. People continue to move around the UK in search of employment and different life styles in the twenty-first century.

Investigating why people moved to Britain can be investigated over a long period of time and this is possibly a helpful way for understanding recent immigration in the twentieth and twenty-first centuries. The search for a better life has been a key motivating factor across time: Viking settlers looked for land to farm and peoples to trade with. Huguenots escaping persecution in the sixteenth and seventeenth centuries fled from France and contributed to the Bedfordshire lace industry and the weaving industry in London. Dutch engineers helped drain the Fens in the seventeenth century. In the nineteenth century Jewish refugees fled from pogroms in Eastern Europe and Russia. Following the Second World War, Polish exiles established communities in Britain and workers from the Commonwealth responded to the labour shortage and came to work in Britain. (See Hann (2004) for discussion on Commonwealth migration post Second World War.)

Questions for beginning investigations

Key investigations for children can develop from some of the following questions:

- Who moved? Why did they move? What social/economic/personal factors were involved and which factors were the most important? Who made the choice to move and who stayed behind?
- How did people reach their destinations? What was the journey like? Was it dangerous? Did it take long? What happened to people on their journeys? How did people feel? Did they miss the people they had left behind? What were their feelings about reaching their new destination? How can we find out about the journeys which people made? What sources of information may be useful?
- What was it like for people when they arrived? Did they feel welcomed? What did they do? What challenges did they meet? How did they adapt to their new lives? Which aspects of lives changed and which remained the same? Did their lives improve?
- Do you think that they felt that they had made the right decision? Did they maintain links with their old homes? Did they want to return? What happened to the people who remained at home? How did the movement of people away change their lives and communities?

Studying the movements of people in the past

This may raise many sensitive and controversial issues and involve children in considering human rights and issues of fairness and social justice. For example, the story of the native American princess, Pocohantas raises questions concerning the fair treatment of people and thinking about laws which protect human rights (Harnett 2010). The arrival of the Europeans in Australia may be used to introduce children to notions of social justice and citizenship (Harnett 2006a).

Studying the transatlantic slave trade

The history of the transatlantic slave trade raises many painful and sensitive issues. Children may learn different versions of the trade from their families, from their teachers and from different media. Traille draws attention to the emotional responses which children from African-Caribbean descent sometimes felt in their history lessons, concerning the Atlantic trade and suggests that teachers need to try to understand how their children might think and feel. She concludes by emphasising the importance of providing children with 'the tools for exploring and challenging their preconceptions' and advises that in teaching the trans-Atlantic slave trade the following may be helpful for planning:

■ Present the topic of slavery as an important phenomenon of human history.
■ Highlight that it was to be found in all major civilisations from the ancient world to the present day.
■ Remember and emphasise that African-Caribbean history starts centuries before the Middle Passage and continues long after (Traille 2007: 37).

Evidence of the transatlantic trade remains in many of the British cities which were involved. In Bristol, buildings, memorials and street names all provide evidence of Bristol's past involvement (see National Archives at www.nationalarchives.gov.uk/pathways/blackhistory/journeys/virtual_tour_html/bristol/bristol.htm).

Bristol

Much of Bristol's wealth was based on this trade and ways in which this trade should be remembered within the city is a continuing source of debate. Edward Colston (1636–1721) was a wealthy merchant and derived much of his wealth from the slave trade and plantations in the West Indies. He was also a great philanthropist and donated much of his money to hospitals, schools and other good causes in Bristol. Smart suggests some creative ways in which children can be encouraged to learn about Colston and to explore how different communities may have different perspectives on what he achieved (Smart 2008).

THINKING CREATIVELY ABOUT BRITISH HISTORY; WHAT DO CHILDREN KNOW?

It is interesting to explore children's views of 'Britishness' and of the peoples who live in the United Kingdom. Living in England, seven-year-old Iona makes the following observations about people from the four nations, in her illustrations and captions (Figures 10.3(a)–(d)).

Looking at the pictures which Iona has drawn we can note that clothing is significant for her in distinguishing different nationalities. All her people are dressed very differently. The Scottish man is carefully drawn with buttons on his jacket and detailed features on his sporran. Iona has represented the plaid on his kilt and evidently has a view that Scottish men are quite hairy! Her picture represents many ways in which Scottish people are characterised and is a reminder of the powerful influence of the

Figure 10.3 Seven-year-old Iona's observations about 'the four nations': (a) English girl; (b) Irish woman; (c) Welsh woman; (d) Scottish man

media in shaping young children's views and consequently the important role which education must play in encouraging children to question what they encounter.

The illustrations also remind us of the different funds of knowledge derived from very varied experiences which children draw on as they approach their learning. A Welsh teacher had told Iona that microwaves were *popty ping* in Welsh; Iona had remembered seeing different flags on the television in Ireland and from personal experience she knew what garments to wear when it is cold and had dressed her Welsh woman in hat, scarf and gloves. An awareness of children's existing understandings and misconceptions therefore is key to planning for their future learning and Traille reminds us how this is important in facilitating 'an inclusive ethic of care within history classrooms' (Traille 2008: 20).

Although children in England are currently expected to learn the *National History Curriculum for England* (DfEE/QCA 1999) there is an expectation that they will learn about the histories of all four nations which comprise the United Kingdom. In fact the selection of topics which are taught most regularly in English primary schools suggests that this is not the case (Nichol and Harnett 2011) and children have limited opportunities for learning about the histories of Wales, Scotland and Ireland. However, the histories of these countries are all interlinked and it is worthwhile considering ways in which children's awareness of their British heritage might be extended.

The resources from Ireland in Schools provide opportunities to include an Irish dimension within selected topics of the English history curriculum (Ireland in Schools, www.iisresource.org) They also promote activities which enable children to develop understanding of Irish culture, literature and music. Various research studies have analysed the contribution which inclusion of an Irish dimension might make to children's historical understanding (Gove-Humphries *et al.* 2008; Bracey 2010; Bracey *et al.* 2011). The website, Education Scotland provides useful information and resources (www.educationscotland.gov.uk/scotlandshistory/index.asp) and a history of Wales can be found at www.bbc.co.uk/wales/history/sites/themes/guide.shtml.

The *Diversity and Curriculum Review*, led by Sir Keith Ajegbo in 2007 recommends that all secondary-aged children should learn about the histories of peoples within the United Kingdom. It argues for the place of history in helping children understand the country in which they live today and advocates that a curriculum strand should be developed entitled *Identity and Diversity: Living Together in the UK*. This strand would bring together critical thinking about ethnicity, religion and race, explicit links to political issues and values and the use of contemporary history. The following areas to include were recommended:

■ Contextualised understanding that the UK is a 'multinational' state, made up of England, Northern Ireland, Scotland and Wales;
■ Immigration;
■ Commonwealth and the legacy of Empire;
■ European Union;
■ Extending the franchise (e.g. the legacy of slavery, universal suffrage, equal opportunities legislation) (DfES 2007: 12).

DEVELOPING CREATIVE CONNECTIONS WITH THE EUROPEAN UNION

History is a particularly useful subject to develop children's awareness of their common European heritage. This is not always easy since the notion of Europe has been forged by conflict and bloodshed as much as by peaceful endeavours. The Council of Europe has sponsored projects providing older children with opportunities for learning about the histories of other countries within the European Union and to understand a range of histories contributing to European consciousness. A recent project focuses on 'The Image of the Other in History Teaching' and emphasises the objectives and methodology for teaching history of cultural diversity of European societies and globalisation (Council of Europe 2008). 'Shared Histories for a Europe without Dividing Lines' is a current project creating teaching materials relating to significant historical examples of interactions and convergences within Europe, within specific themes such as: the consequences of the industrial revolution; the development of education; human rights as they appear in Art and the relations between Europe and the world (Council of Europe 2010).

Little research has explored the knowledge and understanding of primary-aged children towards European history. Cooper investigated what children from Finland, England, Greece, Holland and Romania knew about the past and how they acquired that knowledge (Cooper 2000). She found that children were aware of many aspects of the past over a very long time span, but often saw these aspects as fragmented pieces of information. There were similarities in some of the topics studied by children from the different countries and family, visits and books were all key sources of information.

Younger children too may learn the history of Europe through folk tales set in the past. The website www.eurotales.eril.net offers examples of different folk tales from a range of European countries with English translations and provides a useful reminder of the power of good stories to develop understanding of ways of life in the past. There are similarities between many folk heroes and heroines; for example the story of Robin Hood and his resistance against oppression may be contrasted with the stories associated with William Tell, the Swiss huntsman's resistance to Austrian rule. Cooper argues that folk tales support young children in thinking historically, by introducing them to similarities and differences in past lives, by encouraging them to sequence events and through the exploration of motives for events and the appreciation of different interpretations (Cooper and Ditchburn 2009: 58). In research conducted with English pupils she concludes that as the children rewrote a Turkish folk tale they began to 'develop the kind of understanding that is essential for plural democracies within a multinational and interdependent international world' (ibid.: 69).

Case study: France and England

Another way of supporting children's learning is through identifying specific European events and linking them with history taught in school. This was an approach adopted by Christchurch Junior School in Bristol. The children were learning about the Tudors in their history lessons and their teacher was looking for an opportunity to include a European dimension in her teaching. The teacher was part of a network of teachers integrating foreign language teaching within their work with primary-aged children and was investigating ways in which languages might be taught through different curriculum subjects.

In 1520, Henry VIII of England met Francis I of France at the Field of the Cloth of Gold near Calais in France. This was a meeting between two powerful monarchs, young men wanting to show off their magnificence and to try and outshine each other. There was a dazzling array of tents and pavilions, and people dressed in fine clothes; there was music, feasting and jousting to entertain all those who attended. The picture, *The Field of the Cloth of Gold* (www.royalcollection.org.uk) is a very good starting point to introduce children to the story.

Children were introduced to key events in the story and encouraged to research more details, following teaching sessions. They learned how to dance a pavane and perform a French song. Jousting rules were explained and the children created their own shadow puppets to enact the jousts. English and French competitors were cheered by supporters in their own language. Reflecting on children's learning, the teacher emphasised how making learning fun and vivid had motivated the children and how the children had remembered both the historical content and 'the language and structures taught because they learnt the new language in context and for a real purpose' (Hughes with Wright 2007: 31).

Some starting points

Investigating social and cultural histories promotes opportunities to consider aspects of common European heritages, which unite peoples in Europe. Exploring everyday objects encourages reflection on people's similar experiences and the universality of some of the approaches which different societies adopted to meet the challenges of their everyday lives (Harnett 2006: 169). One way of developing children's awareness of common threads in everyday life across Europe is to encourage their exploration of museum web-sites across Europe. For example the Comenius Pedagogical Museum in Prague, in the Czech Republic, has a reconstruction of a nineteenth-century school room; children might be interested in comparing this reconstruction with their own knowledge of education at that time in the UK (www.praguecard.biz/attraction.php?id-521).

SOME POINTS FOR CONSIDERATION IN DEVELOPING CHILDREN'S UNDERSTANDING OF LOCAL, NATIONAL AND GLOBAL HISTORIES

We conclude with an overview of suggestions for developing the dimensions of history which have been discussed in this chapter.

1   Look for connections between the locality and the wider world as starting points – children and their families: a local person, an event, an object, street names, the community – anything which will arouse children's interest and curiosity and encourage them to explore connections with elsewhere.

2   Support children in framing enquiry questions to support their learning.

3   Consider how different peoples in the past are represented. Do children's assumptions need to be challenged? For example, children may assume that life was simpler and people less intelligent in less technologically advanced societies. Enquiries which encourage children to focus on how different communities/societies resolved challenges in their everyday lives develops respect for the technologies which they were able to employ.

4   Encourage children to investigate different societies throughout the world before the arrival of the Europeans (e.g. the Aztecs; the Mughal Empire). Do children assume that Europeans brought civilisation to different parts of the world?

5   Look for a range of perspectives on similar events. Explore the feelings of all peoples involved in cultural encounters.

6   Encourage children to identify appropriate sources of information and to ask questions about which sources they don't have and why.

7   Draw children's attention to geographical links, which influence people's histories (e.g. the climate and terrain).

8   Use resources to help children appreciate what was happening in different parts of the world at the same time and construct time lines, which take into account events and developments in other places of the world. History World is a useful resource to explore world history events and developments and provides information, time lines and pictures (www.historyworld.net).

REFERENCES

BBC *A History of Wales,* www.bbc.co.uk/wales/history/sites/themes/guide.shtml (accessed 1 May 2012).

Bracey, P. (2010) Perceptions of the contribution of an Irish dimension in the English history curriculum, *Educational Review* 62(2): 203–213.

Bracey, P., Gove-Humphries, A. and Jackson, D. (2011) Teaching diversity in the history classroom, in I. Davies (ed.) *Debates in History Teaching*, London: Routledge.

Catling, S. (2006) Geography and history: Exploring the local connection, *Primary History* 42: 14–16.

Claire, H. (1996) *Reclaiming our Pasts. Equality and Diversity in the Primary History Curriculum*, Stoke on Trent: Trentham Books.

Cooper, H. (2000) Primary History in Europe: a staple diet or a hot potato? In J. Arthur and R. Phillips (eds) *Issues in History Teaching*, London: Routledge.

Cooper, H. and Ditchburn, E. (2009) Folk tales – universal values, individual differences, *International Journal of History Teaching Learning and Research* 8(1): 58–70.

Council of Europe and Research Centre for Islamic History, Art and Culture (2008) Globalisation and images of the other: Challenges and new perspectives for history teaching in Europe?, www.coe.int/t/dg4/education/historyteaching/Source/Projects/DocumentsImage/RAPSymposium Istanbu2008en_fr.pdf (accessed 1 May 2012).

Council of Europe (2010) Shared histories for a europe with dividing lines, www.coe.int/t/dg4/education/historyteaching/projects/sharedhistories/oslo2010intro_EN.asp (accessed 1 May 2012).

DfEE/QCA (1999) (Department for Education and Employment/Qualifications and Curriculum Authority) *National Curriculum for England and Wales: handbook for primary teachers in England*, London: DfEE/QCA.

DfES (2007) *Curriculum Review. Diversity and Citizenship*, London, DfES, www.education. gov.uk/publications/eOrderingDownload/DfES_Diversity_and_Citizenship.pdf (accessed 28 April 2012).

Gove-Humphries, A. Bracey, P. and Jackson, D. (2008) Here come the Vikings! Making a saga out of a crisis, *Primary History* (50): 31–35.

Hann, K. (2004) Migration: the search for a better life, *Primary History* (37): 5–9.

Harnett, P. (2006a) Exploring the potential for history and citizenship education with primary children at the British Empire and Commonwealth Museum in Bristol, *International Journal of Historical Learning, Teaching and Research* 6: 34–39.

Harnett, P. (2006b) Shared Heritages? Investigating Ways of Life in the Past to Promote European Consciousness with Children in Primary Schools, in Ross, A. (ed.) *Citizenship Education: Europe and the World*, London: CiCe, pp. 169–174, http://learning.londonmet. ac.uk/cice/docs/2006-169.pdf (accessed 1 May 2012).

Harnett, P. (2010) *T.E.A.C.H. (Teaching Emotive and Controversial History) at Key Stage 1, Case Study – the Story of Pocahontas*, www.history.org.uk/resources/resource_view.php?resource_ type=about&id=4912&subid=4955&cid=152&print=1 (accessed 1 May 2012)

Hughes, S. and Wright, J. (2007) Case Study 4: Harry met Francis – the Field of the Cloth of Gold. An inspirational and authentic context for teaching aspects of history, dance, drama, design and technology through French, *Primary History* 47: 30–31.

Maddern, K. (2010) How overseas links mean well, but, *TES Connect* 13 March, www.tes. co.uk/article.aspx?storycode=6038085 (accessed 1 May 2012).

Nichol, J. and Harnett, P. (2011) History Teaching in England and the English National History Curriculum 3-11: past, present, into the future, *International Journal of History Learning, Teaching and Research* 10(1):106–119.

Smart, D. (2008) *Memorials: Linking the Local to the National and the Global*, www.euroclio. eu/.../789=memorialslinking-the-local-to-the-national-a... (accessed 1 May 2012).

Traille, K. (2007) 'You should be proud about your history. They made me feel ashamed': teaching history hurts, *Teaching History* 127: 31–38.

Traille, K. (2008) Primary history and the curriculum. The perspectives of students of African-Carribean origin and their mothers, *Primary History* 50: 19–21.

Websites

Comenius Pedagogical Museum: www.praguecard.biz/attraction.php?id=521(accessed October 2012).

Education Scotland: www.educationscotland.gov.uk/scotlandshistory/index.asp (accessed 1 May 2012).

Eurotales: www.eurotales.eril.net (accessed 1 May 2012).

Ireland in Schools: www.iisresource.org/Pages/primary_history.aspx (accessed 1 May 2012).

National Archives: www.nationalarchives.gov.uk/pathways/blackhistory/journeys/virtual_tour_ html/bristol/bristol.htm) (accessed 1 May 2012).

Royal Collection: www.royalcollection.org.uk (accessed 1 May 2012).

CHAPTER 11

CREATIVE APPROACHES TO WHOLE SCHOOL CURRICULUM PLANNING FOR HISTORY

Linsey Maginn

INTRODUCTION

Historical enquiry skills and progression

The primary history curriculum identifies a set of key knowledge and skills which children are expected to achieve by the end of Key Stage 2. In addition to this it outlines the content and breadth of what we teach through the program of study. When implementing whole school planning, it is essential that it should promote the five key areas of primary history curriculum:

- Chronological Understanding
- Knowledge and Understanding
- Historical Enquiry
- Historical Interpretation
- Organization and Communication.

It is also crucial that progression within the strands of enquiry is evident across each key stage and each year group. The attainment targets in the primary history curriculum suggest a pattern of progression in history from Key Stage 1 to Key Stage 2.

Key Stage 1

Pupils begin to develop in their understanding of chronology by placing artefacts, photographs and events in order and begin to use vocabulary associated with the passing of time. Pupils begin recounting past events in their own lives and progress to showing knowledge and understanding of aspects of the past beyond living memory. Pupils distinguish between fact and fiction and then begin to compare pictures or photographs of people in the past. They begin to discuss the reliability of different sources, including stories, to find out about the past. Children use a range of artefacts and sources and sort them into 'then' and 'now'. They begin to ask and answer questions about different sources, including where, when, why, what and how? Children communicate what they have learned through drama, drawing, displays and presentations.

Key Stage 2

In Key Stage 2 pupils progress to using dates and times, including AD and BC (CE and BCE) and begin placing these on a time line. They begin to make links between periods studied and compare and contrast different events on a time line. They are expected to show a more accurate understanding of the past and over a range of periods, including AD and BC. Pupils will link sources and work out how conclusions were made about the past. Children compare different accounts and sources and begin to consider the ways of checking the accuracy of different sources. Children describe, give reasons for, and results of the main events and changes. Children begin to evaluate different sources and explain why some are more useful for particular tasks. Children use a variety of ways to communicate their ideas including the use of information and communication technologies (ICT), extended writing, displays and presentations.

Cross-curricular approaches

The emphasis on raising standards in literacy and in numeracy has resulted in subjects including history becoming less of a priority in many schools. This has led to teachers, including myself, finding it more of a challenge to ensure coverage of the key knowledge and skills within Key Stage 1 and Key Stage 2. Harnett (2000: 34–35) recognised the pressures on schools, in delivering all aspects of the curriculum and identified that 'for space linking subjects together becomes more attractive, and a return to greater emphasis on topic work becomes more of a possibility'. The primary history curriculum, however, lends itself to cross-curricular work, as explicit links are made with the core subjects. Cooper (2000: 34) identified how 'history is an umbrella discipline' and highlighted how the different areas in literacy, numeracy and science can be related to historical content. It has also been argued that an integrated approach to the primary curriculum is more 'congruent with the process of learning' as 'almost all issues in lives, the community and the world require a multi perspectival and multi disciplinary approach' (Skelton and Reeves 2009). It could be argued therefore that an integrated approach to teaching history could address the issues associated with a crowded curriculum and in addition, provide children with a multi-perspectival view of the world, which underpins the values promoted in the history curriculum.

In the Ofsted report *History for All* (2011) it was found that 'pupils progress in history tended to be slower in the schools visited that did not teach history as a discrete subject than in those that did'. However 'integrated work succeeded when emphasis was placed on the knowledge and skills the subject aims to promote'. It is easy to lose sight of the discrete concepts of different disciplines when integrating the curriculum and this must be considered when planning units of work. It is essential therefore that when considering a thematic approach to history teaching and learning the integrity of the subject is maintained. Perhaps a solution within an integrated approach 'seems to be to teach a core study unit during one term of each year through an integrated topic with a strong history focus' (Cooper 1995: 41).

A good example of how an integrated curriculum meets learners' needs and fosters the key knowledge and skills within each discipline is by looking at the structure of the International Primary Curriculum (IPC). The IPC is based on a thematic approach to help children achieve their learning goals and succeed in all areas of the curriculum. It is largely based on the constructivist view of learning, where children internalise and construct new knowledge based on past experiences. They see subjects as interdependent and children are taught to make connections across subject areas to consolidate learning. In one international school they found that their curriculum no longer met the needs of their culturally diverse rolls and so adopted the IPC. During each unit of work, the school used a home country/host country approach to support a topic about explorers. The children learned about the home country of the explorer and then about the adventures from the country explored through linking different areas of the curriculum. By integrating the curriculum, children were able to make connections between learning and begin to develop a multi-perspectival view of the world, which underpins many of the values and aims within the primary history curriculum (Skelton and Reeves 2009: 142).

In the rest of this chapter I shall exemplify how an integrated approach to the primary history curriculum was implemented in an inner city Manchester school to meet the needs of children from multi-faith and multi-cultural backgrounds. I shall discuss how a review of the curriculum was essential to deepen children's knowledge and understanding, develop historical skills and enhance creativity and enjoyment in learning. The process of implementing the new initiative and an analysis of its outcome will follow.

PLANNING AN INTEGRATED APPROACH TO HISTORY FOR CHILDREN FROM DIFFERENT CULTURES IN AN INNER CITY SCHOOL

Rationale for a new initiative

The school in which I teach is a Community School. It is a larger than average school, situated just north of the Manchester city centre. Almost all of the pupils are from multi-cultural and multi-ethnic groups and the majority of children have English as an additional language. There are over 28 different languages spoken; most frequently spoken are Urdu, Punjubi and Arabic. Many of the children who joined the school during the Reception Year with no English are bilingual by Year 2. Despite the rich diversity of cultures within the school, the primary history curriculum did not reflect this. Prior to implementing the new initiative, history was taught as a discrete subject over a block of two weeks. The children did experience depth in the subject and teachers made some good links with literacy, numeracy and ICT, when possible. However, the Qualification and Assessment Authority (QCA) support materials seemed to dominate the curriculum across Key Stage 1 and Key Stage 2 and lacked real meaning for children from diverse cultural backgrounds. This can be seen in Table 11.1, which shows the topics taught.

■ **Table 11.1** History topics taught prior to the new curriculum initiative

Year Group	Term 1	Term 2	Term 3
1	How are toys different to those in the past?	What were homes like a long time ago?	What were seaside holidays like in the past?
2	What are we remembering on remembrance day?	How do we know about the Great Fire of London?	Why do we remember Florence Nightingale?
3	Why have people invaded and settled in Britain in the past? The Romans	Why did Henry VIII marry six times?	How did life change in our locality in Victorian times?
4	Why have people invaded and settled in Britain in the past? The Vikings	What were the differences between rich and poor Tudors?	What was is like for children in the Second World War?
5	Who were the Ancient Greeks?	What were the effects of Tudor exploration?	How has life in Britain changed since 1948?
6	How can we find out about the Aztecs?	What can we learn about recent history from studying the life of a famous person?	SATS

Following lesson observations, pupil interviews and work scrutinies, it was evident that children were curious about the past and most of them enjoyed history lessons. Coverage of the key knowledge, skills and understanding within history units of work was good. However, this was not being transferred to other curriculum areas, nor were other curriculum areas being used to enhance the knowledge and skills in history. As the school was moving towards a more thematic approach to the curriculum, I used this opportunity to introduce a new initiative that would celebrate the diversity of cultures in the school and provide children with purposeful learning experiences across the primary history curriculum.

The idea was that each year group would take on one of the continents of the world and use this as their theme for a term. Over a term, all year groups across Key Stage 1 and Key Stage 2 would study their continent in depth by exploring the cultural aspects of the continent through music, drama and citizenship and the geographical aspects including climate, weather, landscapes and globalization. This would then lead on to the study of an historical person or episode that took place in that continent in the past. By using the continents as a context for learning, we hoped that children would be able to make stronger connections between curriculum areas and use this to develop historical knowledge and skills relevant to their own experiences.

The process of creating the new initiative

Whole school planning

Implementing the continent-themed initiative involved cooperation and discussion from the whole school staff. It was essential that staff were clear about the aims and outcomes of the new initiative, to ensure effective whole school planning. These were:

- ■ to introduce new history units of work based on a continent theme;
- ■ to ensure that Knowledge, Skills and Understanding (KSU) of the primary history curriculum are emphasised throughout the theme;
- ■ to link the history unit of work with other curriculum areas;
- ■ to use a range of teaching and learning strategies;
- ■ to make history teaching and learning more relevant to the children.

Staff were split into six groups and given Africa, Australasia, Europe, Asia, South America and North America as themes to work on. In groups the staff brainstormed different historical figures or episodes that could be associated with their continent and noted these on diagrams, which were later put on display at the front of the room. Next the staff joined up with their year group partners and discussed which continent and associated history study would best fit their existing curriculum and year group. The continents and associated units of study were then distributed to each year group. The next step in the planning stage was to roughly break down the history study into six to eight lessons and then select which history knowledge and skills lend themselves to the unit. After each year group had planned their history study, they started thinking about links to other curriculum areas, which would provide the history unit with deeper, more meaningful purpose. The staff then created a cross-curricular map for their year group which was then transferred to the whole school planner (see Table 11.2).

Table 11.2 Cross-curricular plans outlined for each year group

Year	Continent	Literacy	ICT	History	Geography	Art and Music
1	Africa	Write diary entries and recounts in role as David Livingstone	Use textease to plot events on timeline of David Livingstone's life	David Livingstone	Barnaby Bear in Africa – explore food, animals, climate and weather	African masks African jewellery African Drums African Dance
2	Australasia	Non-chronological reports based on Aboriginals	Create aboriginal art using Dazzle programme	Aboriginals	Compare (passport the world/Barnaby Bear)	Aboriginal art
3	Europe	Use ICT to create Roman newspaper headlines and stories	Create mosaic patterns using ICT software	The Romans	Tourism in different countries in Europe, compare weather patterns	Build Roman villas, create mosaic patterns
4	Asia	Explanation texts Newspaper writing	Internet research on Gandhi Powerpoint presentation for Assembly	Gandhi	Compare village in India to Manchester/ How are we connected?	Rangoli Patterns, bollywood dance, origami sculpture, fabric and tie dying
5	South America	Historical recounts in character/ information texts	Powerpoint presentation on the Aztecs	The Aztecs	Compare/How are we connected?	Ceremonial masks, jewellery Geometric design printing
6	North America	Write a play based on witch trials/ historical recounts	Create own webpages on witch trials	The Witch Trials	Compare landscapes, terrain, climate	Totem poles Wigwams

Responding to the learning needs of the children

Whole school planning was a significant step towards implementing the new initiative. However, it was essential that consideration was given to the diverse cultural and learning needs of the children.

- ■ Parental involvement was an important factor in fostering the cultural aspects of the new initiative and an invaluable resource in supporting the teaching and learning of the history units. Since the children within the school were from culturally rich backgrounds, parents could be used to provide first-hand experiences of what places are like and the effects different periods in history had on them.
- ■ Availability of resources to support the new history units was initially an issue and budgets for teaching resources vary from school to school. Books, internet and video resources contained some very useful teaching material to support the units and the local museums contained a wealth of information and artefacts that could be adapted for the new history units.
- ■ Using a range of teaching methods was also essential in ensuring that learning needs were being met and that that children were given a range of experiences in which to explore their continent. The use of artefacts, drama, role-play, books, videos and ICT were all considered when planning the unit.

The development of year group plans

Using a continent as a theme for delivering the history curriculum across a term was effective in all year groups. Good links were made across subject areas to enhance historical knowledge, skills and understanding, and children were able to make confident links between the cultural, geographical and historical aspects of their history study.

In Year 4, the children explored Indian culture and traditions through art, dance and music and the beliefs and practices of the Hindu and Buddhist faiths through Religious Education (Figure 11.1).

Learning about the beliefs and cultures in India today helped place the unit in context for the children and also provided children with an opportunity to share their own experiences of India, which acted as a great motivator for the rest of the unit. In geography children studied aspects of the QCA unit 'A Village in India', which allowed them to identify Asia and India on the world map. The children also learned about the economic diversity of India by comparing what it is like to live in different parts of the country. Exploring India in different subject areas allowed children to make more confident enquiries in history. Children were able to apply their knowledge of the geographical and cultural features of India to explain Britain's imperial role in developing trade around the world. Children were also able to explain what life would have been like for workers in India at this time and the significance this had on Gandhi's motivation for Independence. This was enhanced by parent volunteers who offered to share their own personal experiences of growing up in India.

In Year 1, children learned about the explorer David Livingstone as part of their Africa theme (Figure 11.2). Links to other curriculum areas supported children in finding

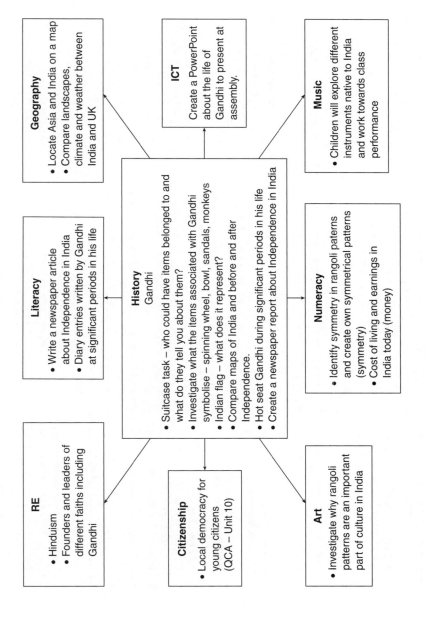

Figure 11.1 Year 4 cross-curricular planner: Asia

Geography
• Locate Asia and India on a map
• Compare landscapes, climate and weather between India and UK

ICT
Create a PowerPoint about the life of Gandhi to present at assembly.

Music
• Children will explore different instruments native to India and work towards class performance

Literacy
• Write a newspaper article about Independence in India
• Diary entries written by Gandhi at significant periods in his life

History
Gandhi
• Suitcase task – who could have items belonged to and what do they tell you about them?
• Investigate what the items associated with Gandhi symbolise – spinning wheel, bowl, sandals, monkeys
• Indian flag – what does it represent?
• Compare maps of India and before and after Independence.
• Hot seat Gandhi during significant periods in his life
• Create a newspaper report about Independence in India

Numeracy
• Identify symmetry in rangoli patterns and create own symmetrical patterns (symmetry)
• Cost of living and earnings in India today (money)

RE
• Hinduism
• Founders and leaders of different faiths including Gandhi

Citizenship
• Local democracy for young citizens (QCA – Unit 10)

Art
• Investigate why rangoli patterns are an important part of culture in India

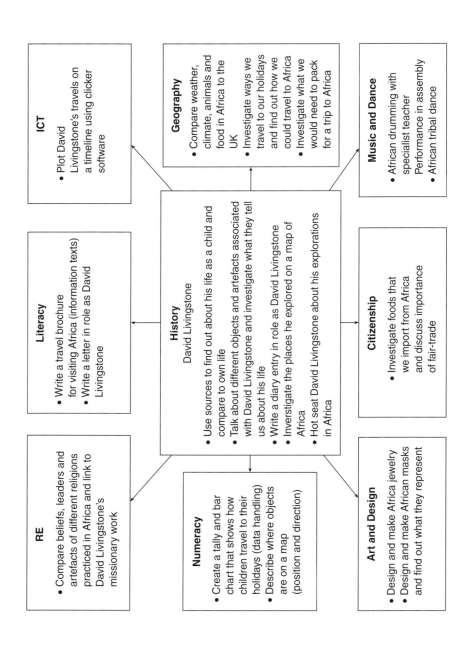

ICT
- Plot David Livingstone's travels on a timeline using clicker software

Geography
- Compare weather, climate, animals and food in Africa to the UK
- Investigate ways we travel to our holidays and find out how we could travel to Africa
- Investigate what we would need to pack for a trip to Africa

Music and Dance
- African drumming with specialist teacher Performance in assembly
- African tribal dance

Literacy
- Write a travel brochure for visiting Africa (information texts)
- Write a letter in role as David Livingstone

History
David Livingstone
- Use sources to find out about his life as a child and compare to own life
- Talk about different objects and artefacts associated with David Livingstone and investigate what they tell us about his life
- Write a diary entry in role as David Livingstone
- Inverstigate the places he explored on a map of Africa
- Hot seat David Livingstone about his explorations in Africa

Citizenship
- Investigate foods that we import from Africa and discuss importance of fair-trade

RE
- Compare beliefs, leaders and artefacts of different religions practiced in Africa and link to David Livingstone's missionary work

Numeracy
- Create a tally and bar chart that shows how children travel to their holidays (data handling)
- Describe where objects are on a map (position and direction)

Art and Design
- Design and make Africa jewelry
- Design and make African masks and find out what they represent

Figure 11.2 Year 1 cross-curricular planner: Africa

out about his expeditions to Africa and helped them make sense of different sources to explain what it would have been like. The unit was introduced by sharing a story set in Africa with the children. This led onto discussion about the differences in weather, food and animals in the UK and in Africa, which linked well with geography where children explored each of these aspects in much more depth. In Religious Education, children learned about Christianity and compared this with their own beliefs. This was explored further as children then compared different cultures and traditions and took part in African drumming and dance lessons. A parent volunteer from Africa was able to come in and share her experiences of growing up there. The face-to-face contact with someone from Africa allowed children to ask about what they had been learning in geography and more importantly, helped to place the unit in a real-life context. The thematic approach to teaching and learning had a significant impact on the children's ability to make confident enquiries, ask and answer relevant questions and to accurately explain the experiences of David Livingstone.

Implementing the plan for Year 1, Africa

Lesson 1. The history unit was introduced through a suitcase task. An old suitcase filled with different objects associated with David Livingstone, including maps of his expeditions, a first-aid kit and a Bible was placed in front of the classroom. Children were told that it had been found in an old house in Scotland but no one knows to whom it belongs. The children became curious about its contents and were excited when it was revealed that we could open it.

Adam: It's a map of Africa with lines on it. Maybe the person travelled in Africa.

Aleesha: Yes and they would have needed the water bottle because it's very hot.

Teacher: That's interesting. Why would the person travelling have a Bible?

Adam: Maybe they are a Christian. Maybe they went travelling in Africa to tell about being a Christian!

In small groups, children had the opportunity discuss the objects inside the case and to whom they might have belonged. Children made connections between subject areas and applied what they had learned in RE and in geography to form confident enquiries about the mystery person. Cooper (2000) highlighted that where children struggle to make inferences, it is often the result of lack of knowledge or experience. Here, children learned that objects can provide clues about people and the past and their existing knowledge about Africa allowed them to cross-reference the evidence to make powerful deductions. In addition it stimulated children's curiosities about David Livingstone and children were motivated to find out more.

Lesson 2. During the next lesson, the children were introduced to photographs as a way of finding out about the past. The children were asked to bring in photographs of themselves participating in activities they enjoyed doing outside school. This was used to stimulate discussion about what information photographs can tell us and how they could be a useful source of evidence for finding out about the lives of other people. The children were then split up into groups and looked at photographs of 'the person's' house (taken by the teacher after visiting the David Livingstone museum) and photographs of the cotton mills where he used work. An adult helped each group of children to compare the childhood of David Livingstone with their own lives, by asking questions about how the photographs compare with the activities in their own photographs.

Lesson 3. In this lesson, the children were introduced to another source of evidence that would unlock more clues about the mystery person. The lesson began with a discussion about what has been discovered about the person so far and what sources of evidence had helped children reach their decisions. Using their knowledge, gained in literacy lessons, about the purpose and features of diary entries, children were introduced to copies of the original diary entries written by David Livingstone. After exploring what more clues the diary entries could reveal, the children were split into mixed-ability groups, to look at the diary entries adapted by the teacher to suit the ability levels of the class. Each group learned about a different event David Livingstone experienced in Africa, including the discovery of Victoria Falls, the discovery of Lake Ngami and being attacked by a lion. Each group then presented what they had learned from the diary entries to the rest of the class and this was recorded on a class timeline.

Lesson 4. In this lesson, the children used ICT software to help them plot what they had learned about David Livingstone so far, in chronological order. The teacher had made differentiated clicker grids with sentences and pictures of significant events in his life, which included his childhood, missionary work in Africa and the discovery of Victoria Falls. The children then placed these events in chronological order.

Lesson 5. The focus of this lesson was to develop children's ability to ask and answer questions and use these skills to find out about and explore the thoughts and feelings that could have been experienced by David Livingstone at different times. As a class, the children formed questions they would ask him, based on the knowledge they had gained so far, using the headings Who, What, Where, When, Why, How, as prompts. The children then had the opportunity to use these questions in a hot-seating activity with a child in role as David Livingstone (D.L.):

Ryan: How long did it take you to get to Africa?

D.L.:   Well, it took me a few months because there were no aeroplanes a long time ago so I had to get on a ship.

Saman: Were you scared of the tigers and lions?

D.L.:   Yes! A lion attacked me. I was so scared, because it was growling and I thought it was going to eat me, but it just bit my shoulder, it was really painful.

The hot-seating activity really helped to bring the unit to life as children had the chance to question the person they had been investigating for the past few weeks. The children's existing knowledge of Africa helped them form effective questions that would elicit a detailed response. The child in role as David Livingstone gave impressive answers to the class questions. He was able to make connections between what he had learned across the curriculum to explain the reasons for different events and actions, which contributed well to the children's writing task in the next lesson.

Lesson 6. In literacy, children were exploring the features and purposes of letter writing and had written letters to children in a school in Africa. Throughout the unit, children were applying their knowledge and skills from other curricular areas to make enquiries in history and make sense of the events and actions experienced by David Livingstone. This provided children with a context in which to write letters in role as David Livingstone. The class brainstormed different events and experiences he would have had in Africa and this was used in a role-play simulation game. Following planning time and shared writing, the children wrote their own letters.

Writing in role as David Livingstone gave children a clear purpose for writing and this stimulated the more reluctant writers in the class to produce high-quality work. The children combined their knowledge and experience of Africa, built up over the unit, to communicate what they had learned. In this example, the children used their geographical knowledge to explain how David Livingstone might have felt during his explorations (Figure 11.3).

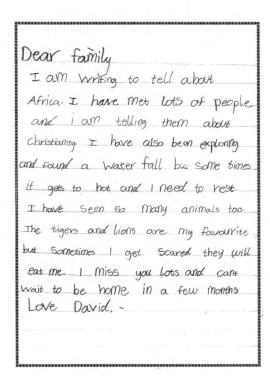

Figure 11.3 'David Livingstone' writes about how he felt during his explorations

CONCLUSION

There have been many approaches to whole school planning in history. Many believe that history should be a taught as a discrete subject, in its own right. However, with more demands in raising standards in literacy and in numeracy, more schools are adopting the thematic approach to teaching and learning. This, however, comes with the risk that history will become lost within a topic approach and that children will miss out on developing knowledge and skills specific to history. It is suggested that during whole school planning, history remains the focus for at least one of the themes across a term.

Using a thematic approach to teaching and learning can help to place learning in a purposeful context and help children develop a multi-perspectival view of the units of study. In this whole school approach, children were provided with richer, wider experiences, which helped them underpin the main principles of history: cause, continuity and change. Children were becoming more secure at making connections between subject areas and were using these to make more confident enquiries. In Year 1, children were able to apply their existing learning to new contexts in history which helped them develop a deeper understanding of what life might have been like for an explorer in Africa. Writing standards across the school had also improved significantly in both Key Stage 1 and Key Stage 2, as children's experiences across the curriculum gave them a powerful and meaningful context on which to base their writing.

By the time children reach Year 6 they would have explored the lives, actions and beliefs of people in every continent of the world. It is important that the curriculum reflects the ethnically diverse population today and that it is inclusive of the experiences and beliefs of the children in the school. This can help make learning more purposeful for children and provides an opportunity to celebrate the range of cultures represented in a school.

REFERENCES

Arthur, J. and Phillips, R. (2000) *Issues in History Teaching*, London: Routledge.

Cooper, H. (1995) *The Teaching of History in Primary Schools*, London: David Fulton.

Cooper, H. (2000) *The Teaching of History in Primary Schools: Implementing the Revised National Curriculum*, London: David Fulton.

Harnett, P. (2000) Curriculum decision making in the primary school, in J. Arthur and R. Phillips (eds) *Issues in History Teaching*, pp. 24–38, London: Routledge.

Ofsted (Office for Standards in Education) (2011) *History for All*, London: Ofsted.

Skelton, M. and Reeves, G. (2009) What it means for primary aged children to be internationally minded: the contribution of geography and history, in C. Rowley and H. Cooper (eds) *Cross-curricular Approaches to Teaching and Learning*, pp. 141–62, London: Sage.

CHAPTER 12

AWAKENING CREATIVITY

Hilary Cooper

SYBIL MARSHALL

It has been said throughout this book that creative teachers engage in creative thinking at their own level, and that this enables them to transmit creativity to their pupils. Sybil Marshall describes how the way she taught history changed dramatically when she began teaching in a village school in Cambridgeshire in the 1950s (Marshall 1963). Her story is an inspiring one with which to end this book.

> As the village got used to me and I to it I recognised the presence. It was the past, not the glorious epic past nor the grievous and oppressed past of an agricultural community, such as one might have expected. Nor was it the dead-and-gone-for-ever past, not even the loved and regretted past. The past I felt was a ghost with the spirit and soul of some mischievous child which hid somewhere along my way and popped out suddenly to tickle my consciousness and tap on my memory and be gone again, before I had time to put a name to it. It crept up slyly and pretended to be the present and then nipped away again, leaving me wondering if there really were any way of telling one from the other.
>
> (p. 43)

She became immersed in local history.

When an elderly village lady discovered that Sybil Marshall liked 'old things', she 'took me inside her cottage and showed me the shawl in which her great grandmother had been married'. They were married at the church, here, in the morning', she said, 'but after that they didn't know how to spend the rest of the day. So they walked into Cambridge to see a man hung.'

She finds later, 'with a sense of skin prickling', that her own experience is echoed in T.S. Elliott's *Four Quartets* (1943):

> Time present and time past
>
> Are both perhaps contained in time future
>
> And time future contained in time past.

Marshall reviewed, in the light of her new awareness,

> my previous, mistaken attempts to teach history, and for the first time I saw ...
> what the teacher's function with regard to history really is. Once a child has
> understood that history is now and always the details of the story of the past are
> his for the taking.
>
> (p. 45)

Marshall and her children became enthusiastic in finding out about the past
together; first about their familiar environment, then making links with similar communities elsewhere and with national events. They became confident and independent
in their enquiries, in using a variety of sources, asking questions about them and
exploring them through book-making, art, models and role-play.

Marshall encouraged the children to use visual sources, the murals in the church,
buildings (including a cottage with a beam where the medieval mural painter tried out
his colours) and written sources (including an account of an Elizabethan May Day).
Continually the children asked questions, researched and speculated. Who was
Dowsing? (Reformation iconoclast.) Why did he want to cover up our pictures? Could
we find bits of all the statues that were smashed if we dug in the churchyard? Or discover the stained glass from the windows that were taken out and hidden, according
to village rumour?

One girl's question about a document describing an Elizabethan May Day
Celebration, which the children were interpreting in detail as a mural, 'Mrs Marshall,
what are courtpies?' led to research with the university librarian. They found that they
are a kind of bodice.

I was inspired by Sybil Marshall and I hope that you will be too – and by our book!

REFERENCES

Elliott, T.S. (1943) *Burnt Norton*, in *Four Quartets*, New York: Harcourt, Brace and Company.
Marshall, S. (1963) *An Experiment in Education*, Cambridge: Cambridge University Press.

APPENDIX

Key features of creative pedagogy identified in the literature which are embedded in the process of historical enquiry: a checklist for evaluating creativity in this book and in your teaching

Enquiry Learning how to ask and investigate historical questions: framing questions; open-ended questions.	
Generation of possibilities Probabalistic thinking: speculation, ability to defend an argument, an interpretation, an inference, to listen to views of others, possibly change viewpoint. Ability to accept that history is dynamic, that interpretations vary new evidence is found, because of times in which account is written.	
Historical imagination Speculation based on evidence, according to what seems likely, is in accordance with what is known at the time, and cannot be contradicted.	
Ability to see from different perspectives See event, person from different perspectives. See period from different perspectives (ethnicity, gender, group, individual, art, music etc., local/ national/global).	
Concept development through use, trial/error Language specifically (e.g. villain) or generally used in historical enquiry (e.g. castle, weapon, communication, power, belief), or concepts invented by historians (e.g. Victorian).	
Make connections Chronology and time concepts: connections within and between periods.	

Generic aspects of creativity involved in teaching history

Autonomy	
Ownership	
Originality	
Teachers as co–participants	
Identify children's creative strengths and foster their creativity; giving them confidence to take risks	
Time and space to experiment	
Flexibility of style and pace	
Desire to give each child opportunity to excel	
Encourage children to identify and share their own questions, brainstorms, partnerships	
Stand back and observe learner engagement	
Opportunities to take part in small groups	
Reflect back questions children ask	
Use metaphor, anecdote, analogy to make connections	
Capitalise on the unexpected without losing the objective	
Non-judgemental	
Whole class and group discussions	
Knowledge about and interest in children's ideas	
Respect for children's emotional comfort	
Teachers model creativity; act spontaneously shifting focus of a lesson	
Playing with ideas	
Key features of imaginative play	

INDEX